Faculty Development by Design

Integrating Technology in Higher Education

a volume in
Research Methods for Educational Technology

Series Editor:
Walter F. Heinecke, *University of Virginia*

Research Methods for Educational Technolgy

Walter F. Heinecke, Series Editor

Technology and Assessment: The Tale of Two Interpretations (2006)
edited by Michael Russell

*Qualitative Research Methods for Education and
Intstructional Technology* (2004)
edited by Mukta Jost and Rema Nilakanta

*What Should Teachers Know About Technology:
Perspectives and Practices* (2003)
edited by Yong Zhao

Methods of Evaluating Educational Technology
edited by Walt Heinecke and Laura Blasi (2001)

Falculty Development by Design

Integrating Technology in Higher Education

edited by

Punya Mishra

Matthew J. Koehler

and

Yong Zhao
Michigan State University

INFORMATION AGE
PUBLISHING

Charlotte, NC • www.infoagepub.com

Library of Congress Cataloging-in-Publication Data

Faculty development by design : integrating technology in higher education /
edited by Puny Mishra, Matthew J. Koehler, and Youg Zhao.
    p. cm. -- (Research methods for educational technology)
  Includes bibliographical references.
  ISBN-13: 978-1-59311-582-1 (pbk.)
  ISBN-13: 978-1-59311-583-8 (hardcover)
  1. Education, Higher--United States--Computer-assisted instruction. 2.
Educational technology--United States. 3. Teachers--Training of--United
States. I. Mishra, Puny. II. Koehler, Matthew J. III. Zhao, Youg.
  LB2395.7.F32 2007
  378.0071'5--dc22

                      2006033092

ISBN 13: 978-1-59311-582-1 (pbk.)
        978-1-59311-583-8 (hardcover)
ISBN 10: 1-59311-582-2 (pbk.)
        1-59311-583-0 (hardcover)

Printed in the United States of America

For our parents

Kanan & Benoy
Mary, John, Karen, and Dan
Guangming and Guangzheng

Who taught us that…
Design is not for philosophy—it is for life.
—Issey Miyake

As with most media from which things are built, whether
the thing is a cathedral, a bacterium, a sonnet, a figure or
a word processor, architecture dominates material. To
understand clay is not to understand the pot. What a pot
is all about can be appreciated better by understanding
the creators and users of the pot and their need both to
inform the material with their meaning and to abstract
meaning from the form
—Alan Kay

CONTENTS

ACKNOWLEDGMENTS

It is good to have an end to journey toward, but it is the journey that matters, in the end.

—Ursula K. LeGuin

The coming together of this book has been like a long distance run. When we first taught a faculty development course back in the spring of 1999, little did we know that we had initiated a process that would take years to unfold, (and, in fact, it continues even today). We had no idea that this small group of 5 faculty members and 18 graduate students would soon encompass dozens of faculty members, staff and students, involving almost every department in the College of Education. Clearly this book (and the project on which it is based) has been a collaborative effort, the result of years of work by many people—and, in fact, is a fine example of the very philosophy it preaches. This large cast of characters means that our debts are many, and naming them all, an onerous and possibly impossible task. It is to be expected that we will miss naming some, and for that we apologize in advance.

To start, we would like to thank the person who initiated this whole thing 5 years ago—Carole Ames, the dean of the College of Education at Michigan State University. She came up with the idea of the faculty development course, and has supported it with both money and encouragement over the years. She has been a strong advocate of thoughtful technology integration in higher education and this project would not have gotten off the ground without her unstinting guidance and support.

This project would have stayed at a relatively small scale without the U.S. Department of Education's Preparing Tomorrow's Teachers to Use Technology (PT3) grant that we received in 2000. This grant allowed us to expand the project and reach and include many more faculty members and graduate students. We are also grateful to Bob Floden and Bertram "Chip" Bruce, the external evaluators for the grant for their feedback.

Faculty members are the heart and soul of this project. Their ideas, their concern for quality teaching and their wish to improve their pedagogy sustained the design teams and led to what has been achieved. They generously gave of their time and energy to this project, often receiving little in return (except possibly the gratitude of their students). If there is one thing we have learned through this project, it is just how dedicated to quality teaching our faculty members are. We came into this project primarily as learning technologists, interested and passionate about design and technology. However, working with these talented and dedicated faculty members showed us just how little we knew about the actual dynamics of teaching and pedagogy. This has been a wonderful journey and would not have been possible without them.

You will meet some of these faculty members in these pages, describing their journey, in their own words. But there are many others who, for pressures of time and prior commitments, could not write chapters for the book. This book would not be complete, however, without mentioning all the faculty members who participated in the design teams. They are, in alphabetical order: Dorothea Anagnostopoulos, Linda Anderson, Laura Apol, Jean Baker, Tom Bird, Dan Chazen, Cleo Cherryholmes, Chris Clark, Sandra Crespo, Jenny Denyer, John Dirkx, Pat Edwards, Sharon Feinman-Nemser, Robert Floden, Joyce Grant, John Kosciulek, Tim Little, Troy Mariage, Wanda May, Matthew Mayer, Susan Melnick, Evelyn Oka, Cindy Okolo, Linda Patriarca, Susan Peters, John Powell, Cheryl Rosean, Kathy Roth, Kris Renn, Christina Schwartz, Avner Segall, Ed Smith, David Stewart,[1] Steve Weiland, and Sandy Wilcox.

Our thanks also to certain key members of the project team, without whose hard work this project would never have gotten off the ground. Key among them is Rick Banghart. Rick, more than anybody else, embodies the new generation of learning technology experts, knowledgeable about technology yet sensitive to the complex and often conflicting demands of actual classrooms and teaching. We would also like to thank members of the College of Education technology support team (Laurence Bates, Kate Baird, Charlie Ruggiero, and Ken Dirkin) for their help and support through the duration of this project.

We would also like to thank all the doctoral and master's students, K-12 teachers, and in certain cases, K-12 students (too numerous to name individually) who were members of the various design teams. We could have achieved little without their help and support. We would like to thank the teaching assistants for the faculty development course (Aparna Ramchandran and Aman Yadav) as well as Kurnia Yahya, our research assistant, for their dedication and hard work.

Thanks are also due to Gail Nutter, without whose knowledge of budgets and other administrative details, this project would never have gotten off the ground. Thanks also to Lisa Roy and Lisa Payne, successive administrative assistants who helped keep graduate students paid, equipment ordered and tracked, reimbursements made, and in ways large and small, kept the wheels oiled and running.

We would in particular like to thank the authors of the chapters. When they began this project, writing a chapter about it was not a part of the deal. We appreciate the fact that they took on this additional load (and our demands for rewrites, and re-rewrites within tight deadlines) in good grace. We would also like to thank Bertram "Chip" Bruce and Martin Oliver for taking time out of their hectic schedules to write the two concluding chapters for this book. They wrote these chapters even as the other chapters were being assembled, which made their task of determining common themes akin to flying an airplane while building it. We are glad they agreed to do this because this book would have been incomplete without their perspectives.

A heartfelt thanks to Lisa Peruski for hours of work in converting what was a set of ideas and a collection of papers into a coherent, thematically integrated book. Thanks are also due to Sue Barratt for her careful proofreading of the manuscripts.

The fruits of our academic labors are often quite personal, though the costs are often born by our families and friends. We are grateful to our spouses and children and friends and colleagues for allowing us to work odd and often late hours as we struggled with the projects and the book.

One of the greatest pleasures of academia is playing with ideas. Finding the right colleagues is extremely important in that regard, and we are lucky to have found each other. A wonderful consequence of writing this book has been the close friendship we (the editors) have developed with each other. We have talked, argued, and discussed these issues of design, technology, and teaching over the years, over coffees and beers (and the occasional chai), in classes and in corridors, in conferences and in living rooms. These ideas have been poked and prodded, examined and finessed, many many times, so much so that they have become a part of our being.

Finally, it is customary in the acknowledgments to absolve all those involved in the book (apart from the editors) of any guilt regarding any errors that may have remained. We agree, all credit for anything good and useful in these pages goes to the authors of the chapters and the other individuals listed above. However, each of us individually (Punya, Matt, and Zhao) also would like to quite emphatically declare that any mistakes and errors that appear in this book are clearly the responsibility of the other two editors.

Punya, Matt, and Zhao
East Lansing, May 2006

NOTE

1. Just as this book was getting ready to be sent to the publishers came news of the sudden and tragic death of David Stewart. David had been a member of our faculty development course in 2003, and represented in his grace and dedication, in his love for teaching, and in the high level of scholarship, the highest ideals of this project. He will be missed.

EDITOR'S PREFACE

Technology is on its way to becoming ubiquitous in education. In addition, more and more evidence is suggesting that technology, when properly infused into teaching and learning, has a significant and positive effect on student learning. In a national study examining the relationship between pedagogical approach and technology use based on National Assessment of Educational Progress (NAEP) test scores as the outcome variable, Wenglinsky (2005) found that students perform better in classrooms taught by teachers employing technology with constructivist teaching methods. Didactic teachers are prone to use technology for drill and practice, while constructivist teachers are more likely to use technology for real-world, problem solving. He concludes: "When technology is used in concert with constructivist teaching practices, students tend to perform well; and when it is used in concert with didactic practices, they do not" (p. 78).

However, one of the most significant stumbling blocks to the integration of technology into American public schools has been a lack of training for teachers. Many teachers do not feel confident or prepared to integrate technology into their content teaching. Currently we are in a period of significant turnover in the population of our nation's teachers (National Center for Education Statistics, 1998). Teacher education programs in colleges of education will continue to serve as the nexus for teacher preparation, change and innovation in education. New teachers trained in teacher education programs will be faced with significant challenges to innovate with technology. What are we doing to prepare teachers to effectively integrate technology into instruction?

The Preparing Tomorrow's Teachers for Technology (PT3) program was the largest federal program ever to address this problem. Since 1999 it has funded innovative approaches to train preservice teachers to use technology in instruction. There were several strands of technology innovation pursued by grantees such as course redesign, e-portfolios, statewide systemic approaches, provision of technology tools including video learning, and faculty development. Faculty development approaches developed through PT3 initiatives included: mentoring, workshops, design teams, and one-on-one tutoring approaches (PT3.org, 2006). I am happy to introduce two contributions to this series, *Faculty Development By Design: Integrating Technology in Higher Education*, edited by Punya Mishra, Matthew J. Koehler, and Yong Zhao, and *Faculty Mentoring: The Power of Students in Developing Technology Expertise*, edited by Ann Thompson, Hsueh-Hua Chuang and Ismail Sahin. The approaches you will read about in these books are excellent examples of the way in which colleges of education are implementing design teams and mentoring initiatives in order to promote the integration of technology in teacher education.

While there were many approaches to technology integration funded in the PT3 program, the mentoring of teacher education faculty received significant attention in many projects. The theory upon which these innovative approaches were based is a sound one. If teacher education faculty could be prepared to integrate technology into their courses, preservice teachers would be seamlessly exposed to technology enhanced; there would be a multiplier effect as faculty influenced the practice of thousands of teachers every year. The challenge is to find an approach to effectively encourage faculty to integrate technology into their instruction of preservice teachers. This requires significant thought and a theoretically reasoned approach to the task.

In *Community of Designers* the editors have established an essential cornerstone for further development in the field. In addition, the contributors to this volume take a refreshing sociological approach to technology integration in this collection of chapters. The authors have built a model of technology integration based on Shulman's (1987) notion of pedagogical content knowledge. They have added technology into the equation that balances content knowledge with pedagogical knowledge. They state:

> This suggests a possible restructuring of professional development experiences for instructors so that they might develop the kind of nuanced understandings called for in our TCPK framework. Our approach to professional development is called, Communities of Designers, and is based on an active engagement with authentic problems of pedagogy. By participating in these communities of design, teachers build something that is sensitive to the subject matter (instead of learning the technology in general) and the specific instructional goals (instead of general ones). Therefore, every act of design is always a process of weaving together components of technology, content, and pedagogy. (p 18)

Developing and describing this concept is a significant step forward in our understanding of technology integration in education. A future challenge will be to operationalize it and to measure it. Mishra and his colleagues at Michigan State University remind us that technology integration should always be content based. The book provides us with important principles for technology integration. For instance they state:

> *Principle 1.* Teachers' ability to use technology must be closely connected to their ability to teach.... Their understanding of technology must be grounded in their understanding of teaching and learning in subject-specific and learner-specific contexts. (p. 19)

This advice comports with work conducted here at the Center for Technology and Teacher Education about the need to view technology integration within the context of subject and content specific applications (see http://www.teacherlink.org/content/). The authors remind us that technology is a tool that should help teachers make pedagogical decisions. Teachers need to be an active participant in the reinvention of technology in teaching. The authors also assert that the relationship between technological innovation and educational practice is a dialogical relationship. They state: "Technological innovation pushes pedagogical change, but it is also selected and redefined by existing pedagogy. Technological innovation should be anchored in thoughtful pedagogical practices while serving as a catalyst for change" (p. 20). The book contains a series of chapters in which these principles are applied.

Sadly, the PT3 program has been discontinued and the funding for technology integration and preparation has been continually cut in the Enhancing Education Through Technology (EETT) provision of the No Child Left Behind Act (NCLB). The support for technology in education reflected in the EETT provisions of Title II, Part D of NCLB is itself at risk as this introduction is written. It is particularly sad when, as presented in this volume, efforts to develop innovative ways of changing faculty practice and therefore provide modeling of effective technology integration for thousands of teachers have been so successful, thanks in part to federal funding through such programs as PT3. Children will be left behind if policy makers fail to make the commitment to technology training for educators at all levels of the system. As Mishra and his colleagues illustrate in this volume, teacher educators are doing their part to turn federal funding into successful practice.

Walt Heinecke
Series Editor
Center for Technology and Teacher Education

Charlottesville, VA
June, 2006

REFERENCES

National Center for Education Statistics. (1998). *The Baby Boom Echo Report.* Retrieved June 7, 2006, from http://www.qualityteachers.org/shortage/stats.htm

Shulman, L. S. (1987). Knowledge and teaching: Foundations of the new reform. *Harvard Educational Review, 57*(1), 1-22.

Wenglinsky, H. (2005). *Using technology wisely: the keys to success in schools.* New York: Teachers College Press.

CHAPTER 1

COMMUNITIES OF DESIGNERS

A Brief History and Introduction

Punya Mishra, Matthew J. Koehler, and Yong Zhao

Indeed, the best books have a use, like sticks and stones, which is above or beside their design, not anticipated in the preface, not concluded in the appendix.

—*Henry David Thoreau*

This is a book about technology integration in higher education. It documents the stories of a group of faculty members and graduate students at Michigan State University as they struggled to learn about, and implement, technology in their own teaching. They did this through their participation in an ongoing project (6 years and counting) that we call "communities of designers." This has been an eventful journey as the chapters in this book testify. If there is one important lesson we can learn from these chapters, it is that technology integration is not about technology alone, it is not just about boxes and wires and interfaces and software programs: Successful technology integration is a sociological issue, intimately connected to institutional cultures and practices, to social groups (formal and informal), and to individual intention, agency and interest. Most importantly, appropriate use of technology in teaching requires the

Faculty Development by Design: Integrating Technology in Higher Education, 1–22
Copyright © 2007 by Information Age Publishing

thoughtful integration of content, pedagogy, and technology. This book attempts to offer not just a bird's-eye view of the communities of designers project, but also to help identify broad themes and issues that can inform discussions and policies of technology integration at other institutions.

THE BACKGROUND

Integrating technology into instruction is one of the most important issues faced by institutions of higher education (Green, 1998). The 2001 (Green, 2001) survey conducted by the Campus Computing Project showed that over 31% of the respondents believed that assisting faculty with integrating technology into instruction was the single most important information technology (IT) issue faced by 2 and 4-year colleges. Other studies (Albright, 1997; Caffarella & Zinn, 1999; Parker, 1997; Schwieso, 1993) show that faculty does not often use technology in systematic or pedagogically sound ways.

These issues gain a greater significance when we consider that faculty members in colleges of education are responsible for preparing the next generation of K-12 teachers. K-12 teachers are under increasing pressure to meet state and national technology standards and mandates. However, faculty members at colleges of education are often underprepared to offer their teacher education candidates the required experiences and knowledge to meet these mandates. For instance, the 2001 Campus Computing (Green, 2001) survey noted that faculty in colleges of education were often less prepared than their colleagues in science, business, engineering, mathematics, and occupational programs to integrate technology into their teaching. The relative lack of faculty preparedness around technology and consequent lack of technology integration means that teachers graduating from these colleges are often ill-equipped to integrate technology into their own teaching. This is particularly troubling when we consider recently implemented standards and technology competencies that all K-12 teachers are supposed to meet. It has been argued that institutions of higher education need to develop and implement similar technology competencies for higher education faculty (Rogers, 2000). However, merely requiring a set of skills or technology competencies for instructors does not in any way insure that technology will be used in the classroom, or that it will be used appropriately and effectively. Moreover, issues of academic freedom and the relative autonomy enjoyed by university faculty often deter the uniform implementation of such requirements.

There are certain fundamental problems faced by higher education faculty as they attempt to integrate technology into their teaching. We list some of them below:

1. *Lack of experience in teaching/learning with technology.*   Most faculty members in higher education gained their knowledge and skills without educational technology, or at a time when educational technology was at a very different state than it is today. It is not surprising that many do not necessarily see the value of using technology for teaching, consider it irrelevant to good teaching, or see themselves as insufficiently prepared or skilled to use technology.

2. *The rapid rate of technology change.*   Technology changes so fast, causing hardware, software, and knowledge to become outdated every couple of years. Training instructors on specific software packages is particularly troublesome, because any given software release is unlikely to be used just a few years down the road. Any attempt to keep educators up to date on the latest and greatest hardware or software (especially if it focuses on specifics), is doomed to create outdated professionals.

3. *Inappropriate design of software.*   Most software tools available today are designed for the world of business and work, not education (Zhao, 2003). Converting general-purpose tools created for the world of business (e.g., spreadsheet programs) for use in the world of classroom teaching is neither trivial nor obvious. Doing so requires teachers to have deep knowledge of their content area, pedagogy, and the constraints and affordances of various technologies. Of course, a teacher could decide not to repurpose tools, but then students would simply be learning technologies (for the sake of learning technology) instead of more pressing subject-matter concerns.

4. *The situated nature of learning.*   Teacher knowledge is situated and local (Ball & Cohen, 1999; Putnam & Borko, 2000; Zeichner, Melnick & Gomez, 1996). Teachers' knowledge about technology is also situated in the context where technology is used. This knowledge is not only about what technology can do, but also (and perhaps more importantly) what technology can do for them. General one-size fits all approaches to technology skill development only encourage inappropriate generic solutions to the problem of teaching. Although there are some useful all-purpose technologies (e.g., grade books, knowledge-management systems, etc.), we argue that the full potential of technology can only be realized in the teaching of specific subject matter that is sensitive to the values,

experiences, teaching styles, and philosophies of individual teachers.

5. *An emphasis on "what" not "how."*   A potential guide to the development of technology skills in teachers are offered by the ever-burgeoning lists of state and national technology standards for teachers. In an attempt to codify, in standards, the knowledge that teachers need to have, there has been an emphasis on *what* teachers need to know, without paying much attention to *how* they are to learn it. An unfortunate consequence of this emphasis is the introduction of skills-based interventions such as professional development workshops and seminars. Teaching instructors how to use specific software and hardware configurations without also showing them how it applies to their own instruction, often leads to trial-and-error experimentation by teachers (Kent & McNergney, 1999). We argue that instructional methods, values, and goals need to be developed that lead to deeper understandings of technology integration.

6. *The time intensive nature of technology integration.*   Faculty members are often overworked and keep a very busy schedule. They have little time or interest in learning about technology unless it is directly applicable to what they do. This demand for immediate use often leads to the delivery of simplistic skills-oriented technology workshops. However, such workshops have rarely been found effective in promoting sustainable changes, nor have they been successful in actually attracting faculty. Thus, to develop a program that sustains faculty interest and results in significant changes, we need an approach to training that is both directly connected to the professional needs of the faculty, and rich and complex enough to enable intellectual engagement beyond simple skills. Part of the problem, we argue, has been a tendency to only look at the technology and not at the broader context of its use. It has become clear, over time, that merely introducing technology into the educational process is not enough. Rather, it is *how* technology is used that should become our primary focus when thinking about training (Carr, Jonassen, Litzinger, & Marra, 1998).

7. *The SEP syndrome.*   A significant part of the problem of technology integration has been, what we have called the "Somebody Else's Problem" (SEP) syndrome (Koehler, Mishra, Hershey, & Peruski, 2004). Technology and pedagogy are often seen as being domains ruled by different groups of people—teachers and instructors, who are in charge of pedagogy; and technologists, who are in charge of the technology. Similar to C. P. Snow's (1959) idea of two cultures,

teachers and techies live in different worlds and often hold curiously distorted images of each other. On one hand, the technologists view the nontechnologists as luddites, conservative, resistant to change, and oblivious to the transformative power of technology. On the other hand, the nontechnologists tend to view technologists as being shallowly enthusiastic, ignorant of education and learning theories, and unaware of the reality of classrooms and schools. Clearly, this gulf of mutual incomprehension needs to be bridged. Let's not forget that the educational technology world is dominated by instructional design paradigms that promote behaviorist and skills-based approaches to training.

Undoubtedly, overcoming the above list of problems is no easy task. However, over the past 5 years at the College of Education at Michigan State University, we have developed a systematic program of research and development around technology integration in higher education that we assert makes several inroads toward addressing these problems. The approach, which we have called "Communities of Design for Faculty Development," is the focus of this book.

Before describing the process of design communities, however, we briefly explain our underlying theoretical framework for teaching with technology that focuses on the role of different types of knowledge.

TPCK: A FRAMEWORK FOR TEACHER KNOWLEDGE FOR TECHNOLOGY INTEGRATION

The question of what teachers need to know has received a great deal of attention recently. It has been argued that teaching is a complex activity that occurs in an ill-structured dynamic environment and requires the context sensitive and flexible access to different knowledge bases such as knowledge of student thinking and learning, and knowledge of subject matter (Glaser, 1984; Leinhardt & Greeno, 1986; Putnam & Borko, 2000; Shulman, 1986, 1987; Spiro, Coulson, Feltovich, & Anderson, 1988; Spiro, Feltovich, Jacobson, & Coulson, 1991).

Shulman (1986) argued for a critical component of teacher knowledge that he called Pedagogical Content Knowledge (PCK). He argued that characterizing the complex ways in which teachers think about *how particular content should be taught*, requires teachers to develop "ways of representing and formulating the subject that make it comprehensible to others" (p. 9). Shulman did not include technological knowledge in his conceptualization of PCK, partly because, at that time, technologies had not become as integral a part of education as they have today. These new information technologies include both hardware and software, ranging from desktop machines to hand-held computers, from multimedia programs and educational games to the Internet. The rapid rate of evolution of these technologies distinguishes them from earlier, relatively stable technologies, and forces teachers to continually update their skills and knowledge as current technologies become obsolete. With these new technologies have come new challenges and requirements for their thoughtful application to pedagogy.

Over the past few years we have attempted to extend Shulman's idea of PCK to include technology (Koehler, Mishra, Hershey, & Peruski, 2004; Mishra, & Koehler, 2006). At the core of our argument is the idea that knowledge of technology cannot be treated as being context free. Moreover, the prevalence of information technologies in classrooms today requires teachers to develop an understanding of how technology relates to pedagogy and content.

PCK has been described as representing "a class of knowledge that is central to teachers' work and that would not typically be held by non-teaching subject matter experts or by teachers who know little of that subject" (Marks, 1990, p. 9). Extending that to include technology we can define Technological Pedagogical Content Knowledge (TPCK) as follows: TPCK is a class of knowledge that is central to teacher's work. It is a form of knowledge that typically would not be held by technologically proficient, subject matter experts, by technologists who know little of the subject or of pedagogy, or by teachers who know little of that subject or about technology.[1]

In our model of technology integration in teaching and learning we assert that good teaching requires a thoughtful interweaving of all three key sources of knowledge—technology, pedagogy and content (see Figure 1.1). We argue against simplistic conceptualizations of the relationships between content (the actual subject matter that is to be learned/taught), pedagogy (the process and practice or methods of teaching and learning), and technology (which include both commonplace technologies, such as chalkboards, and more advanced technologies such as digital computers and the Internet).

One of the important aspects of our model is that it includes and extends Shulman's (1987) idea of PCK. As Figure 1.1 shows, PCK lies at the intersection of pedagogical knowledge and content knowledge. What our model adds is three other forms of knowledge (represented by three other intersections): Technological Content Knowledge (TCK) as the overlap between technological knowledge and content knowledge; Technological Pedagogical Knowledge (TPK) at the intersection of technological knowledge and pedagogical knowledge; and finally, Technological Pedagogical Content Knowledge (TPCK) at the intersection of all three.

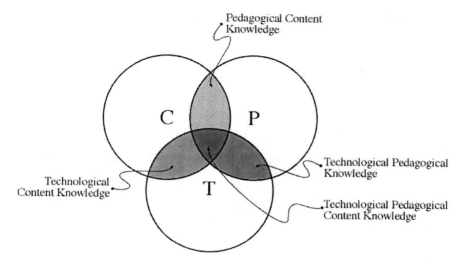

Figure 1.1.   Three circles of knowledge (content, pedagogy, and technology) overlap to lead to four more kinds of interrelated knowledge.

The value of content and pedagogical knowledge is something most educators will understand right away (based on Shulman's pioneering work). However, the addition of technology as an independent knowledge base may seem more controversial to some. The traditional view of the relationship between the three aspects argues that content drives most decisions: the pedagogical goals and technologies to be used follow from a choice of what to teach. Matters are rarely that clear cut, particularly when newer technologies are considered. We argue that technologies often come with their own imperatives and constraints that can change or modify the manner in which content is covered and/or the process of pedagogy that may be most appropriate. The choice of a technology can often lead to changes in the way in which we conceptualize content and pedagogy.

We argue that viewing any of these components in isolation from the others represents a real disservice to good teaching. Teaching and learning with technology exists in a dynamic transactional relationship (Bruce, 1997; Dewey & Bentley, 1949; Rosenblatt, 1978) between the three components in our framework—a change in any one of the factors has to be "compensated" by changes in the other two. These interactions go both ways, deciding on a particular technological tool will offer constraints upon the representations that can be developed, the course content that can be covered and delivered, which in turn effects the pedagogical process as well.

Consider, for instance, the advent of online learning. Constructing an online course is more then merely moving lectures and assignments online. Choosing to teach via the Web has a ripple effect on both how the content is represented and how it is to be conveyed to the learners (the pedagogy). The argument here is not whether the change is good or bad, but rather that effective online teaching requires instructors to think deeply about the relationship between all three knowledge bases—not individually but in a coevolutionary and coconstructed manner. The addition of a new technology reconstructs the dynamic equilibrium between all three elements forcing instructors to develop new representations of content and new pedagogical strategies that exploit the affordances (and overcome the constraints) of this new medium.

Similarly, changing pedagogical strategies (say moving from a lecture to a discussion format) necessarily requires rethinking the manner in which content is represented, as well as the technologies used to support it. To continue the argument, a change in the content to be taught (say from high school English to high school mathematics, or from middle-school biology to undergraduate biology) would perforce lead to changes in pedagogical strategies and technologies used.

We must add that separating these three components is not straightforward and at one level must be seen as an analytic act. Content, pedagogy, and technology are intimately related to each other and separating them out (as our model does) may be difficult to achieve in practice. Quality teaching requires developing a nuanced understanding of the complex relationships between technology, content, and pedagogy, and utilizing this understanding to develop appropriate, context specific strategies, and representations. Productive technology integration in teaching needs to consider all three issues not in isolation, but rather in the complex relationships in the system defined by the three key elements. Thus, our model emphasizes the complex interplay, connections, and interactions between these three bodies of knowledge, without privileging any of them specifically.

TPCK AND FACULTY DEVELOPMENT: THE COMMUNITIES OF DESIGN APPROACH

Current research on teacher learning, teacher adoption of technology, and cognitive sciences as well as our own experiences suggest that the ability to teach with technology is much more complex than mere acquisition of mechanical skills. Viewing teacher knowledge for technology integration as being a transaction between the three factors of content, pedagogy, and technology has significant implications for teacher education and teachers' professional development. We argue (Mishra & Koehler, 2003; Mishra & Koehler, 2006) that an overemphasis on skills-based training (e.g., workshops) puts too much focus on the technology (the "T") in our model, without developing knowledge about its relationships to content and pedagogy (the "P" and "C" in our model). In short, the development of flexible understanding of and generative ability to use technology requires intensive, meaningful, and authentic interactions with technology.

In order to go beyond the simple "skills instruction" view offered by the traditional workshop approach, it is necessary to teach technology in contexts that honor the rich connections between technology, the subject matter (content), and the means of teaching it (the pedagogy). This suggests a possible restructuring of professional development experiences for instructors so that they might develop the kind of nuanced understandings called for in our TCPK framework. Our approach to professional development is called, *Communities of Designers*, and is based on an active engagement with authentic problems of pedagogy. By participating in these communities of design, teachers build something that is sensitive to the subject matter (instead of learning the technology in general) and the specific instructional goals (instead of general ones). Therefore, every act of design is always a process of weaving together components of technology, content, and pedagogy.

In a traditional workshop or technology class, teachers are trained to use the latest tools with the hope that they can apply them to their practice. In contrast, in the *Communities of Design* approach, teachers focus on a problem of practice and seek ways to use technology (and thereby learn about technology) to address the problem. Because their explorations of technology are tied to their attempts to solve educational problems, teachers learn "how to learn" about technology and "how to think" about technology. Hence, teachers go beyond thinking of themselves as being passive *users* of technological tools and begin thinking of themselves as being *designers* of technology; that is, they learn to use existing hardware and software in creative, novel, and situation specific ways to accomplish their teaching goals.

This conception of proficiency and its attainment suggests the following several principles that have guided the development of the *Communities of Designers* approach:

Principle 1. Teachers' ability to use technology must be closely connected to their ability to teach; that is, good-teachers-with-technology must be good teachers. Their understanding of technology must be integrated with their understanding of teaching and learning in subject-specific and learner-specific contexts. Promoting such understanding is a high priority and strength of our teacher preparation program; we should build on it.

Principle 2.   Technology, like language, is a medium for expression, communication, inquiry and construction that can help teachers solve pedagogical problems in classrooms. The most effective environment for teachers to learn to teach with technology is one that provides ample opportunities to engage in authentic uses.

Principle 3.   The implementation of technology is the reinvention of technology. The realization of technological potential in educational settings is socially constructed and highly situational. Therefore, teachers should actively participate in the construction and reinterpretation of technology in their own teaching within a visible community of practice and inquiry that is both dedicated to and engaged in standards-based teaching and learning.

Principle 4.   The relationship between technological innovation and established educational practices is dialogical. Technological innovation pushes pedagogical change, but it is also selected and redefined by existing pedagogy. Technological innovation should be anchored in thoughtful pedagogical practices while serving as a catalyst for change. Thus, an effective environment should encourage the exploration of the dialogical process between pedagogy and technology.

Building on these principles, and our experience and success in using design-based approaches to foster teacher knowledge, we developed the *Communities of Designers* approach. In a nutshell, a design community is a group of individuals (teacher education faculty, educational technology specialists and students, preservice teachers, and in-service teachers) working collaboratively to design and develop technological solutions to authentic pedagogical problems faced by the teacher education faculty. The essence of this approach lies with four key words: *community, design, products/solution,* and *authentic problems.*

"Community" defines the social arrangement of the approach. A community, especially a purposefully constructed one, should include individuals with a diversity of expertise and expectations, making it possible for all members to contribute to and benefit from community activities. Within the context of social constructivism (Cole, 1996; Vygotsky, 1978) or constructionism (Harel, 1991; Harel & Papert, 1991), design projects lend themselves to sustained inquiry and revision of ideas.

"Design" specifies the activity dimension of the approach. Thus, building upon ideas grounded in situated cognition theory (Brown, Collins, & Duguid, 1989), learning is contextualized in the process of doing—solving an authentic problem of practice. Design-based activity provides the rich context for learning, sustained inquiry, and revision and is well-suited to develop the deep understanding needed to apply knowledge in the complex domains of real world practice. This emphasis on design is informed by long-standing research on the use of design for learning complex and interrelated ideas (Blumenfeld, Soloway, Marx, Krajcik, Guzdial, & Palincsar, 1991; Brown, 1992; Perkins, 1986; Harel & Papert; 1990, 1991; Kafai, 1996), with many theoretical and pragmatic connections to project-based learning (Blumenfeld, Marx, Soloway, & Krajcik, 1996; Blumenfeld, Soloway, Marx, Krajcik, Guzdial, & Palincsar, 1991; Dewey, 1934; Papert, 1991; Roth, 1995; Roup, Gal, Drayton, & Pfister, 1993). In constructing a product/solution, the learning of a design community is located at the intersection of theory and practice, technology and pedagogy, and designer and audience. Design communities also can transform members by encouraging them to take control of their own learning, as they take the necessary steps toward reaching the solution to their authentic problem.

This focus on authentic problems provides the connection between what the faculty may *learn* and what they *actually do*. These problems also provide the opportunity for the faculty to explore technology as a solution to teacher education problems in a situated manner (Barab & Duffy, 2000; Marx, Blumenfeld, Krajcik, & Soloway, 1997; Pea, 1993). Teacher knowledge, including knowledge about how to use technology, is situated and local (Ball & Cohen, 1999; Borko & Putnam, 1996; Cochran-Smith & Lytle, 1993; Lampert & Ball, 1999; Putnam & Borko, 2000; Zeichner, Melnick, & Gomez, 1996). The knowledge is not only about what technology can do, but also (and perhaps more importantly) what technology can do for them. The process of learning to use technology is thus a translation process whereby teachers understand the meaning and implications of a technology and translate it into a solution for a local problem. Moreover, they need opportunities to apply what they are learning in a variety of contexts over time—including classroom contexts—in order to develop sufficient confidence and skill to adapt new ideas to future situations (Bosch & Cardinale, 1993; Brown, 1992; Willis & Mehlinger, 1996). They also need opportunities to grapple with authentic pedagogical issues related to standards-based subject matter teaching, and explore potential technological responses to those issues (Rosaen, Hobson, & Khan, 2003). It is, thus, essential for teachers to engage in experimenting with technology in response to authentic problems that they are likely to encounter in their teaching.

Consistent with other research in this area (Barab & Duffy, 2000), design team participants contend with authentic and engaging ill-structured problems that reflect the complexity of the real world (Marx, Blumenfeld, Krajcik, & Soloway, 1997; Pea, 1993). Learners have to actively engage in active practices of inquiry, research and design, in collaborative groups (that include higher education faculty members and graduate students with an interest in educational technology) to design tangible, meaningful artifacts as end products of the learning process (Blumenfeld et al., 1991). The actual process of design is the anchor around which learning happens. This evolving artifact is also the test of the viability of individual and collective understandings as participants test theirs, and others', conceptions and ideas of the project. Learning in this context involves becoming a *practitioner*, not just learning about *practice* (Brown & Duguid, 1991). We see learning by design as the foundation for building a beginning repertoire (Feiman-Nemser, 2001) where repertoire is defined as "a variety of techniques, skills, and approaches in all dimensions of education that teachers have at their fingertips" (Wasley, Hampel, & Clark 1997, p. 45).

IMPLEMENTING COMMUNITIES OF DESIGN

The College of Education (COE) administers programs in Teacher education (TE) at the undergraduate and graduate levels; higher, adult, and lifelong education (HALE) at the graduate level; counseling and educational psychology at the graduate level; and special education at the undergraduate and graduate levels. The programs function relatively independently but faculty regularly cross boundaries to collaborate when interests and research intersect. Educational psychology, unlike the other degree programs, includes a technology specialty and many faculty are employed because of their technological pedagogical expertise. These faculty had worked with, engaged, and supported other COE faculty informally for several years as technology continued to change and more and more faculty members strove to integrate technology into their teaching in meaningful ways. The support from educational psychology faculty became more formalized when the dean of the COE asked two of the authors (Mishra and Zhao) to offer a course for faculty development. The communities of design approach was first implemented in this course in 1999. The result combined faculty development with a regular masters course in educational technology.

Prior to the beginning of the course, the dean issued a call for proposals to the teacher education faculty, to which over 20 faculty members responded. Six faculty members were selected to participate in the program. The selection criteria included the significance of the problem proposed, the potential impact of the finished solution, and the potential impact on the faculty at large. Six faculty members then joined the class. Six design teams were formed around each of the faculty members. The students enrolled in the class were asked to select a design team to join according to their own interests. The problems the design teams worked on were diverse but all significant and real. They included: the design of a Web site for teaching an introductory teacher preparation course; developing strategies for using classroom digital video for training collaborating teachers in K-12 districts to work with pre-service teacher interns; developing a database of lesson plans for learning elementary level science; the design of technologies for literacy instruction and evaluation in elementary reading; and, an online course on immigrant issues for pre-service teachers and development of a Web-based interface for preservice teachers to construct and share their teaching videos.

The results of the first faculty development course appeared to be very positive in a number of ways. First, the faculty developed a deeper and more flexible understanding of technology. Many of them describe the experience as transformative. Second, the teams produced products that were subsequently used in the teacher education program, which is a good indication of technology integration and transformed teaching practices. Third, the participating graduate students learned more about the complexity of technology integration and teacher education.

Capitalizing on the success, the College decided to continue and expand the program to faculty in other departments within the College. The College has offered the program every year for 4 years since the first one. By every measure, the faculty development course has become an integral part of the faculty development plan in the college and part of the educational technology masters' program. For example, this effort was a key means for helping the college develop faculty skilled at teaching online as part of the new online masters' program (e.g., Koehler et al., 2004).

Later, with support from the U.S. Department of Education's Preparing Tomorrow's Teachers for Technology (PT3) grant, we took the *Communities of Designers* approach even further. As part of our efforts, we set up opportunities for faculty to pursue year-long funding for design projects that integrated technology into the college, the teacher education program, or into the surrounding educational communities. We were widening the scope of problems that could be investigated through the design approach, which provided longer and more kinds of support than could be delivered during a semester long course, in essence. We were expanding the role of the various participants (graduate students, teacher education students, teachers in the schools, and other partners could be part of the team). Over the past 5 years, over 30 faculty members have led these communities of designers and the work continues today.

Implementing a *Community of Designers* breaks down into four stages that each design team experienced over its lifecycle: identifying participants and problems, forming communities, providing leadership and support, and working on the problems. We briefly describe the four stages below.

1. *Inviting proposals and identifying authentic problems.*   Key to the success of this approach is to identify authentic problems. To identify potential participants and authentic problems, the dean issued an open call for proposals to all of the faculty members at the college. The call described the program and invited interested faculty members to propose the problems they face and would like to work on in the faculty development program. The call made it clear that prior technology proficiency was not a requirement. What was considered important was the significance and authenticity of the problem, as well as its potential for exploring technology as a solution. Later, as the PT3 grant developed, additional design teams were supported by a similar proposal and awarding structure led by the grant leaders.

2. *Forming communities.*   The faculty member served as the head of the design community. Other members of the community included experts in educational technology, who were often graduate students in educational technology or graduate assistants who had expertise in using technology. In addition, depending on the situation, preservice and in-service teachers, who were often the potential audience of the design products, were also included in the design community.

3. *Providing leadership and support.*   One or two educational technology faculty members were often needed to provide overall leadership and serve as resources to all the design communities at any given time. Other general support included graduate students and undergraduate students with special expertise in technology. These students often served as consultants to design communities.

4. *Working on the problems.*   Once the design community was formed, members of the community began to explore technology as a solution to the problem over a period of time, during which they may have attended classes led by the educational technology faculty and or consulted with the educational technology faculty and other technology specialists. This was where the bulk of the professional development really happened, where the participants encountered the boundaries and intersections of content, pedagogy, and technology.

We have learned some significant lessons over the past 5 years, most of which will be revealed in the chapters that follow. We have also used these communities of designers as sites for research. This has resulted in a series of publications and conference presentations, as well as the theoretical framework that guides our work today. That said, there are some key metalessons that might be useful to present here.

One of the most important lessons we have learned is to base the design team idea on an authentic pedagogical problem as identified by faculty members who teach these courses. We have also learned that it is important to trust the faculty members and not monitor them too closely. The fact that these are concerns raised by faculty members is an automatic motivator. Moreover, design problems often changed and mutated as the design teams learned more about the work they were engaged in. Trusting the faculty members and design teams meant that we were open to their reconceptualizations and redesigns. We have learned that going hand in hand with trusting the faculty members is the need for strong institutional support-both financial and technological. Finally, we have learned that it is important to have a good mix of people in the design teams. Our design teams were quite eclectic in nature, including technology novices, technology experts, graduate students, faculty members, in-service teachers, preservice teachers, and in certain cases, K-12 students. We have found that each of these stakeholders brings a different perspective to the design process, enriching it and making the solutions more robust and applicable.

This is not to say that all design teams were successful and that all technology projects were completed without frustration or even completed at all (at least as originally envisaged). This will be revealed in the chapters that follow.

ABOUT THE CHAPTERS

This book is a collection of reflective papers on the experiences and learning of some of the faculty members who participated in the faculty development program. Even though their accounts all document and analyze the design community approach, the authors have diverse backgrounds, interests, viewpoints, and authentic problems they engaged in. Each chapter helps to add detail to the *Community of Designers* framework, and highlight the nuances as well. Collectively, the chapters reinforce two main themes. First, faculty development does not happen in a vacuum. Rather, it is connected to pedagogical problems and concerns faculty members face as they attempt to integrate technology in their teaching. Second, a focus on community indicates that technology integration is a sociological issue rather than a psychological one or a technical/administrative one.

Chapters 2-8, written by faculty and graduate student designers, are quite different from each other, appropriately reflecting contextual and local influences on the design of technology for teaching and learning. Each of these chapters is a reflective piece on one (or more) community member's experience in learning about technology, particularly as it played out through their participation in the design community experience. Each of the authors brought an immense body of scholarly and practical experience with pedagogy in the area of higher education to their design communities. Each of these chapters explores and documents their learning and changes in thinking about pedagogy and technology through their participation in the design communities. That said, each chapter broadly follows the following framework:

1. The chapters start with a description of *the authentic problem the project intended to address*. Too often technology integration is driven by the imperatives of the technology—cool tools in search of a solution. A key aspect of our approach is that the prime driving force for learning and implementing technology have been authentic pedagogical problems identified by practicing teacher educators. Thus, the first part of the chapter addresses why the individual project was important, the problem it attempted to address.

2. The next section of the chapter offers an *analysis of the various roles of participants in the community*. It describes the nature and process of collaboration with other stakeholders and participants, and how the community facilitated (or did not facilitate) the design/problem solving process. Technology integration cannot take place in a vacuum. Nor can it occur by just one individual acquiring technical knowledge. It often requires collaboration with other people. For instance, we know that different design teams formed different kinds of communities. Most of them included graduate students, other faculty members, technology-experts, practicing teachers, interns, and so on. Of course, all this happened within a broader college and university level institutional context. The support offered by these teams, groups, institutions, and individuals was both material (such as laptops, software, money etc.), and intangible, though no less important (such as faculty development courses, summer support, informal consultancy, and so on).

3. The third section of the chapters provides *documentation and analysis of the process of seeking a technology solution*. This section usually offers a description of the process of developing a technological solution to the original problem. Learning a new technology can often be quite frustrating and time consuming. Too often descriptions of technology integration do not describe the "actual" process of technology development and integration. This section

describes the nature of problems faced (technological, structural, social), how they were overcome, and what technologies were learned and used. Some of the chapters talk not just of the ideas that the faculty started with, but also ideas that were discarded. The descriptions are not just of what worked, but also what did not, and how these disruptions, disturbances, and contradictions led to learning.

Too often design is seen as the application of abstract scientific principles to technology, what Schon (1983) has called "the myth of technical rationality." However, as these chapters reveal design is a messy and complex process. It is not a linear movement toward a specific goal, but rather a zig-zag, iterative process in which goals and plans are in a constant state of negotiation. These chapters show that design is most fruitfully seen as a dialogue between constraints and tradeoffs, between theoretical and pragmatic concerns, and between the artifact being created and the evolving conceptions of the designers. There is a constant play between the triad of content, pedagogy, and technology, and the best solutions are ones that respect the imperatives of all three.

4. Finally, the chapters end with a *final reflection and summing up of the process by the author/participant*. This section provides a description of where things stand today and tentative descriptions of where they see it going in the future.

Although each chapter addresses these four common themes each of them is also grounded in specific contexts, offering a diversity of viewpoints and approaches through the content to be covered, the pedagogies supported and the technologies employed. Briefly, chapters two through five focus on uses of various technologies in literacy education. Cheryl Rosaen and Sharon Hobson (chapter 2) describe their 4 year journey to explore and understand the large variety of ways that technology, guided by considerations of learning, can infuse literacy education in both teaching and teacher education. Laura Apol and Sheryl Rop's (chapter 3) story begins with their concerns about children's literature response in literacy education. They find that the use of videotape of selected classroom episodes depicting exceptionally thoughtful and talented teachers makes literary response come alive for future literacy teachers. Leslie David Burns and Stephen Koziol (chapter 4) seek ways to help students develop and use their own video in an English methods course while Dorothea Anagnostopoulos, Jory Brass, and Dipendra Subedi (chapter 5) work with high-school students to explore "new literacies." They investigate the various literacy practices that digital technologies make available to and demand of adolescents and in the process explore their own understandings of literacy.

Chapters 6 and 7 focus on integrating technology to further students' and teachers' understanding in social studies. Both chapters also explore design teams comprised mainly of university faculty and practicing teachers. Avner Segall and Bettie Landauer-Menchik (chapter 6) work with teachers to design ways to foster critical reading of maps by developing a Web-based series of curricular modules for teachers, student teachers, and students. Timothy Little (chapter 7) explores collaborative development of social studies materials and shows how PowerPoint can be a powerful tool compared to the ways it is typically used.

Chapters 8 and 9, written by faculty members in the Higher, Adult and Lifelong Education Program, present more in-depth personal journeys into learning about technology within diverse design communities. John Dirkx (chapter 8) integrated problem-based learning and online technology in his efforts to address teaching highly theoretical content that students would have to apply within the world of educational practice, while also respecting students' needs and interests. Ann Austin (chapter 9) writes openly about the challenges both she and her students faced in incorporating Web-based technology into face-to-face courses. Dr. Austin's goal in using this technology was to provide her doctoral students with ways to extend the learning community beyond the physical confines of the classroom walls where they met for 3 hours, one time per week.

The last two chapters in the book are by Dr. Bertram "Chip" Bruce (chapter 11) and Dr. Martin Oliver (chapter 10). Dr. Bruce has been partially involved with the project (he was an external evaluator on the part funded through the PT3 grant) and offers an insider/outside perspective on the chapters. Dr. Martin Oliver was not involved in the project and provides an "outsider's" view of the project.

We hope that you have as much fun and learn as much from reading these chapters as we had in living through these experiences.

NOTE

1.   The idea of TPCK is not entirely new. A precursor to the TPCK idea, within the context of educational software design, can be found in Mishra (1998). Others who have discussed TPCK and related ideas include Keating and Evans (2001), Margerum-Leys and Marx (2002), Niess (2005), Pierson (2001), and Zhao (2003). Our conception of TPCK has developed over time through a series of publications and presentations the most definitive of which is Mishra and Koehler (2006). An updated reference list is maintained at http://punyamishra.com/tpck/references.html

REFERENCES

Albright, L. P. (1997). The information technology imperative for higher education: A report. *Library Acquisitions: Practice and Theory, 21*(3), 268–270.

Ball, D. L., & Cohen, D. K. (1999). Developing practice, developing practitioners: Toward a practice-based theory of professional education. In G. Sykes & L. Darling-Hammond (Eds.), *Teaching as the learning profession: Handbook of policy and practice* (pp. 3-32). San Francisco: Jossey Bass.

Barab, S. A., & Duffy, T. M. (2000). From practice fields to communities of practice. In D. Jonassen & S. Land (Eds.), *Theoretical foundation of learning environments* (pp. 25 – 56). Mahwah, NJ: Erlbaum.

Blumenfeld, P. C., Marx, R. W., Soloway, E., & Krajcik, J. (1996). Learning with peers: From small group cooperation to collaborative communities. *Educational Researcher, 25*(8), 37-40.

Blumenfeld, P. C., Soloway, E., Marx, R., Krajcik, J., Guzdial, M., & Palincsar, A. (1991). Motivating project-based learning: Sustaining the doing, supporting the learning. *Educational Psychologist, 26* (3&4), 369-398.

Borko, H., & Putnam, R. (1996). Learning to teach. In D. C. Berliner & R. C. Calfee (Eds.), *Handbook of educational psychology* (pp. 673-708). New York: Macmillan.

Bosch, K. A., & Cardinale, L. (1993). Preservice teachers' perceptions of computer use during a field experience. *Journal of Computing in Teacher Education, 10*(1), 23-27.

Brown, A. L. (1992). Design experiments: theoretical and methodological challenges in creating complex interventions in classroom settings. *The Journal of the Learning Sciences, 2*(2), 141-178.

Brown, J. S., Collins, A., & Duguid, P. (1989). Situated cognition and the culture of learning. *Educational Researcher, 18*(1), 32-42.

Brown, J. S., & Duguid, P. (1991). Organisational learning and communities of practice: Towards a unified view of working, learning, and innovation. *Organisational Science, 2*(1), 40-57.

Bruce, B. C. (1997). Literacy technologies: What stance should we take? *Journal of Literacy Research, 29*(2), 289-309.

Caffarella, R. S., & Zinn, L. R. (1999). Professional development for faculty: A conceptual framework of barriers and supports. *Innovative Higher Education, 23*(4), 241 - 254.

Carr, A., Jonassen, D., Litzinger, M. E., & Marra, (1998). Good ideas to foment educational revolution: The role of systematic change in advancing situated learning, constructivism, and feminist pedagogy. *Educational Technology, 38*(1), 5-14.

Cochran-Smith, M., & Lytle, S. L. (1993). *Inside/outside: Teacher research and knowledge.* New York: Teachers College Press.

Cole, M. (1996). *Cultural psychology: A once and future discipline.* Cambridge, MA: Harvard University Press.

Dewey, J. (1934). *Art as experience.* New York: Perigree.

Dewey, J., & Bentley, A. F. (1949). *Knowing and the known.* Boston: Beacon.

Feiman-Nemser, S. (2001). From preparation to practice: Designing a continuum to strengthen and sustain teaching. *Teachers College Record, 103*(6), 1013-1055.

Glaser, R. (1984). Education and thinking: The role of knowledge. *American Psychology, 39*(2), 93-104.

Green, K. C. (1998). Colleges struggle with IT planning. *The 1998 National Survey of Information Technology in U.S. Higher Education.* Retrieved July 19, 2006, from http://www.campuscomputing.net/summaries/1998/index.html

Green, K. C. (2001). *The 2001 National Survey of Information Technology in US Higher Education.* Retrieved July 19, 2006, from http://www.campuscomputing.net/summaries/2001/

Harel, I. (1991). *Children designers.* Norwood, NJ: Ablex.

Harel, I., & Papert, S. (1990). Software design as a learning environment. *Interactive Learning Environments, 1*(1), 1-32.

Harel, I., & Papert, S. (1991). *Constructionism.* Norwood, NJ: Ablex.

Kafai, Y. (1996). Learning design by making games: Children's development of design strategies in the creation of a complex computational artifact. In Y. Kafai & M. Resnick (Eds.), *Constructionism in practice: Designing, thinking and learning in a digital world* (pp. 71-96). Mahwah, NJ: Erlbaum.

Keating, T., & Evans, E. (2001, April). *Three computers in the back of the classroom: Pre-service teachers' conceptions of technology integration.* Paper presented at the annual meeting of the American Educational Research Association, Seattle, WA.

Kent, T. W., & McNergney, R. F. (1999). *Will technology really change education? From blackboard to web.* Thousand Oaks, CA: Corwin Press.

Koehler, M.J., Mishra, P., Hershey, K., & Peruski, L. (2004). With a little help from your students: A new model for faculty development and online course design. *Journal of Technology and Teacher Education, 12*(1), 25-55.

Lampert, M., & Ball, D. L. (1999). Aligning teacher education with contemporary K-12 reform visions. In L. Darling-Hammond & G. Sykes (Eds.), *Teaching as the learning profession: Handbook of policy and practice* (pp.33-53). San Francisco: Jossey-Bass.

Leinhardt, G., & Greeno, J. G. (1986). The cognitive skill of teaching. *Journal of Educational Psychology, 78*(2), 75-95.

Lundeberg, M. A., Bergland, M., Klyczek, K., & Hoffman, D. (2003). Using action research to develop preservice teachers' beliefs, knowledge and confidence about technology. *Journal of Interactive Online Learning, 1*(4). Retrieved July 19, 2006, from http://ncolr.uidaho.com/jiol/archives/2003/spring/toc.asp

Margerum-Leys, J., & Marx, R. (2002). Teacher knowledge of educational technology: A study of student teacher/mentor teacher pairs. *Journal of Educational Computing Research, 26*(4), 427-462.

Marks, R. (1990). Pedagogical content knowledge: From a mathematical case to a modified conception. *Journal of Teacher Education, 41*(3), 3-11.

Marx, R. W., Blumenfeld, P. C., Krajcik, J. S., & Soloway, E. (1997). Enacting project-based science: Challenges for practice and policy. *Elementary School Journal, 97*(4), 341-358.

Mishra, P., & Koehler, M. J. (2003). Not "what" but "how": Becoming design-wise about educational technology. In Y. Zhao (Ed.), *What teachers should know about technology: Perspectives and practices* (pp. 99-122). Greenwich, CT: Information Age Publishing.

Mishra, P., & Koehler, M. J. (2006). Technological Pedagogical Content Knowledge: A new framework for teacher knowledge. *Teachers College Record, 108*(6), 1017-1054.

Neiss, M. L. (2005). Preparing teachers to teach science and mathematics with technology: Developing a technology pedagogical content knowledge. *Teaching and Teacher Education, 21,* 509-523.

Papert, S. (1991). Situating constructionism, In S. Papert & I. Harel (Eds.), *Constructionism* (pp. 1-11). Norwood, NJ: Ablex.

Parker, D. R. (1997). Increasing faculty use of technology in teaching and teacher education. *Journal of Technology and Teacher Education, 5*(2 & 3), 105-115.

Pea, R. D. (1993). Practices of distributed intelligence and designs for education. In G. Salomon (Ed.), *Distributed cognitions* (pp. 47-87). New York: Cambridge University Press.

Perkins, D. N. (1986). *Knowledge as design.* Hillsdale, NJ: Erlbaum.

Pierson, M. E. (2001). Technology integration practice as a function of pedagogical expertise. *Journal of Research on Computing in Education, 33*(4), 413-429.

Putnam, R. T., & Borko, H. (2000). What do new views of knowledge and thinking have to say about research on teacher learning? *Educational Researcher, 29*(1), 4-15.

Rogers, D. (2000). A paradigm shift: Technology integration for higher education in the new millennium. *Educational Technology Review, 1*(13), 19-33. Retrieved July 19, 2006, from http://dl.aace.org/6256

Rosaen, C. L., Hobson, S., & Khan, G. (2003). Making connections: Collaborative approaches to preparing today's and tomorrow's teachers to use technology. *Journal of Technology and Teacher Education, 11*(2), 139-172.

Rosenblatt, L. M. (1978). *The reader, the text, the poem: The transactional theory of literary work.* Carbondale, IL: Southern Illinois University Press.

Roth, W. M. (1995). *Authentic school science.* The Netherlands: Kluwer.

Roup, R., Gal, S., Drayton, B., & Pfister, M. (Eds.). (1993). *LabNet: Toward a community of practice.* Hillsdale, NJ: Erlbaum.

Schon, D. (1983). *The reflective practitioner.* London: Temple Smith.

Schwieso, J. (1993, February). Staff usage of information technology in a faculty of higher education: A survey and case study. *Educational & Training Technology International: ETTI, 30*(1), 88-94.

Shulman, L. (1986). Those who understand: Knowledge growth in teaching. *Educational Researcher, 15*(2), 4-14.

Shulman, L. S. (1987). Knowledge and teaching: Foundations of the new reform. *Harvard Educational Review, 57*(1), 1-22.

Snow, C. P. (1959). *The two cultures and the scientific revolution. The Rede lecture.* New York: Cambridge University Press.

Spiro, R. J., Coulson, R. L., Feltovich, P. J., & Anderson, D. K. (1988). Cognitive flexibility theory: Advanced knowledge acquisition in ill-structured domains. In V. Patel (Ed.), *Tenth annual conference of the cognitive science society* (pp. 375–383). Hillsdale, NJ: Erlbaum.

Spiro, R. J., Feltovich, P. J., Jacobson, M. J., & Coulson, R. L. (1991). Cognitive flexibility, constructivism, and hypertext: Random access instruction for advanced knowledge acquisition in ill-structured domains. *Educational Technology, 31*(9), 24-33.

Vygotsky, L. S. (1978). *Mind in society: The development of higher psychological processes*. Cambridge, MA: Harvard University Press.

Wasley, P., Hampel, R., & Clark, R. (1997). *Kids and school reform*. San Francisco: Jossey-Bass.

Willis, J., & Mehlinger, H. (1996). Information technology and teacher education. In J. Sikula, T. J. Butter, & E. Guyton (Eds.), *Handbook on research in teacher education* (pp. 978-1029). New York: Simon and Schuster Macmillan.

Zeichner, K., Melnick S., & Gomez, M. (1996). *Currents of reforming preservice teacher education*. New York: Teachers College Press.

Zhao, Y. (Ed.). (2003). *What teachers should know about technology: Perspectives and practices*. Greenwich, CT: Information Age Publishing.

CHAPTER 2

INFUSING TECHNOLOGY IN TEACHER EDUCATION

How Does Learning Guide Design?

Cheryl L. Rosaen and Sharon Hobson

Good design begins with honesty, asks tough questions, comes from collaboration and from trusting your intuition.

—Freeman Thomas

INTRODUCTION

Like many teacher educators who are attempting to infuse technology within a teacher preparation program (Brush, Igoe, Brinkerhoff, Glazewski, Ku, & Smith, 2001; Dawson & Norris, 2000; Morrow, Barnhart, & Rooyakkers, 2002; Rademacher, Tyler-Wood, Doclar, & Pemberton, 2001; Thomas & Cooper, 2000), we have many questions about whether and how such integration supports our students' immediate and long term professional learning. Consider, for example, Miranda's comments about her learning during our integrated language arts and mathematics methods course:[1]

Faculty Development by Design: Integrating Technology in Higher Education, 23–47
Copyright © 2007 by Information Age Publishing
All rights of reproduction in any form reserved.

I hadn't thought about technology until the first day [of class] when we walked in and you said that we were getting laptops and would be integrating computers into the classroom. I was so excited. The most I thought [is] that the kids work on computers and do educational software. That was technology in the classroom. So I had no idea to the extent that your students could search the Internet for answers and go other places, electronic portfolios, but what a tool it could be in my own teaching; in both organization of a resource file, my own Web page, to market myself to future employers, as well as a tool to use in my own lessons like PowerPoint and presentations for every lesson. It's incredible. I know that there are so many more ways to use it that I want to keep exploring. (Miranda, Interview #1)

When Miranda shared these thoughts 3 months after she completed the senior-level course, we wondered whether her enthusiasm would be sustained. During her year-long internship in a first grade classroom, she continued to develop the Web site she developed during our course into a professional portfolio, and she found ways to integrate technology into her teaching of social studies and language arts. She explained,

[In language arts] the students wrote an acrostic poem and then we took those poems into the computer lab and they had to use Kids Pix to illustrate the background and then we pasted the poem on top of it. [In social studies] we were learning about Stanleys all around the world and I was teaching about families in France and the culture in France and so we pulled up Internet sites and showed the Eiffel Tower and you could take a walk through the Louvre and see different pictures in the Louvre. (Miranda, Interview #2)

More recently, we received an e-mail message from her letting us know how excited she was, as a first-year teacher, to create a PowerPoint presentation of her class to show at an open house and to help her colleagues do the same. She commented that if it had not been for our class, she would not have known how to do that. Her current Web page showcases her professional learning regarding the teaching of diverse learners, standards-based curriculum development, technology in the classroom, classroom management, professional development, and fostering home-school connections.

It appears that our teacher education course and related classroom experiences started Miranda on a path of thinking seriously about the potential of technology to support her professional work in and out of the classroom. At the same time, we are struck by how much we have to learn about the work that we set out to do. We have been designing and redesigning our team-taught methods course for the past 4 years to figure out how to address a key pedagogical issue in teacher education: *How can we embed meaningful uses of technology within course offerings and school-based field work such that teacher candidates learn to use technology in support of their own professional learning and in support of the learning of elementary students?* In today's world where advances in technology are taking place faster than most of us are able to keep up with or even imagine, a second question emerges that is of equal importance: *How can we design our instruction to push teacher candidates to think forward to technology's uses in tomorrow's world while their current experiences are limited to today's knowledge?* That is, we want our students to develop the capacity to make wise and sensible choices in the future for technologies that do not yet exist (International Society for Technology in Education [ISTE], 1999; National Council for Accreditation of Teacher Education [NCATE], 1997).

This chapter describes a 4-year design process focused on infusing technology into a fall semester senior-level teacher education methods course that is situated in a teacher education program where a separate technology course is not offered. Upon formal acceptance into the Michigan State University Teacher Preparation Program in their junior year, students enroll in a course titled Learners and Learning. In the authors' teacher preparation team, this course focuses on classroom management and lesson planning, and has students in the field classroom about 2 hours per week. During their senior year, students take block methods courses in literacy and math, and science and social studies, while also spending about 4 hours per week in classrooms. During the postbaccalaureate internship year, novices work with collaborating teachers in classrooms 4-5 days per week. Simultaneously they take two master's-level courses per semester that continue to support them in planning and teaching in the four subject matters emphasized in earlier courses. These courses also emphasize inquiry and professional roles.

As we saw it, the design problem for our senior-level methods course was to develop specific tasks and assignments that were intended to support our students' professional learning within the course and to enable them to try out and critically appraise pedagogical uses in elementary classrooms. During Year 1, with modest support from an Eisenhower grant, we worked with teachers in three schools to agree on appropriate field assignments and provided professional development in using technology. During Year 2 we had support from a Preparing Tomorrow's Teachers to Use Technology (PT3) project funded by the U.S. Department of Education. We provided more intensive professional development to teachers in two schools where our seniors did their fieldwork and collected data to document our students' learning. During all 4 years, Michigan State University's College of Education provided each of our students with a well-equipped laptop computer that they continued using during that academic year and throughout their year-long internship, and the Office of Teaching and Technology provided on-demand technical support for our students.

Even with that support, along with careful and systematic attention to the design process, it is still complicated to understand the professional learning that occurs when technology is present in university classrooms or in schools. As Wenger (1998) so aptly reminded us, "*Learning cannot be designed*: it can only be designed *for*—that is, facilitated or frustrated" (p. 229, emphasis in original). Our design process was iterative, where "each move is a local experiment that contributes to the global experiment of reframing the problem" and "a reflective conversation with the situation" (Schon, 1987, pp. 57-58). Our understanding of key pedagogical issues, tensions, and questions deepened as we reflected on each semester's approach to the technology infusion issue. Design, as Wenger (1998) described it, is "a systematic, planned, and reflexive colonization of time and space in the service of an undertaking" (p. 228). We engaged in cycles of inquiry where we tried out various approaches to infusing technology into our course, documented and analyzed our students' experiences and learning, reflected on what we learned, and made further adjustments in the course (Elliott, 1991; Oja & Smulyan, 1989).

The three questions that guided our design process also provide the organization for this chapter:

- What are teacher candidates learning about the potential (and constraints) of technology to support their professional learning and the learning of the students in the elementary classroom?
- How does student learning guide the design process?
- What can be learned about technology infusion in teacher education from the design process?

We begin with a brief portrait of ways our students used technology to support professional and classroom-based learning. Then, we describe how explicit attention paid to designing *for* teacher candidates' learning informed the course development process over a 4-year period. We discuss the general principles and conceptual frameworks that guided our planning decisions as well as how students' experiences and feedback on their learning influenced our course design. We conclude by highlighting what we have learned from the design process about infusing technology in a teacher education methods course.

LEARNING ABOUT THE POTENTIAL AND
CONSTRAINTS OF TECHNOLOGY

The fast-paced development of an exciting and complex array of technologies provides both opportunities and challenges for teacher educators who are responsible for preparing teachers for today's and tomorrow's world. Bruce and Levin (1997) refer to technologies as "media" to place an emphasis on the learner, on learning processes, and the capacity of technology to connect learners to other people, other technologies, and the world. Burbules and Callister (2000) argued that technology is more than a conduit for information or a tool. They explained that technologies create "an environment—a space, a cyberspace—in which human interactions happen" (p. 4) and our relationship with technology is two-way, in that as we interact with it, it has the potential to change us. When a technology environment is infused into a teacher education course, certain "affordances for the negotiation of meaning" (Wenger, 1998, p. 229) become available to the teacher educator and her students.

Thus, our design process began with a vision of providing a balance between structured opportunities for exposure to technologies, and choices regarding when and how technologies would be used in university and classroom settings (Brush et al., 2001; Dawson & Norris, 2000; Morrow et al., 2002; Rademacher et al., 2001; Thomas & Cooper, 2000). We thought students should learn to appraise the potential and constraints of various technologies for fostering meaningful professional and classroom-based learning. Since variation and choice were designed into our course structure, we could not predict exactly which technologies our students would choose to interact with, or the meaning they would derive from their interactions.

We have written elsewhere about our study of one cohort ($n = 26$) regarding increases in our students' basic skills and expansion of technology uses, and we have described examples of our students' technology uses in and out of the classroom (Rosaen & Bird, 2003; Rosaen, Hobson, & Khan, 2003). Below we portray ways in which teacher candidates interacted with technologies that were available to them for professional and classroom uses to provide a context for closer examination of how student learning guided our design process.[2]

Supporting Professional Learning

Windschitle and Sahl (2002) argued that the presence of laptop computers in schools introduces new elements into the educational environment that distinguish them from other environments where desktop computers are pervasive: laptops are portable; they can more easily become students' personal tools; and, "'places and spaces' for learning can become more fluid" (p. 170). We were curious about whether and how our students' ubiquitous access to well-equipped laptops might influence how technology would support their professional learning.

As we might have predicted, the laptops provided an important medium for writing and communication. Students described how the laptops almost became an "appendage" that was with them wherever they went for use in e-mail communication, doing research, and writing papers. Moreover, they began to use the computer for composing, which reduced their workload and, as they worked their way through the revision process, helped them identify the areas in which their thinking changed over the course of the semester. They were changed by their access to and use of the laptop (Burbules & Callister, 2000). As predicted by Windschitle and Sahl (2002), the laptop became their personal and central place to keep everything they needed to do all their coursework, and expanded the "places and spaces" for communication and learning (p. 170).

Many educators have written about the potential of the Internet to connect users to information, technologies, and people outside the regular classroom (e.g., Bitter & Pierson, 1999; Bruce & Levin, 1997; Burbules & Callister, 2000; Burnishke & Monke, 2001; Hird, 2000; Sandholtz, Ringstaff, & Dwyer, 1997; Valdez, McNabb, Foertsch, Anderson, Hawkes, & Raack, 1999; Waugh & Handler, 1997). Our students welcomed opportunities to learn how to access teaching resources via the Internet and appraise their value. While all students were asked to create an organizational structure for a physical teaching resource file, we also suggested they bookmark key language arts and mathematics Web resources and organize an electronic Web-based resource file. Teacher candidates showcased their professional learning on their own Web pages. Many students went beyond course requirements and added their resumes and examples of their professional writing from other courses to their sites, uploaded their bookmarks to their site, made links to Web sites for their K-12 students to access, and made links for their own professional use.

Our learning community was also influenced by the presence of technologies during class, such as laptops equipped with standard productivity software. For example, during the second week of class we asked our students to create "All About Me" PowerPoint presentations to introduce themselves to one another and to the children in their field placement classroom. This prompted many forms of collaboration. They helped one another learn to use the software, and find resources on the Internet. They shared resources and design ideas and provided feedback to their colleagues about the emerging products. They brought in "virtual helpers" by sharing what they learned at home on the weekend from a relative or friend when they returned to class. Teacher candidates helped one another solve technological problems with the laptops and software. Within each cohort, we saw a sense of community blossom and mature, and in follow-up interviews our students described repeatedly how that sense of community continued to evolve as their cohort remained together in the program.

Supporting Learning in the Classroom

Teacher candidates spent 4 hours per week in a field placement classroom. The only assigned use for technology was to use a set of criteria we developed together in class to appraise the assets and limitations of one piece of educational software in language arts or mathematics. Otherwise, students were free to negotiate with their collaborating teachers (CTs) other options to use technology.[3] Across four cohorts, the following additional uses were reported during their senior year:

- software for writing and publishing
- Web-based interactive software
- computer use during center time (educational software)
- digital camera to create class booklets
- digital camera to document class events (field trips)
- newsletters with digital photos
- Internet with students
- electronic pen pal
- lesson presentation using PowerPoint
- PowerPoint to record student ideas (K-W-L chart)
- PowerPoint to prepare for parent conferences
- keyboarding, use of mouse
- electronic portfolio
- preparing teaching materials (assessments, worksheets, play money)

Students also provided support for their collaborating teachers, thus shifting roles regarding who was considered to be an expert or novice. These efforts included: helping a teacher set up and use her e-mail; demonstrating how to put digital photographs into a newsletter; searching the Internet for lesson plans; creating PowerPoint presentations; helping prepare electronic portfolios; and, assisting in evaluating educational software and Web sites.

MAINTAINING A CRITICAL STANCE AND CREATING VISIONS FOR THE FUTURE

While we are quite encouraged to see the variety of classroom technology uses, one of our main concerns throughout the design process has been with the stance our students are developing about technology. We want our students to ask whether and how various technologies afford negotiation of meaningful learning, and found ample evidence that they do think carefully about this issue. Kalie, for example, went into detail about her earthquake miniunit she taught to fourth graders:

> They earned money for the victims. I used a PowerPoint presentation to introduce different aspects of the earth core. I used animated Web sites to show how the earth and faults move. They had paper models that they were working with at the same time.

In this instance, technology brought information into the classroom that might not be available otherwise, and it provided visual images to demonstrate scientific knowledge. At the same time, paper models provided hands-on examples to reinforce what was presented visually.

Alex also raised key questions about meaningful technology uses in the classroom. During his internship he collaborated with a fellow intern to write a proposal to the College of Education. They proposed to create technology-supported educational materials for classroom use and to study the pros and cons of technology implementation in elementary and middle school classrooms. They wanted to understand the practicality and cost effectiveness of technology for classroom teachers. Alex and his colleague were granted the use of a computer projector and other technology needed to create teaching materials. With this additional equipment and software, they used technology to enhance a daily instructional routine, observed the effects of using educational software in the classroom, created PowerPoint presentations for use throughout various units, and created customized games that served as reviews and assessments. After documenting and reflecting on these experiences, Alex maintained the viewpoint that technology must be used only when it has the potential to serve educational goals effectively, and concluded that it must be worth the energy and time required of the teacher.

Like Kalie and Alex, all students we interviewed expressed a desire to remain open to the affordances of technology while also holding a firm commitment only to adopt uses that promote meaningful learning for themselves and their students. Many realized these technologies afford ways to: represent ideas and processes that are hard to represent without technology; provide access to data and content; change the nature of tasks in which students might engage; and, facilitate communication and collaboration with peers and experts (Wallace, 2002). They experienced using technology as media for inquiry, communication, and expression (Bruce & Levin, 1997). These students seemed to be aware that there will always be more to learn.

How Does Student Learning Guide the Design Process?

If technology is something with which users interact and have a relationship, then we also need to recognize that choices about technology "always stand in relation to a whole host of other changing practices and social processes" (Burbules & Callister, 2000, p. 7). That is, the decision to infuse technology into a teacher education course is not independent of factors such as broader decisions about the course (e.g., its content, activities, participation structures and assignments), the teacher preparation program, and the university context in which the program is situated. Moreover, our design process needed to be guided by the realization that, "what is most 'new' may not be the technology, the thing itself, but a whole host of other changes that accompany it" (Burbules & Callister, 2000, p. 7).

In this section we describe the context of our course within the teacher education program and explain our understanding of our obligations and commitments. Next, we discuss enabling conditions for using technology and two conceptual frameworks that guided our course development. Finally, we discuss principles that guided our design process and explain the progression of course developments across four semesters.

UNDERSTANDING OUR OBLIGATIONS AND COMMITMENTS

Our design arose from the Michigan State University (MSU) faculty decision to infuse technology into existing courses instead of offering a separate course, so that technology could be linked with the substance of the program (Gillingham & Topper, 1999). The majority of students came to our senior-level with prior technology experience during their junior year course in four areas: basic uses of e-mail; book marking Internet Web sites; basic features of word processing; and, the creation of a database that the candidate designed to organize and work with text from the professional literature (Rosaen & Bird, 2003). Senior-level course instructors were responsible for creating opportunities for teacher candidates to work with educational software. Therefore, in Year 1 we asked teacher candidates to use and appraise one piece of educational software.

We believed that we had a broader obligation also to provide structures, guidance, and support to our students in learning to use technology for professional and teaching purposes (ISTE, 1999; Morrow et al., 2002; NCATE, 1997; Thomas & Cooper, 2000). Teacher candidates needed opportunities to consider whether and how technology affords opportunities to construct understandings and develop necessary skills associated with standards-based development of curriculum, teaching, and assessment in mathematics (National Council of Teachers of Mathematics [NCTM], 1991 and 2000) and English language Arts (National Council of Teachers of English & International Reading Association [NCTE/IRA], 1996).

KEY ENABLING CONDITIONS FOR SUCCESSFUL TECHNOLOGY INFUSION

Technology uses necessarily develop in context. Throughout the design process, we paid attention to three key *enabling conditions* (Dewey, 1938) for successful technology infusion: enhancing our own technology knowledge; enhancing collaborating teachers' knowledge of professional and classroom uses of technology; and garnering teacher education program resources and support.

Enhancing our own technology knowledge. Given our belief that we should do more than simply assign our students to fulfill a specified technology requirement, each of us set out to learn about the affordances and constraints of technology in teacher education. We also wanted to explore how we might create a "community of practice" that could span the boundaries of the university and the schools in which seniors do field assignments in our methods course.

The second author (Sharon) took a course in 2000 that was designed to help graduate students begin exploring ways in which they could use the World Wide Web and other technologies in teaching. Sharon developed her own Web page and started to upload the syllabi, assignments, and other relevant class materials to her Web site for the classes that she taught. She also began to link relevant mathematics sites to her page to increase her efficiency and the efficiency of her students.

In the spring of 1999, Cheryl took an educational technology course that was offered by the College of Education to support "design teams" comprised of faculty and graduate students to explore educational uses of technology in teacher education.[4] This course provided her with a laptop computer and introduced applications such as PowerPoint, basic Web page design, and use of the digital camera. It also provided a context for exploring ways to create a "community of practice" among teacher candidates, the course instructors, and collaborating teachers with whom teacher candidates work in schools.

Enhancing collaborating teachers' knowledge of professional and classroom uses of technology.   Our work began with 15 collaborating teachers (CTs) in three schools during the summer of 1999. We shared what was happening with technology in each building, identified technological challenges within each school site, and tried out some field assignments that were closely connected to the classroom curriculum and the content of our course. During the next 2 years, two graduate assistants collaborated in the design process, provided technical support to classroom teachers, and documented teachers' and teacher candidates' perceptions of their learning. Classroom teachers had reallocated time to participate in professional development and work with us. Our approach to working with approximately 15 CTs in two buildings included three components.[5]

First, course assignments were agreed upon with collaborating teachers to increase the likelihood that technology uses were authentic and connected to the classroom curriculum (e.g., drafting and sharing lesson plans; using the Internet to find high quality teaching resources; use of PowerPoint presentations; appraisal of educational software; assisting in using a variety of technologies). Second, a graduate assistant offered weekly "on demand" professional development to assist CTs in solving technical and classroom-based pedagogical problems. Third, seniors shared what they were learning about technology with their CTs and assisted them in creating special projects such as PowerPoint presentations for use at parent conferences. CTs learned to use technology for a variety of pedagogical uses (e.g., educational software; use of Internet with students; digital camera; scanner) and professional uses (e.g., use of Internet for resources and lesson ideas; use of software to create newsletters; use of e-mail).

Garnering teacher education program resources and support.   Just as it was essential to build capacity within the schools, we found it essential to assure our own resources on campus. Each fall cohort was equipped with laptop computers to provide access to technology within and outside our classroom. Nevertheless, during Year 1 we had to use a computer lab that was equipped with desktop computers to access the Internet because we did not have a way for all students to access the Internet with their laptops within our regular classroom. By Year 3 the College equipped the classroom in which we taught with Internet access for 20 computers. Even with such efforts, we have experienced times when all students could not access the Internet simultaneously for in-class Web page development. Over the 4-year span, we have found it essential to work, in advance, with our technology support people in MSU's Office of Teaching and Technology, to assure that all equipment is in good working order and that adequate support is provided to our students for problem solving and troubleshooting.

CONCEPTUAL FRAMEWORKS THAT GUIDE INFUSION

The design of any course must be guided by key concepts and ideas that are organized within clear conceptual frameworks so as to lend clarity and coherence to its content and methods. Two frameworks were especially helpful in guiding our thinking about technology infusion.

Subject matter framework. We articulated a common framework that allows us to compare and contrast language arts and mathematics learning goals: content, processes, and attitude goals.[6] Content goals include the knowledge, concepts, and information associated with mathematics (e.g., knowledge of number and operation, geometry, measurement) and English language arts content (e.g., knowledge of literary genres, literary elements, and knowledge of the grammar of the English language). Process goals in mathematics include communication, problem solving, reasoning and proof, making connections, and representation. The language arts—reading, writing, speaking, listening and viewing—are processes in which learners engage to make sense of the world around them and are foundational to learning in all subject matters (Pearson, 2001). Critical thinking and reasoning are core processes for making sense of oral, visual, and written texts. Attitudes in either subject matter might include such things as enjoyment, motivation to learn, perseverance, flexibility, or the willingness to take risks.

This subject matter framework organizes our discussion of how the *Michigan Curriculum Framework* (Michigan Department of Education, 1996) guides curriculum development, teaching, and assessment in local schools. In addition, it guides our students' development of learning goals during the lesson planning process. It also allows our students to explore themselves as learners in math and English/language arts. Moreover, when technology enters the picture as a resource, as a medium for communication, or as an environment or a space in which human interactions take place, the subject matter framework allows us to locate what sort of subject-specific learning it does or does not afford. For instance, when looking at an example of educational software in mathematics, teacher candidates are encouraged to ask not only whether the software is entertaining or keeps students' attention, but which mathematical content (e.g., core concepts) and processes (e.g., problem solving, reasoning, communication) are represented. If technology-driven exercises only ask children to provide answers to problems without delving into conceptual understanding or mathematical processes, teacher candidates are encouraged to identify those limitations.

Professional learning framework.   We also aim to promote a range of professional processes and habits that are likely to support teacher candidates when engaging in immediate and long-term goal-directed learning.[7] We want our students to engage in: disciplined curiosity about teaching, learning, and their contexts; thoughtful goal setting; deliberate acquisition and application of knowledge and skills; generating and demonstrating new knowledge with colleagues; and, engaging in self-assessment. Many teacher educators have begun to think of professional processes and habits as being achieved partly through portfolio processes (Rosaen, Hobson, & Kahn, 2003). In our course syllabus, we made explicit how each assignment is an opportunity to work toward: (a) our teacher preparation program standards;[8] (b) satisfying the program's technology requirements; and, (c) engagement in portfolio processes.

DESIGNING AND REDESIGNING FOR MEANINGFUL INFUSION

As described above, we interpreted our design problem as that of developing specific tasks and assignments that were intended to support our students' professional learning within the course and to enable them to try out and critically appraise pedagogical uses in elementary classrooms. First and foremost, we wanted to model principles of good teaching in the way we designed, taught, and redesigned the course.

Creating authentic tasks.   We tried to create tasks that were focused, purposeful, and authentic so our students would be involved in the real work that teachers do for professional development, and preparing for and teaching in the classroom. For example, creating an "All About Me" PowerPoint presentation had several purposes. As teacher candidates used their presentation to introduce themselves to the children in the classroom, they began to understand it as a powerful medium for interactive communication. At the same time, our students also learned to use the software, discovered its capabilities, and began to take advantage of other technologies to create presentations.

Exploration, immersion, and collaboration for learning.   We thought of learning to use software such as PowerPoint as similar to learning to write within a writer's workshop (Calkins, 1994). We promoted free exploration of PowerPoint as a communication medium, immersion in learning its use, and collaboration in teaching one another how to use it. Students quickly taught one another that they could find Internet resources such as images, graphics, and sound effects to include in their presentations. Some learned to use the digital camera so they could insert photographs. One student wrote her philosophy statement using PowerPoint and inserted video clips of herself discussing key ideas. She also included digital photos of working in her field placement classroom with an ESL student, where they were using PowerPoint as a language experience activity (Tompkins, 2003). Other students began to use PowerPoint in a variety of ways in their classroom as they developed and taught other units during the spring semester. Students built upon what they learned from that beginning exposure and constructed their own professional and classroom uses.

Building the professional learning community.   As described earlier, our approach to introducing and working with PowerPoint helped build our professional learning community. We learned about each other's background, interests, and goals through sharing the PowerPoint presentations during class. As students shifted from being a novice in one area to being an expert in another, they began to understand more deeply the power of collaborative learning. Knowing our students and helping them know one another are critical elements of building a professional learning community.

Modeling technology uses and ongoing learning.   We modeled various uses of technology, and participated as fellow learners of technology in the process. Few of our students came to the course with knowledge of how to construct a Web page, and even those who did had limited exposure to its potential for supporting their professional learning. In 2000, we, too, had limited experience in Web page design and construction, so we were open about our limited knowledge and our attempts to learn more. We presented some sample Web sites that could provide images of how a professional might use a Web site as a resource file, including one that Sharon had recently created. All students were taught the basics of developing a web page that could become an electronic resource file. Simultaneously, we required our students to create a resource file with which they were more familiar—a physical file where they could organize and store teaching resources and materials. We offered the option of helping them further develop their web page as an electronic resource file. This was a voluntary design opportunity that did not specify an exact product, because we assumed that we could learn more from seeing what our students could create than from assigning a product that might be limited by our own knowledge or vision.

Adopting a critical stance.   We also modeled a critical stance toward the use of teaching approaches and resources, including technology. Key questions about how any resource supports meaningful learning were embedded throughout our course. We used specific criteria for making decisions about the use of high quality children's literature, authentic reading and writing tasks, meaningful mathematical tasks, and the promotion of problem solving and critical thinking (Tompkins, 2003; Van de Walle, 2000). Our class developed criteria for appraising educational software, taking into account the instructional importance of the program, the subject matter content emphasized, its ease of use, the type of interaction promoted, motivational aspects, and how adaptable it is to a range of students.

Using student feedback to redesign.   Finally, we asked our students to provide written feedback about the usefulness of tasks and assignments in supporting their learning and we also learned a great deal from follow-up interviews (see Rosaen & Bird, 2003; Rosaen, Hobson, & Khan, 2003, for more details). Student feedback from one semester was used to redesign assignments for subsequent semesters. For example, based on student feedback and questions, we began to offer more structured introductory sessions during laptop distribution. Several of the benefits of the "All About Me" project were articulated by our students, so we continued to assign that introductory project.

We were particularly curious, and cautious, about how to proceed with Web page development. We wanted it to become a valuable and meaningful support for our students' professional learning, and therefore thought we should let them take the lead and show us what was possible to achieve. In Year 2 we showed sample Web pages created by practicing professionals and offered support in helping our students create one, but we did not make Web page development a requirement. During interviews of seniors from the Year 2 cohort, we showed a Web page created by one student, Miranda (who was introduced at the beginning of this chapter) and asked them if they thought we should require students in subsequent semesters to create one. They overwhelmingly said we should, as long as we built in support along the way. That feedback encouraged us to require the Year 3 cohort to develop a Web site organized around the course goals. We also required them to "showcase" one aspect of their learning on one of their linked pages to get them started in thinking about how they might represent their professional learning in an electronic portfolio. By Year 4, based on continuing feedback, we maintained that requirement, and found ways to further scaffold the Web page development across the semester. Meanwhile, we were also collecting a rich set of sample Web sites that could be used as examples in subsequent semesters. In addition, we began to use our own course Web site to document many of our class events with digital photos so those would be available to our students to help them showcase their learning.

Student comments from the Year 1 and Year 2 cohorts about the limited access of high quality educational software at the school sites prompted us in Year 3 to provide a list of URLs (uniform resource locators) where students could search and download examples to use for their software appraisals. We also asked students to bring their laptops to class and to discuss the qualities of their educational software. Student comments helped us realize that they learned as much from viewing their colleagues' software as they learned from using their own, so we reserved more time in Year 4 for sharing and discussion.

There were other ways in which our technology uses progressed in response to student feedback. In the first 3 years we primarily used e-mail as a means to communicate with our students. By the fourth year, we began to send students electronic versions of their assignments to complete (e.g., analysis of lessons taught; educational software appraisal) and return to us electronically. By the third year we used a course Web site to post our syllabus and major assignments. In the fourth year we added photos and links to provide access to PDF files of lengthy documents such as a class book of poetry. We organized several of our assignments (e.g., lesson planning, drafting and revising philosophy statements, poetry writing) to require use of the laptops in and out of class. Our intent was to encourage our students to move from using word processing only to type a final product from drafts that were written by hand, to using the affordances of word processing (cutting, pasting, copying, creating tables, and charts) to represent and develop their ideas throughout the writing process. We have found that as our own uses of technology have increased-through modeling and through what we ask our students to do it has become increasingly feasible to ask our students to do more (Kinslow, Newcombe, & Goss, 2002; Rosaen, 2005).

Teacher Educators Learning About Technology Infusion

Throughout the design process, we also have changed and grown. We share some of our insights to bring this chapter to a close and to suggest that the technology integration process is never finished.

TECHNOLOGY INTEGRATION REQUIRES TIME AND ORGANIZATION

Our iterative design process required regular, ongoing collaborative activities. We planned during summers to make major decisions about course organization, content, and assignments. Throughout each semester we exchanged electronic drafts of assignments, communicated regularly over e-mail, and planned together. We engaged in ongoing reflective conversations, shared information we learned about our students with one another, raised questions, and offered comments about how we thought things were going. Considerable time was spent between semesters analyzing student feedback and figuring out how to use that feedback to head in new directions during subsequent semesters. We also found ourselves pushing one another to step out of our comfort zones and provided mutual support to take risks and try new ideas. While some may question whether this type of collaborative work is worth it, we think the leverage gained by working together far outweighs the time and energy expended. The feedback from our students affirms our thinking. From the Year 2 interviews, we found that nearly all of the 13 students interviewed initiated a comment about our collaboration, such as, "I think that a lot of [my own learning in our class] is the collaboration that you [Sharon] and Cheryl have. It is non-stop. We can't tell where Cheryl stops and Sharon begins, besides the subject matter." Even 1 year later, Miranda said,

> I really liked the way that you and Cheryl started off together, that is the first that I had ever had of a class where two teachers were teaching together and I really liked seeing that, especially because that is what goes on in innovative, great classrooms outside the college level. (Miranda, Interview #2)

TECHNOLOGY INTEGRATION FOLLOWS PRINCIPLES OF TEACHING AND LEARNING

Maintaining a focus on key principles prevents technology from driving course content and organization. Most importantly, technology infusion has helped us know our students in ways that we have not attained before and, therefore, helps us to be increasingly responsive to their learning needs. We asked our students to join us in exploring the affordances and constraints of technology, in expanding the "places and spaces" for communication and learning (Windschitle & Sahl, 2002, p. 170) in the context of two different subject matters. Each teacher candidate brings different combinations of strengths and areas needing further work in mathematics and English/language arts and each brings different ideas about the roles technology can play in supporting professional and classroom-based learning. Collaborative exploration provides occasions to make explicit how each of us can be novices, experts, or somewhere in-between, depending on the learning context.

TECHNOLOGY INTEGRATION IS GUIDED BY CONCEPTUAL FRAMEWORKS

We are continuing to clarify and refine our guiding conceptual frameworks used to organize our course. For example, how might we place technology more explicitly within our subject matter framework? Should we treat technology as yet a third subject matter that has its own content, process and attitude goals? Or does technology become one of the "processes" within mathematics and English/language arts? Alternatively, should we expand the three types of learning goals in our subject matter framework (content, processes, and attitude) to include technology as a fourth learning goal? What's more, if technology is more than a tool, and instead conceived of as various forms of media (Bruce & Levin, 1997), or an environment in which human interactions happen (Burbules & Callister, 2000), where does it belong within our professional learning framework? These are questions we are addressing as we plan for subsequent semesters.

TECHNOLOGY INTEGRATION DEEPENS OUR UNDERSTANDING OF TECHNOLOGY

Our conception of what technology is, can be, and should be has grown and changed throughout the design process. The language we used earlier in the design process (e.g., thinking of technology as a learning tool) revealed the limitations of our initial understanding. Fortunately, we began the design process with an openness to what we could learn about it and from it. In those early days we were not able to articulate that we were entering into a *relationship with* technology, or anticipate how technologies might *change us*. We entered with relatively narrow views of the affordances of certain technologies and did not anticipate their full malleability (Mishra & Koehler, 2003). Our students, through their own design work, have helped us learn about uses that we had not thought of ourselves. Moreover, we did not enter this collaborative work with a clear view of the full range of what there is to be learned about technology—for example, how important it is to prepare teacher candidates to think forward to technology uses in tomorrow's world while their (and our) current experiences are limited to today's knowledge.

TECHNOLOGY INTEGRATION HAS INTENDED AND UNINTENDED CONSEQUENCES

We are learning from the challenges we continue to face as well. Our course has a highly complex structure that places demands on our students to juggle multiple requirements at one time. Some feel overwhelmed enough without adding the demands of learning to use various technologies. We must question whether new ideas for embedding technology within the course will actually enhance learning. For example, our university is adopting a new Web-based technology for course management that seems to have some attractive features. If we invest in making all of our course materials accessible through this new technology, will the demands of using it overwhelm our course content or be perceived as efficient and helpful?

TECHNOLOGY INTEGRATION REQUIRES KEY ENABLING CONDITIONS

Our college provides an array of resources and support structures for such efforts, but it is challenging to find the time to stay current about the latest technological advancements. As technology uses become more embedded in our own and our colleagues' courses, there is a greater demand for computer facilities and well-equipped classrooms that were once easy to reserve. There is increased wear and tear on hardware, and sometimes we cannot count on specific resources being available on the day and time we need.

Additionally, there has been less collaboration and interactive dialogue among CTs and teacher candidates than we envisioned. More development work is needed to foster a culture of collaboration and reciprocity, where teacher candidates and CTs work together to use and appraise technology and to think critically about meaningful technology integration into the K-5 curriculum (Rosaen, Hobson, & Khan, 2003). Complicating matters, the CTs who use technologies in schools continue to face challenges with maintaining reliable access to the technologies they are learning to use. Some CTs who wished to work with seniors were not invested in learning to use technology, and some did not attend any workshops, even when they could do so during regular school hours. It has been difficult to maintain a stable group of CTs whose knowledge of and skill in using technology for pedagogical and professional purposes might grow and deepen over time.

TECHNOLOGY INTEGRATION REQUIRES ONGOING EXPLORATION

These challenges notwithstanding, we are eager to continue to try to design for learning—to figure out whether and how technology might enhance our teacher candidates' and K-5 students' opportunities to learn. By bringing together what we have learned about our students' learning, enabling conditions for successful infusion, conceptual frameworks that guide infusion, and principles that guide our design of the course, we look forward to future design processes. We agree with our former student, Miranda, that technology is incredible, and we know there are so many more ways to use it. We, too, want to keep exploring.

Design Challenges for Infusing Technology in Teacher Education

This detailed examination of one pair of instructor's experiences with technology infusion points out some longstanding challenges that all educators face when they attempt to design integrated curriculum. First and foremost, when integrating technology or any combination of subject matters, they should be relevant to the overall educational goals for a course or program and not merely included as an add on (Alleman & Brophy, 1993; Jacobs, 1989; Lapp & Flood, 1994). That is, there is a delicate balance to be achieved, and as our work shows, the use of conceptual frameworks and principles of teaching and learning can help educators make focused decisions regarding what to include (or not). Second, technology integration requires equal attention to content and processes (Pearson, 1994), especially because some subject matters such as language arts are process oriented. Along similar lines, Reinking (1995) and Labbo and Reinking (1999) argue for a convergence in how we conceive of technology and literacy. They suggest that technology should not be considered as a topic because,

> considering technology merely as a topic belies the breadth of literacy issues affected by new technologies, its increasing influence in daily literate activity, and the wide range of unprecedented questions of research and practice it generates, let alone the conventional questions and issues it threatens to make moot. (Labbo & Reinking, 1995, p. 479; Reinking, 1995)

As our story shows, our understanding of technology expanded from viewing it as a tool, to understanding it as an environment for communication and inquiry and these new insights enabled us to think in more complex ways about what technology integration means. Finally, our experiences highlight the human and organizational factors associated with technology infusion. Without a commitment of time and effort on our parts and on the part of the College of Education, we would not have been able to offer rich learning opportunities for our teacher candidates. Thus, technology integration is not a solitary endeavor, but rather a complex social design process that must be examined and improved continually as technologies themselves become transformed and afford new possibilities.

NOTES

1. Pseudonyms are used when referring to all students.
2. We are drawing from 19 follow-up interviews (11 from cohort 2 and 8 from cohort 3) to develop this description.
3. This negotiation included the opportunity to share their "All About Me" presentation with the class. In some cases this was not possible because the collaborating teacher did not have technology available to project the display for the class to see. In other cases, teachers found innovative ways to accomplish the display such as placing the laptop on a chair so all students could see the computer screen. See Rosaen, Hobson, and Khan (2003) for a discussion of successes and challenges associated with our attempts to support collaborating teachers in their learning to use technology with the intent to eventually provide technology-rich classroom environments for teacher candidates' field experiences.
4. Although the 1999 version of this course is not discussed specifically in Mishra and Koehler (2003), the "learning by design" approach is described, and the organization of the 1999 course was similar to the description for Case I in the chapter.
5. See Rosaen, Hobson, and Khan (2003) for a more detailed discussion of our collaborative approach to working with collaborating teachers and their learning.
6. This subject matter framework is discussed in Rosaen, Schram, and Herbel-Eisenmann (2002) and draws upon work done by Cantlon (1994) and national standards in mathematics (NCTM, 1991 and 2000) and English/language arts (NCTE/IRA, 1996).

7. This conceptual framework was piloted initially in our course and during the internship year to guide interns' portfolio development. It draws heavily upon the work of Lyons (1998) and Wilcox and Tomei's (1999) *Professional Portfolios for Teachers* and on some of our own work (Bird, 1990; Rosaen, 2002). It is discussed in more detail in Rosaen and Bird (2003).

8. MSU's Program Standards are organized around four categories: (1) knowing subject matters and how to teach them; (2) working with students; (3) creating and managing a classroom learning community; and (4) working and learning in a school and profession.

REFERENCES

Alleman, J., & Brophy, J. (1993). Is curriculum integration a boom or a threat to social studies? *Social Education, 57*(6), 287-291.

Bird, T. (1990). The schoolteacher's portfolio: An essay on possibilities. In J. Millman & L. Darling-Hammond (Eds.), *Handbook of teacher evaluation: Elementary and secondary personnel* (2nd ed., pp. 241-256). Beverly Hills, CA: Sage.

Bitter, G., & Pierson, M. (1999). *Using Technology in the Classroom*. Needham Heights, MA: Allyn & Bacon.

Bruce, B. C., & Levin, J. (1997). Educational technology: Media for inquiry, communication, construction, and expression. *Journal of Educational Computing Research, 17*(1), 79-102.

Brush, T., Igoe, A., Brinkerhoff, J., Glazewski, K., Ky, H., & Smith, C. (2001). Lessons from the field: Integrating technology into preservice teacher education. *Journal of Computing in Teacher Education, 17*(4), 16-20.

Burbules, N. C., & Callister, T. A. (2000). *Watch IT: The risks and promises of information technologies for education*. Boulder, CO: Westview Press.

Burniske, R. W., & Monke, L. (2001). *Breaking Down the digital walls: Learning to Teach in a post-modem world*. Albany: State University of New York Press.

Cantlon, D. (1994). Toward authentic assessment: Philosophy and Tools. In P. Schram (Ed.), *Nurturing the freedom to wonder: Vignettes from elementary mathematics classrooms* (pp. 93-119). Lansing: Michigan Council of Teachers of Mathematics.

Calkins, L. (1994). *The art of teaching writing*. Portsmouth, NH: Heinemann.

Dawson, K., & Norris, A. (2000). Preservice teachers' experiences in a K-12/university technology-based field initiative: Benefits, facilitators, constraints, and implications for teacher educators. *Journal of Computing in Teacher Education, 17*(1), 4-12.

Dewey, J. (1938). *Experience and education*. New York: Macmillan.

Elliott, J. (1991). *Action research for educational change*. Philadelphia: Open University Press.

Gillingham, M. G., & Topper, A. (1999). Technology in teacher preparation: Preparing teachers for the future. *Journal of Technology and Teacher Education, 7*, 303-321.

Hird, A. (2000). *Learning from cyber-savvy students: How Internet-age kids impact classroom teaching.* Sterling, VA: Stylus.

International Society for Technology in Education. (1999). *National educational technology standards for students: Connecting curriculum and technology.* Eugene, OR: Author.

Jacobs, H. H. (1989). The growing need for interdisciplinary curriculum content. In H. H. Jacobs (Ed.), *Interdisciplinary curriculum: Design and implementation* (pp. 1-12). Alexandria, VA: Association for Supervision and Curriculum Development.

Kinslow J., Goss, M., & Newcombe, E. (2002). Forming a cadre of learners: Effective educational technology integration in a teacher preparation program. *Journal of Computing in Teacher Education, 18*(3), 81-86.

Labbo, L. D., & Reinking, D. (1999). Theory and research into practice: Negotiating the multiple realities of technology in literacy research and instruction. *Reading Research Quarterly, 34*(4), 478-492.

Lapp, D., & Flood, J. (1994). Integrating the curriculum: First steps. *The Reading Teacher, 47*(5), 416-419.

Lyons, N. (1998). Reflection in teaching: Can it be developmental? A portfolio perspective. *Teacher Education Quarterly, 25*(1), 115-127.

Michigan Department of Education. (1996). *Michigan Curriculum Framework.* Lansing: Author.

Mishra, P., & Koehler, M. J. (2003). Becoming design wise: Going from the "what" to the "why" of learning educational technology. In Y. Zhao (Ed.), *What teachers should know about technology: Perspectives and practices* (pp. 99-122). Greenwich, CT: Information Age Publishing.

Morrow, L. M., Barnhart, S., & Rooyakkers, D. (2002). Integrating technology with the teaching of an early literacy course. *The Reading Teacher, 56*(3), 218-230.

National Council for Accreditation of Teacher Education. (1997). *Technology and the new professional teacher: Preparing for the 21st century classroom.* Washington, DC: Author.

National Council of Teachers of English and International Reading Association (1996). *Standards for the English language arts.* Urbana, IL: Author.

National Council of Teachers of Mathematics. (1991). *Professional standards for teaching mathematics.* Reston, VA: Author.

National Council of Teachers of Mathematics. (2000). *Principles and Standards for School Mathematics.* Reston, VA: Author.

Oja, S., & Smulyan, L. (1989). *Collaborative action research: A developmental approach.* New York: The Falmer Press.

Pearson, P. D. (1994). Integrated language arts: Sources of controversy and seeds of consensus. In L. M. Morrow, J. K. Smith, & L. C. Wilkinson (Eds.), *Integrated language arts: Controversy to consensus* (pp. 11-31). Needham Heights, MA: Allyn & Bacon.

Pearson, P. D. (2001). Learning to teach reading: The status of the knowledge base. In C. M. Roller (Ed.), *Learning to teach reading: Setting the research agenda* (pp. 4-19). Newark, DE: International Reading Association.

Rademacher, J., Tyler-Wood, T., Doclar, J., & Pemberton, J. (2001). Developing learner-centered technology assignments with student teachers. *Journal of Computing in Teacher Education, 17*(3), 18-25.

Reinking, D. (1995). Reading and writing with computers: Literacy research in a post-typographic world. In K. A. Hinchman, D. J. Leu, & C.K. Kinzer (Eds.), *Perspectives on literacy research and practice: 44th Yearbook of the National Reading Conference* (pp. 17-34). Chicago: National Reading Conference.

Rosaen, C. (Ed). (2002). *Guide to the elementary internship, 2002-03: Teacher Preparation Team Two.* East Lansing: Michigan State University.

Rosaen, C. L. (2005). Teacher educators' interactions with technology: How does it change us? In S. Rhine & M. Bailey (Eds.), *Transforming learning through technology: Insights and achievements of the Preparing tomorrow's teachers to use technology program* (pp. 103-114). Washington, DC: International Society for Technology in Education.

Rosaen, C. L., & Bird, T. (2003). Technology-supported portfolio processes designed to promote learning in a teacher preparation program. In Y. Zhao, W. Heneke, & K. Knestis (Eds.), *What should teachers know about technology: Perspectives and practices* (pp. 75-97). Greenwich CT: Information Age Publishing.

Rosaen, C. L., Hobson, S., & Khan, G. (2003). Making connections: Collaborative approaches to preparing today's and tomorrow's teachers to use technology. *Journal of Technology and Teacher Education, 11*(2), 139-172.

Rosaen, C. L., Schram, P., & Herbel-Eisenmann, B. (2002). Using technology to explore connections among mathematics, language and literacy. *Contemporary Issues in Technology and Teacher Education, 2*(3). Retrieved July 20, 2006, from http://www.citejournal.org/vol2/iss3/mathematics/article1.cfm

Sandholtz, J, Ringstaff, C., & Dwyer, D. (1997). *Teaching with technology: Creating student-centered classrooms.* New York: Teachers College Press.

Schon, D. (1987). *Educating the reflective practitioner: Toward a new design for teaching and learning in the professions.* San Francisco: Jossey-Bass.

Thomas, J. A., & Cooper, S. B. (2000). Teaching technology: A new opportunity for pioneers in teacher education. *Journal of Computing in Teacher Education, 17*(1), 13 - 19.

Tompkins, G. (2003). *Literacy for the 21st century* (3rd ed.). Upper Saddle River, NJ: Merrill Prentice Hall.

Valdez, G., McNabb, M., Foertsch, M., Anderson, M., Hawkes, M., & Raack, L. (1999). *Computer-based technology and learning: Evolving uses and expectations.* Chicago and Naperville, IL: North Central Regional Educational Laboratory.

Van de Wall, J. (2000). *Elementary and middle school mathematics: Teaching developmentally* (4th ed.). New York: Addison Wesley Longman.

Wallace, R. M. (2002, April). *Teachers and technology: A new kind of knowledge.* Paper presented at the annual meeting of the American Educational Research Association, New Orleans, LA.

Waugh, M., & Handler, M. (1997). Preparing teachers to teach with technology: The costs and benefits of developing an electronic community of learners. In

K. Westbrook (Ed.), *Technology and the educational workplace: Understanding fiscal impacts: Eighteenth annual yearbook of the American Education Finance Association* (pp. 150-174). Thousand Oaks, CA: Corwin Press.

Wenger, E. (1998). *Communities of practice: Learning, meaning, and identity.* Cambridge, MA: Cambridge University Press.

Wilcox, B., & Tomei, L. (1999). *Professional portfolios for teachers: A guide for learners, experts, and scholars.* Norwood, MA: Christopher-Gordon.

Windschitle, M., & Sahl, K. (2002). Tracing teachers' use of technology in a laptop computer school: The interplay of teacher beliefs, social dynamics, and institutional culture. *American Educational Research Journal, 39*(1), 165-205.

CHAPTER 3

ODYSSEY IN TECHNOLOGY

A Quest to Design Interactive Contexts for Exploring Children's Responses to Literature

Laura Apol and Sheri K. Rop

The universe is made of stories, not atoms.

—Muriel Rukeyser

*I haven't a clue as to how my story will end. But that's all right. When you set out on
a journey and night covers the road, you don't conclude that the road has vanished.
And how else could we discover the stars?*

—Unknown

As instructors of literature, we live in the world of story. We feel acutely
the tug of the narrative line, and in recounting our experience of bringing technology into our teacher education courses, we cannot help but
find the story within the task.

There are elements of stories that readers often come to expect: the
problem to be solved; the characters, major and minor; the setting; and
the plot that unfolds (and often within that plot, the crisis or climax, fol-

Faculty Development by Design: Integrating Technology in Higher Education, 49–69
Copyright © 2007 by Information Age Publishing

lowed by the resolution). Most importantly, in any story worth reading, there is the theme—the point to the telling, the insight that can be acquired.

It is a characteristic of stories that they impose order—narrative structure—on what is, in truth, chaotic, messy, recursive, and ill formed. Stories not only *recount* a tale; they *create* a tale through their telling. They remember selectively. They choose intentionally.

Our story is just such an ordering, making sense, after the fact, of a process that was not linear or tidy—a process that often made little sense except in retrospect. We have titled our story "Odyssey in Technology" because our path through the project was, indeed, a long and wandering journey marked by numerous changes of fortune (as well as by changes in our goals, our students, ourselves, and the technologies involved). It is our sense that this odyssey is ongoing; the project we describe is still in progress, and our goals have been realized only in part.

This, then, is the story of our work.

THE PROBLEM

Our project grew directly from our work with children, literature, and preservice teachers in a college of education. Over the years, we had become convinced that children's responses to literature were an important part of the elementary teacher education curriculum. We knew that the literature written for children plays a central role in the elementary school curriculum, and that both existing research and current standards of practice recognize the importance of children's literature response in literacy education (Marshall, 2000; International Reading Association and National Council of Teachers of English [NCTE], 1996; National Center on Education and the Economy and the University of Pittsburgh, 1999). As instructors of children's literature in a teacher education program, we were committed to teaching our students about children's responses to literature. However, as we did so, it became evident to us that many preservice teachers had little understanding of the range, multiplicity, and complexity of responses of which children are capable. This became the goal for our project: to broaden and deepen our students' understanding of children's responses to literature.

At the start of the project, we had taught (and Laura had supervised the teaching of) multiple sections of an undergraduate children's literature course that we had recently developed in the College of Education at Michigan State University. The course, titled "Reading and Responding to Children's Literature," was designed to help preservice teachers become more skilled and thoughtful in their *reading* of children's literature (so they could enable their future students to become better readers of children's literature) and more capable and self-aware in their *responses* to children's literature (so they could elicit and support varied and complex responses from the students they would teach).

Over the years, we had observed that the preservice teachers in our classes found the "Responding" part of the course to be particularly challenging, and over several semesters we had conducted multiple strands of research in these classes to explore the details and implications of our students' struggles. One set of findings from this research revealed that many preservice teachers:

1. had difficulty understanding what constitutes literature response, substituting "activity" or "craft" for literature response, or imagining response solely in terms of personal reaction to a text;
2. rarely recognized that children are capable of anything but the most superficial of responses, and predicted that children would not understand or be interested in texts that are complicated or that call for complex responses; and,
3. exhibited a limited ability to craft instruction that would facilitate children's responses to literature, but rather tended to design instructional activities that had little to do with the literature itself (Apol, Sakuma, Reynolds, & Rop, 2003).

We saw these tendencies played out during in-class literature discussions and in the writings our students did in and outside class, as well as in the response activities our students designed for children around literature (Apol et al., 2003). This limited understanding frequently resulted in flawed beliefs about the importance and role of literature in the curriculum, in poorly conceived decisions about the selection of books to use with children, and in superficial ideas about how to facilitate children's responses to literature.

Early on we recognized that an obvious corrective to our students' limited understandings of children's abilities to respond to literature would be for these students to observe literature response activities with real children in real classrooms. Indeed, we had incorporated into the course a project that involved our students in reading and talking about a book with a small group of elementary students. However, as novices in classroom practice, our students' attention was most often taken up by a range of new experiences (frequently involving "managing" children's behavior), as well as by concerns for carrying out the details of their assignment. As a result, although our students enjoyed the opportunity to read and talk about books with children, this experience did not allow them the opportunity to see the range and depth of literature responses that are possible for children. Providing our students with such a view was not a realistic possibility; a number of barriers, including time, space, transportation issues, and the disruptive nature of many classroom visits precluded real-time observation. In our case, such visits were even more impractical due to the large numbers of students that were involved—there were more than 120 undergraduates across four or five class sections each semester.

Working within that reality, we gradually came to the conclusion that videotape of thoughtful teachers engaging in literature activities in real classrooms would be the best way of providing a model for our students and of supporting our efforts to broaden and deepen their understandings of literature response. Using classroom video in preservice teacher instruction is not a new idea; however, classroom video had not, to our knowledge, been used in connection with the teaching of children's literature, and also had not, to our knowledge, been used (a) to challenge the assumptions about children and literature held by many preservice teachers and (b) to demonstrate for them the remarkable sophistication of children's thinking about literature.

We wanted to provide for our students carefully selected clips of individual children's responses that could serve as examples to help our students identify and discriminate between various types of literature response (personal, textual, and critical).[1] We also wanted to enable our students to view longer and more complex (or even problematic) segments containing multiple response types and ask students to identify, analyze, and reflect on the responses; and we wanted to help our students move their attention beyond children's responses, paying attention to the ways the teacher worked to elicit and support the children's literature responses.

We had several exemplary teachers available to us—teachers who had studied with Laura in graduate courses—and we began to work on the possibilities of such an undertaking. Through a series of fortuitous events, we were able to obtain videotape of selected classroom episodes (about 30 hours of videotape) in a 3-week literature unit crafted and guided by an exceptionally thoughtful and talented teacher working with her second grade class. In this unit, second graders responded to literature by comparing versions of fairy tales in order to identify literary elements and foreground issues of gender, material wealth, and power. They exhibited a range of responses to literature, moving throughout the unit between personal, textual, and critical response.

Once it became clear that we would have videotape available to us, our attention turned to how to design an effective environment for our own students to work with the material. We realized that this task had many elements: identifying central themes and issues; selecting significant and generative episodes and interactions; editing the video segments themselves; creating a technological delivery system that would enable our goal of student interactions with the material; and, designing the educational context in which these interactions would occur. We understood that to work on all these fronts we would need resources we did not at that moment possess—financial, technical, and conceptual support. The Preparing Tomorrow's Teachers for Technology (PT3) grant, with its funding resources, its community approach to technology implementation, and its focus on the intersection between technology and pedagogical content knowledge in the classroom seemed to us to provide a way to supply all those needs. Thus, our real-world teaching problem led us to become part of a PT3 research team.

THE SETTING

It is important to note that even before we formally began our work with PT3, we already had the advantage of a technology-rich and highly supportive setting in which the work was to take place. At all phases of the project, this setting supported us both tangibly and intangibly in multiple ways. First of all, it provided an atmosphere—a culture—in which technology knowledge and exploration was valued and encouraged. The College of Education at Michigan State University (MSU) is fortunate that the Dean, Carole Ames, has valued and promoted technology in education from the beginning of her time at MSU. As a result of Dean Ames' enthusiasm, technology initiatives have enjoyed strong administrative support. Consequently, faculty members and graduate students are engaged in cutting-edge work in the areas of technology and education, contributing to a climate in which technology innovation is an integral, contagious part of the institutional ethos.

Working within this culture, both of us had been involved, formally and informally, with technology initiatives in MSU. We had seen faculty members make presentations on their technology projects and had participated in colloquia and work sessions in which faculty introduced new software designed for specific pedagogical purposes, discussed technology requirements for undergraduate students, or introduced graduate students to technology products that assisted scholarly work. In addition, Laura was participating in a faculty development course that supported her in creating an online children's literature course, and Sheri was working with another technology team on KLICK! (Kids Learning In Computer Klubhouses!). As a result, although both of us were relative neophytes when it came to technology, we had absorbed a great deal of casual knowledge about technology from our environment, and that knowledge provided us with a valuable foundation for our PT3 work. We also had had the benefit of listening, over time, to some very profound and creative thinking about the potential and the limitations of technology in education—ideas that helped inform our thinking about how our students might interact with our video materials.

Unsurprisingly, this technology-rich culture also provided extensive physical resources that were informally available to us. We had large, well-equipped computer labs that both we, and later our students, could use. There were other research projects from which we could borrow information or technology, and we were surrounded by colleagues who were, for the most part, happy to help us think through and troubleshoot our difficulties when we got stuck.

THE CHARACTERS

From early on, we saw the PT3 grant as a way to supply our project not only with financial and technological support, but also with advice and direction from individuals who had more experience with the possibilities and implementations of technology than did we. What we did not anticipate at the start of the project was the extent of our need for advice and assistance and, as well, the extent of the resources that were available to us. As with any major project, a large number of people came to be involved in our work over time.

We found that there were actually three different categories of participants; in literary terms, there were main characters, supporting characters, and characters that functioned as the deus ex machina[2]—the individuals who intervened suddenly near the end of the project to bring about a satisfying resolution to the story. Although each of these groups of people was a vital part of the process, each made very different contributions and tended to play larger and smaller roles at different times in the work.

Major (Main) Characters

Our initial team consisted of three "main" characters: the two of us, and Matt Koehler, an MSU faculty member who served as our PT3 technical advisor. Due to the nature of our project and the limits of our knowledge of the relevant technology, our technical support needs were probably stronger than the needs of many of the other teams on the grant. As a result, Matt's role as technical advisor was particularly important to us in the early stages, as we developed a plan for the project. We had only the most general sense of how we would get from where we were to where we wanted to be, and Matt led us through the early decision making, helping us refine our ideas about which technology applications could best address both our technical and pedagogical needs. He also provided valuable guidance as we purchased our initial hardware and software.

In the second year of the project, our core team shifted somewhat. While Matt remained a valuable part of the team, available for problem solving and troubleshooting, we needed more hands-on technical help than was reasonable to expect from him with his own full-time faculty load. To help with our technology needs, we hired Yakub Sailanawala, a technology-proficient graduate student in computer science who was able to take over much of the actual computer work—formatting video and designing the computer environment for the project.

Minor (Supporting) Characters

As mentioned before, the commitment of the dean of the MSU College of Education to supporting technology adoption and innovation meant that we had valuable personnel resources available to us as members of the College. When our computer developed a glitch, someone was there to fix it. When we did not know why the DVD burner was not working, someone was able to explain. When the laptop would not work with the overhead projector in a classroom, a support staff member came to troubleshoot. All of this expert help was part of the College's technology support program available to faculty; it is difficult to imagine conducting a project like ours without such people.

The institutional context of support also extended beyond the College to the University itself, and so our cast of characters widened to include many people outside the College of Education. MSU provided and maintained computer labs in our building as well as a tech support hotline that was available to answer questions about common problems with software. The University also maintained a service to support faculty use of technology; from this service, the software coordinator was repeatedly available to troubleshoot problems with the lab.

In addition, there were many technology projects going on in various parts of the University that provided a valuable network of distributed knowledge that we were able to tap into as needed. Helpful people across the institution were willing to answer questions about the best software to use or equipment to buy, or about video editing tricks or DVD formats. Almost always, when someone did not have the answer we needed, they had a suggestion of where else we might go. It is impossible to measure the full impact of these "secondary characters" on both the inception and the development of our project.

These people, who had no formal relationship to our project (indeed, in some cases, they were people we never even met face to face), provided invaluable assistance for our work. They were "recruited" by us on an as-needed basis, often in times of desperation or discouragement. Not all of them were part of the formal structures of the University. Representatives from both hardware and software companies were part of this group, as were students in other parts of the College who we heard might have some knowledge we needed. It is worth noting that in many cases these were one-time contacts—people we contacted by phone or e-mail, or anonymous individuals who provided descriptions of their own technical problem solving on their Web pages. Wherever and however we found them, though, their expertise intersected with our need in timely and vital ways.

Deus Ex Machina

The final group of people that became part of our community of design was entirely unsolicited—a happy surprise that sought us out, and that helped to reshape our project near its end. These characters appeared late in our work, and through their expertise brought a surprising—and satisfying—resolution, functioning as the deus ex machina in our story. These characters were colleagues of ours in the College of Education: Laurence Bates is the Instructional Technology Manager, and Charles Ruggiero is an Information Technology Professional. At a pivotal moment in our project (the "crisis" in the story of our work), Laurence and Charlie introduced us to some of their own work—work that had already been going on in the College, but that had been previously unknown to us. They listened to ways we saw their project intersecting with ours, then reshaped parts of their project to help meet our needs. In this way, Laurence and Charlie became characters in our story, helping to support our goals and resolve our difficulties in completely unexpected ways.

Along the way, then, our project took many forms, and our PT3 team (our "cast of characters") was modified over and over to fit the realities of our technological expertise and the time and resources that were available to us.

It is clear to us that all the people involved in this work—main characters, minor characters, deus ex machina participants—were pivotal to the success of a project that continually shifted as needs, resources, and individuals moved in and out of the scene. It could not have been otherwise. Finding or creating a team that could supply all our needs would have been impossible. We had to learn as we went what kinds of partners we needed, and it became frustratingly clear early on that no one or two individuals—no matter how well intentioned or knowledgeable—could possibly "know it all." The formal structure of the team supported by the PT3 grant provided a base from which to start and a source to which we could return. However, as we went along, we discovered that we needed many more "team members," a fuller cast of characters than the formal structure of the grant provided. The knowledge we needed to tap into was distributed across a wide circle of people who had a wide range of experiences with technology and who possessed multiple ways of thinking about solutions. In the story of our project, we have come to believe that that is the best—perhaps the only—way that technology learning and development can occur.

The Plot/Process

Our story had a problem, a setting, and a cast of characters. As the work unfolded, we also had a plot, a sequence of events that led to a climax and—thankfully—a resolution. Before we began, we knew the history of work such as ours. The gap between the availability of technologies and the development of thoughtful pedagogical applications is a long-recognized problem of technology adoption, and the importance of literature response in the world of literacy education was clear to us as well. This was the starting point for the story of our project.

From a distance, our work had seemed fairly straightforward: our goal was to increase students' understanding of children's responses to literature, and videotape could move us in that direction. We vaguely envisioned our students watching a videotape of brilliant and charming children talking, writing, drawing and acting out brilliant and charming responses to literature, supported and encouraged by their brilliant and charming teacher. This would allow our students to see models of exemplary literature response; as a result, our students would automatically transcend the barriers to their understanding through their thoughtful viewing of and interaction with this classroom video.

In the earliest stages of our thinking, we had not gone much further than this dreaming about the *fact* that classroom video could show our students the varied and nuanced responses of children to literature. However, after we had collected the videotape of a second grade classroom, and the project left the realm of dreams and became a possibility, we began to realize the complexity of the task of utilizing that video effectively. Almost immediately, we recognized that our real challenge would be to decide on teaching goals and then determine the specific *ways* that the video could best be used to accomplish those goals.

Our early pedagogical goals were unequivocally ambitious: we wanted the video materials to allow preservice teachers to examine the various types of literature response of which children are capable, trace individual children's thinking about a particular question or theme, and explore in detail the methods by which an experienced teacher guides children's interactions with literature. To achieve this, we wanted our students to do more than passively view classroom scenes, which could, at best, elicit admiration, motivation, and perhaps a few ideas about the teacher's role in classroom literature response. Rather, we wanted our preservice teachers to look closely and deeply, to compare and contrast, to ask hard questions, to collaboratively develop tentative answers, to reflect on alternative possibilities; in other words, we wanted them to *actively learn* and to facilitate this learning. We wanted them not just to view but to *interact* with the video—to select and track and arrange and challenge. We also wanted to have our students do this work with the video in a range of ways: individually, in small groups, and as a whole class, and we wanted to promote discussion of particularly interesting episodes from various perspectives, which we knew would necessitate multiple viewings of select video clips.

All of these goals, taken together, clearly meant we needed far more sophisticated technology than simple videotape, a VHS player, and a one-way flow of information from the video to the students. The PT3 grant seemed to be the perfect support system for developing this project—an environment explicitly intended to help us think about, design, and create a powerful technological and pedagogical context for our video.

As we created a list of goals for the classroom use of the video, our sense of the technological demands necessary to accomplish those goals became more sophisticated. We believed that the nascent DVD technology might be the best way to enable the kinds of interactions we wanted our students to have with the material, but had very little specific knowledge about the options that were available to us. Early on, Matt helped us understand some of the options with Web-based video, and others in the College worked to help us to understand what we could actually do with DVDs. At the time our project began, there were many technological limitations to a Web-based environment: the small size of the picture, the required downloading time, and students' use of widely differing computers and Web browsers. We knew that a DVD could hold much more video than a CD-ROM; that it could enable a user to move around within and between clips; that it could be used with a projector for whole class use, or on individual computers for small group or independent use. Also, the affordances of DVD technology for enabling multiple representations of classroom practice—integrating video, text, audio and graphic materials in an inquiry-based, learner-centered environment—seemed to provide possibilities not available by other means.

As we worked to refine our sense of the problem and possible solutions, the reality of designing the complete instructional environment presented itself as an extraordinarily complex challenge. We saw that the process of this technology development had three very different components: the design of the entire pedagogical-technological concept, the development of the technology environment for the use of the video, and the process of putting the environment to use—the instructional context. These three components were interrelated, of course, but each held very different challenges. It was also clear that this was not to be a tidy, sequential process. There was a complex, interactive, almost circular relationship between these components. The editing process had to create video clips appropriate for a certain purpose; the interactions with the video were constrained by the technological affordances; and, the instructional context needed to both guide and be constrained by the other two factors. Nevertheless, in many ways we felt that the technology was key—that what we could dream or imagine for our students was determined by what we could do with the available technology.

Even before we arrived at the tough technological questions we would eventually encounter to attain our goals, we knew we faced a daunting task in simply editing the 30 hours of classroom video that we had shot. We needed to determine just which parts of the footage would be most effective for which kinds of learning for our students. This early editing occasioned the first of many collisions we experienced between our dreams and reality. The first time we actually saw the video we were dismayed. While the teacher and students we had videotaped were indeed brilliant and charming, they, like the rest of us, also had off days, unscheduled interruptions, and competing priorities. In addition, the quality of the taping, although professionally done, was disappointing: the sound quality was a serious problem; with the intention of being helpful, the camera person had inserted herself into the children's discussions at times; children turned away or moved out of camera range at crucial moments. In other words, all the problems that naturally characterize a complex human undertaking occurred. We realized that the limitations of the video would greatly exacerbate the already daunting challenge of editing. We not only needed to identify episodes that suited our purposes, but we were limited in our selection to those moments that were clear and audible.

Because we saw how steep our learning curve was going to be, and because we wanted to get the video into our students' hands as soon as possible, we made a decision to create a preliminary set of DVDs, using a basic set of video clips and simple iVideo and iDVD software. Excited and eager to begin, we ordered computers, software, and other supplies. Learning to use the iVideo program proved fairly simple, and creating the clips was a time-consuming but fairly straightforward process. However, small but persistent problems plagued the process. No one seemed to be able to tell us how much video the DVDs would really hold, so it was difficult to decide how long our clips could be. Then, we were stalled for 2 weeks because the video would not load completely into the iDVD program. Numerous phone calls and e-mails for help produced no solution, until finally someone casually asked if the video was already on the machine that was to burn the DVDs. No; in fact we had been trying to import it directly into the iDVD program from the firewire drive where we had it stored. It turned out that the video would not run through the firewire fast enough to import, and therefore needed to be transferred onto the DVD burning machine first. It was a simple solution to a problem no one else had thought to ask about and we had not known enough to mention. These kinds of challenges took up enormous amounts of time and mental energy.

Eventually, in time for second semester classes, we had a full set of DVDs for student use. We had edited the video footage of the children's classroom literature responses into related segments (based primarily on type of response), and we had used these segments to create a set of themed DVDs. Although simple in design, the DVD format enabled the preservice teachers to collaboratively investigate the areas we were most interested in: the particular kinds of literature responses exhibited by the children; the individual children's thinking about a particular question or issue; and the strategies by which an experienced teacher guides children's interactions with literature. We had planned the classroom context for the DVDs very carefully: students would view the sets of clips multiple times in a small group setting, engage in discussions about what they had seen, and collaboratively answer sets of questions that encouraged them to think more deeply about the children's interactions with literature.

The first attempts to use the DVDs with students were an unalloyed disaster. A special classroom in the College held 10 stations with Macintosh DVD players. We planned to begin with a whole-class viewing of a small piece of video in order to introduce students to the teacher and the classroom, followed by independent small-group work at "stations" each containing a computer with a DVD player, where three students—each fitted with headphones—were to view and discuss the video clips. Our difficulties with technology began at the start of the class session; as we began the introduction to the project, the instructor's computer refused to communicate with the overhead projector; once we got the connection functioning properly, the sound was so soft, in spite of extra speakers, that the students could not hear the children's talk. Then, during the rest of the class session (and each time we attempted it after), at least half of the students could not open the players, or there appeared to be no players installed, or the players stuck and skipped, or the sound on the computers refused to function.

When our students encountered difficulties, the students' default assumption was that the DVD disk was bad, or that the computer was not functioning properly, so there was limited commitment on their part to problem solve. As computers failed to play the DVD or to produce sound, students became frustrated, then angry, then disinterested. Time after time, in different labs, or with different support, we tried to use the DVDs. In each case, despite our best efforts to prepare the students, and despite the best efforts of tech support to prepare the labs, old or new problems persisted in turning students' attention from the *content* of the DVDs to the *process* of getting the DVD players to work properly.

Gradually, over time, students' general familiarity with technology in other parts of their lives provided assistance. From one semester to the next, more students were familiar with DVD players and had some idea of how to solve the various problems that arose. In addition, we got better at getting support from the College or University, which included having more readily-available access to the particular rooms that worked best for the viewing of the DVDs, along with support staff on "standby" to problem-solve during class time. Various computer problems continued to plague us, however, and we eventually discovered that students had much better results playing the DVDs on home DVD players connected to televisions than on the computers in the labs. This led to an adaptation of the assignment in which students were released from a class session to meet in small groups to work on the project. This gave them the option of either meeting in their homes and using DVD players to view the clips, or meeting on campus and using computers for the viewing. The students almost invariably chose the former option, and we got fewer and fewer frustrated calls from student groups attempting to view video that would not play for one reason or another.

As the second year of the project began, we reevaluated our progress and our goals. During the DVD segment of the class, we had given our classes a simple questionnaire to help us assess our students' learning and perceptions of children's responses to literature, and we were happy to find that, in spite of the technology problems we encountered, this early research indicated that the first phase had been moderately successful in beginning to reshape students' assumptions about children's capacities for sophisticated responses to literature. However, we realized that the potential of the technology to facilitate multiple means of inquiry and complex understandings of the phenomena had been only partially tapped. We wanted to get beyond the simplicity of the iDVD program format, in which students selected among video clips, discussed what they saw, and then wrote on paper their reactions to their observations and discussions. In the next phase of the project we decided to use the expansive capacities of Final Cut Pro and DVD Studio Pro to create a more complex, flexible, and layered environment which we hoped would result in our students having more complex, flexible and layered interactions with and around the video, audio, and text material and each other. These more sophisticated programs would enable us to design a learning environment in which video, audio, and text materials could be incorporated in ways that could enhance opportunities for individual and group inquiry. We wanted to explore how a more complex utilization of the DVD format could maximize student engagement with and inquiry into multiple representations (Levin & Bruce, 2003) of literature response, encouraging deeper and more nuanced understandings of literature response in children. We also wanted to incorporate the added capacity to link from the DVD to a Web-based environment to further extend the possibilities for inquiry and collaborative learning for our students, adding discussion and workspace features as well as allowing us as instructors to provide students with additional resources about literature response.

This planned restructuring of the project called for a restructuring of the PT3 team as well. While Sheri had taken the lead in the hands-on tasks involved in creating the first set of DVDs, this was possible only because of the simplicity of the software used. Moving from iVideo and iDVD to Final Cut Pro and DVD Studio Pro meant that for the second year of the project we would definitely need some ongoing technical help. This is where Yakub Sailanawala, the graduate student in computer science, came in. As we moved into the actual planning of this new generation of the DVD, Yakub became the lead person on the team for a time. As he worked with the new software, his task was to help us discover how to integrate the specific affordances of the technology with the specific goals we had for our students' interactions with the materials. Then together we created a work plan for moving the project forward and getting it ready for classroom use.

As we reedited the video for the much more complex analysis we wanted to enable with the new DVDs, we struggled with the balance between the "direct instruction" implications of highly focused editing (where we made decisions through our editing of what students should notice and how students should view) and the opportunities we wanted students to have exploring and drawing their own conclusions about what they saw. Early on, we had acknowledged the implicit power of the editing process to shape the viewing experience. We knew that the more straight footage we provided, the less we were constraining our students' viewpoints; however, we also knew that we needed to make the video material manageable in terms of size and focus.

We were nearing the end of the second year of the grant, and although we were pleased with our work so far, we also knew we were still a long way from attaining our early goals. Our limited knowledge of the technology, and the many roadblocks we had encountered along the way, meant that we had moved forward much more slowly than we had hoped, and—even with help from multiple sources—the technologies we were using did not very effectively match our initial goals of student interactivity and engagement. Despite the learning we had already witnessed in our students in their interactions with the DVDs we were creating, we still had a number of ongoing dreams and frustrations—dreams of additional, generative ways that our students could interact with the video materials; frustrations that the technology we were using could not support the interactions we had in mind.

If we view the unfolding of our experiences as the plot of the story of our project, then in the spring we were nearing the point of crisis in that plot. We were scheduled to present our work at a national conference, and we were racing against time to create a product that provided students in our spring semester courses with more interactive capabilities than they currently possessed. Yakub needed faculty access to the University server to store more of our material on University Web space, but since he was a graduate student, he needed to obtain that access through Laurence Bates (mentioned as a deus ex machina character). In the course of a simple meeting about obtaining university server space for our work, Laurence saw in our project an overlap with a technology environment that he and Charlie Ruggiero were already developing in the College of Education. The tool that Laurence and Charlie were creating was just starting to be used in conjunction with other projects in the College, and it was a resource he thought might be of interest to us as well. Laurence requested a meeting to show our "team" (Laura, Sheri, & Yakub) what was already underway with this project, and he and Charlie provided us with an hour-long demonstration of their work, nicknamed IVAN (Interactive Video Access Neighborhood). IVAN represented the development of a suite of integrated, open source, cross-platform tools which would allow educators to organize, select, and present video clips and supporting materials in a compelling and easy-to-use environment.

From the start, Laurence and Charlie were eager to explore with us the intersections between what they had already developed in IVAN and the sorts of technological resources we were seeking for our literature response project, and it was clear from the time of our first meeting that IVAN had much to offer our on-going work. We asked Laurence and Charlie about ways of storing video online so students could access it from across and off-campus. We asked them about ways to allow students to select their own segments from a library of video clips that we would create from the many hours of video that we possessed, then arrange those segments, with commentary, for their peers and instructors to view. We asked them about ways to allow students to select from video to highlight a particular type of response, to follow a particular student, or to identify a particular instructional strategy on the part of the teacher. We asked them about access, since we wanted students to be able to work on this independently and in groups, to be able to save their work, and to be able to move back and forth between written commentary and the videos themselves. Each time, through conversation, Laurence and Charlie were able to imagine ways this could be accomplished, and—within a matter of days—were able to present us with materials that fulfilled our requests. Within a week, they had created links and added capabilities, expanding some of their original program to meet our needs.

The work we did with Laurence and Charlie served as the resolution to the "crisis point" or "climax" to our story. Laurence and Charlie stepped into our story at a critical moment and helped us come as close as we could to our original goals for our students, given both the opportunities and the constraints of time, funding, and expertise that we possessed through PT3 funding. We were able to present this newest iteration of our work at the conference, where it was received with enthusiasm by our colleagues in literature and teacher education.

Throughout this project, we had goals for how the work would unfold; in some remarkable ways, many of those goals were realized. The first of our goals was imagining that we could obtain classroom video that would help our students recognize the powerful responses to literature that children could have; through our connections in the College and in the teaching community, we were able to obtain that video. The second goal was to find the resources to create a technology environment that would enable the use of the video in our classes; the PT3 grant supplied those resources. The final wish, one we thought we had little hope for, since it was by far the most technologically ambitious of the three and we had come so far already, was that our students could go beyond looking at and thinking about video clips *we* had selected, to selecting episodes and creating clips of their own—that is, that our students would go from "reading" the video to "writing" their own understandings of the classroom interactions (Bruce, personal communication, April 3, 2003). Even this was made possible through the creative capabilities of the IVAN suite.

This, then, was the resolution to our story, the "divine intervention" (deus ex machina) that made it possible to realize our deepest wishes for the work. We had the video of children responding to literature; we had the instructional goals and pedagogical contexts for using this video in our classes; and, at last, we had the technological ability to move our students into the world of exploring and creating their own understandings of children's responses to literature.

The Theme/Analysis

In a story worth telling, there is a theme, a point to be made, an insight to be acquired. Sometimes it is a clear, singular point; other times, it is less clear, open to greater interpretation. Sometimes, the author and the reader have a shared understanding of the theme; often they do not, since what is learned is often dependent on need, context, experience, and desire. These themes, then, are our own understandings of what we learned—and what can be learned by others—from the process of our PT3 work.

We learned that what had seemed to us to be a simple idea at the outset—that is, the classroom use of video materials portraying children engaged in literature response, made available in an interactive technological environment—was actually much more complicated than we first imagined. Our setbacks were many. Our limitations often confounded us. The difference between our dreams and the reality of the materials with which we worked often overwhelmed us. The distance between our starting point and our goals for the work grew exponentially as we continued with the project. Very often it was the case that the more we knew, the farther we had to go.

We learned that even the parts of the project that *seemed* simple (burning DVDs, for instance, or having students use headphones in the computer lab to view DVDs individually and in groups) required hours of planning and included many time-consuming complications. While it is true that our skills in technological problem solving were often unequal to the tasks we encountered, it is also the case that the vagaries of technology significantly impeded our progress on several occasions.

We learned that questions open on to more questions, and that each time we felt confident in our direction, we discovered drawbacks and alternate routes that often involved backtracking and major or minor revision. Commitment to an idea or approach often shifted (our decision to use DVDs, for instance), and even before we had fully explored one possibility, more had come into view. The available technologies and their applications developed more quickly than we were able to identify, learn or use, and as a result, there were few predictable outcomes, no matter how carefully we researched or planned.

We learned that learning to use technology in teaching and developing technological applications are not the same thing. Each needed to be negotiated, each was labor-intensive in its own way, and even though these were connected, they were still independent activities. There was a dialogic quality to the process that we discovered through our experience: we brought to the task our subject matter (content) knowledge, as well as our pedagogical knowledge, and each of these not only shaped but (to our surprise) *was shaped by* the technologies involved. While we expected that our pedagogy and content would determine the technologies we chose and developed (and they did), it was also that case that our pedagogy and content shifted and were transformed by the development of the technologies we encountered along the way.

We learned that a team approach—or, as we came to understand it, the "Communities of Design" approach—was integral to our work, and we found that the ways various players contributed to the project were based not only on current knowledge of technology or educational contexts, but also on individual skills, future assignments, and moment-by-moment availability. No one person could, or needed to, know everything, and we could not rely on any particular institutional model or individual for all the answers and guidance we needed. Over and over, we found help where we least expected it, and we learned both where and how to ask questions to lead us to the answers we sought.

At the same time, we learned that the community in which we found ourselves working was much larger than we imagined, and that it shifted throughout the project. Early on, Matt was our resource for technology, while Laura and Sheri—with their knowledge of children's literature and the teaching of it—handled the conceptual and pedagogical components of the work. Later, as our technical needs grew more project specific and Matt could not be expected to know all the details and nuances of the technologies we were using, Sheri took the lead on researching and learning new applications, given her experience with the course and with using technology in other educational contexts. As the project continued to develop and the technology applications became even more sophisticated, the model shifted again, involving Yakub, a highly skilled technician who became a central part—and for a while, a leader—of the team, working with ideas that were at that moment in development within the college and that were taking shape as our project moved along.

We learned that our plan to have video materials portraying children engaged in literature response made available through a sophisticated technological environment was only a beginning step in thinking about using this technology to enhance instruction in our teacher education classrooms. In addition to obtaining video and making it available to students, our challenges included the complex process of designing the instructional context for using these video materials most effectively across multiple sections of our courses. We needed to make certain that the technology we chose supported the fundamental pedagogical goals we had for our students, and that it was embedded in a reproducible but adaptable instructional framework that included a network of support for both students and instructors.

We learned the importance of being satisfied with a less-than-ideal result, of being pleased when *most* (or even *some*) of what we hoped for took place. We learned that the notion of perfection in the world of technology is not only unattainable—it is exhausting, and to insist on "success" in those terms undermines progress that can take place, albeit slowly and with mixed results. In short, we learned to adjust our expectations to fit reality.

And, finally, we learned that designing interactive contexts for our students to work with video was, indeed, an odyssey in technology. It was a long journey from our starting place to the place we arrived. And there were certainly changes of fortune—days we felt we were doomed to wander forever in search of appropriate technologies or approaches; other days we were enthused and amazed by the possibilities a tool, or person, or perspective afforded. In addition to changes of fortune, there were other changes that affected our work as well, for as we approached our goals, we realized that those goals were changing, we were changing, the technologies we were working with were changing, and our students were changing. Things we had not imagined became possible and within reach; things we were committed to moved out of range, or lost their desirability, or both.

And the future of the work? We are moving forward—gradually—toward incorporating these resources into other sections of the children's literature course, taught by other instructors. Without the ongoing support that the PT3 grant provided, our progress is slow. However, we are hopeful that eventually the technology will grow simpler and more reliable, allowing more of the instructors of the course to include it in their teaching without requiring of them some of the time commitments and frustrations we experienced.

This, then, was the story of our project. We have imposed order and tidied much of its chaos in order to create meaning, in order to draw out a narrative line that would move the telling forward in comprehensible ways. We have created a tale with an identifiable problem, a setting, characters, a plot (with a crisis and a resolution), and a theme, drawing on what we know from the world of literature to help make sense of what we are learning in the world of technology and education.

In the experience that became our story, we merged what we knew about our subject, what we knew about teaching, and what we learned about technology, and as we moved deeper into the work we discovered how inseparably related these components are. Our goals changed as we learned more about the available technologies; the technologies changed in response to our goals. We began with an authentic problem that grew from our teaching, and we arrived at a place that both shaped and was shaped by the technologies we created and encountered. We became part of a community that supported our work and that—ultimately—benefited from that work as well. While we would never claim to be "experts" when it came to technology, there is no doubt we became experts on the ways various technologies could enhance the teaching and learning in our children's literature courses.

Ultimately, we know that work such as this requires extraordinary amounts of support (time, technological advice, financial resources), both in its beginnings, as well as in its continuance. It was our good fortune to find ourselves in an environment that encouraged us in our experimenting with technology in our classrooms. It was, as well, our good fortune to have the support (financial, intellectual) of the PT3 communities in which we were involved. It is our goal to continue this work in our classes, and to share these ideas with a wider forum of teachers and learners, making simple and accessible for others what often proved to us to be challenging and labor-intensive.

In the story of our work, we have learned the truth of the anonymous quote that begins our piece:

> *I haven't a clue as to how my story will end. But that's all right. When you set out on a journey and night covers the road, you don't conclude that the road has vanished. And how else could we discover the stars?*

We started this journey, this odyssey, with a fairly clear idea of where we wanted to go, but with few ideas of how to get there. As the project progressed, we found ourselves moving forward, slowly, but we also found ourselves frequently lost, in the dark, unsure of our path. We "wasted" time on detours that were not productive; we discovered happy and productive surprises along the way; ultimately, we accomplished more—and less—than we imagined we would. We were pleased with what we and our students learned; we were disappointed that it took us so long to learn it. Our discoveries were not exactly stars, but they were discoveries nevertheless.

We see much potential in this sort of linking of technology and teacher education, and we look forward to continuing the story that is our work.

NOTES

1.   The course we were teaching was built around three types of response—
     personal, textual, and *critical*—our own structure, based on current research

in the area of literature response. In *personal response,* readers make connections between texts and their own lived experiences (Apol-Obbink, 1992; Many, 1994; Rosenblatt, 1937; Tompkins, 1980). This perspective allows for readers' multiple plausible interpretations of text. In *textual response,* readers closely examine literary elements of texts (i.e., setting, character, plot, theme, style). This is often also termed a "close reading" of the text. In *critical response,* readers see texts and responses as historically, socially and politically situated (Apol, 1998; Nodelman, 1996). Consequently, surfacing and interrogating the assumptions of texts and readers (who do the interpreting) are key aspects of critical response (McGillis, 1996).

2.   Literally, *god out of the machine.* By definition, deus ex machina is an unexpected, artificial, or improbable character, device or event introduced suddenly in a work of fiction or drama to resolve a situation or untangle a plot.

REFERENCES

Apol, L. (1998). "But what does this have to do with kids?": Literary theory in the children's literature classroom. *Journal of Children's Literature, 24*(2), 32-46.

Apol, L., Sakuma, A., Reynolds, T., & Rop, S. (2003). "When can we make paper cranes?": Examining pre-service teachers' resistance to critical readings of historical fiction. *Journal of Literacy Research, 34*(4), 429-464.

Apol-Obbink, L. (1992). Feminist theory in the classroom: Texts, voices and questions. *English Journal, 81,* 38-43.

Levin, J., & Bruce, B. (2003). Technology as media: A learner-centered perspective. In Y. Zhao (Ed.), *What should teachers know about technology? Perspectives and practices* (pp. 45-52). Greenwich, CT: Information Age Publishing.

Many, J. E. (1994). The effect of reader stance on students' personal understanding of literature. In R. B. Ruddell, M. R. Ruddell, & H. Singer (Eds.), *Theoretical models and processes of reading* (pp. 653-667). Newark, DE: International Reading Association.

Marshall, J. (2000). Research on response to literature. In M. L. Kamil, P. B. Rosenthal, P. D. Pearson, & R. Barr (Eds.), *Handbook of Reading Research* (Vol. 3, pp. 381-402). Mahwah, NJ: Erlbaum.

McGillis, R. (1996). *The nimble reader: Literary theory and children's literature.* New York: Twayne.

National Center on Education and the Economy and the University of Pittsburgh (1999). *New Standards: Reading and writing grade by grade.* Pittsburg, PA: Author.

International Reading Association and National Council of Teachers of English. (1996). *Standards for the English language arts.* Newark, DE and Urbana, IL: Author.

Nodelman, P. (1996). *The pleasures of children's literature* (2nd ed.). White Plains, NY: Longman.

Rosenblatt, L. (1937). *Literature as exploration.* New York: Appleton-Century Crofts.

Tompkins, J. P. (Ed.). (1980). *Reader-response criticism: From formalism to post-structuralism.* Baltimore: The Johns Hopkins University Press.

CHAPTER 4

SEXY BEAST

The Integration of Video Technology in an English Methods Course

Leslie David Burns and Stephen Koziol

Problems worthy of attack, prove their worth by hitting back.

— Piet Hein

LUST AT FIRST SIGHT

Technology is a sexy beast. It dresses well. It laughs at your jokes. It winks and flirts, promising you will not be sorry in the morning. It swears it will never hurt you, and it makes you look so much cooler than you probably really are. Yes, technology fills our eyes and hearts with longing, but it is a shallow lover with only as much depth as we are able to lend it. Dinner and a movie might get you lucky, but any long-term relationship can leave you feeling empty. Innuendo aside, this analogy is surprisingly apt in terms of representing the integration of technology in education these days. The look of those new cameras, computers, and software programs may cause lust at first sight, but achieving any long-term benefit from

Faculty Development by Design: Integrating Technology in Higher Education, 71–92
Copyright © 2007 by Information Age Publishing
All rights of reproduction in any form reserved.

their use requires sustained effort and support in a community (Mishra & Koehler, this volume).

The explosion in the capabilities of video technology—its increasing ease of production, its quality, its portability, its transferability, and its novelty—provides educators with an incredible tool for use in preparing teachers to teach well. But beyond the technological advancements, educators must ask how technology can be used as a part of a coherent, long-term program of teacher education (Howey, 1994). Video and computers do not do the work of teaching and learning for us; the knowledge required to use them productively is arguably a kind of literacy unto itself. That is to say, we do ourselves and our students a disservice when we merely plunk preservice teachers down in front of video screens, fire up the DVD-ROMS, and expect that any of them will learn how to teach as a result. The ability to observe teaching does not translate automatically into the ability to teach (Feiman-Nemser, 1985). Rather, learning to use video in order to learn how to teach requires a complex process in a sustained community of learners and designers, and even beginning to engage in such a process requires the preexistence of adequate facilities, infrastructure, and support staff. Four years ago, our goal was to develop a coherent curriculum and pedagogy for using video in teacher education that could help move the development of preservice English teachers toward critical practice and self-reflection oriented around pedagogical competencies while learning to teach.

What follows is the story of one attempt to integrate technology into an English education program; more importantly, it is a story of the day-to-day struggles involved with trying to woo the sexy beast of technology into giving us what we wanted in a large-scale teacher education program. First, we will discuss the problems we perceived we might solve using technology in the English education program at Michigan State University (MSU)—namely, how we could use teaching laboratories more effectively to implement a curriculum of self-study for learning to teach in a subject-area methods course. Second, we will describe the roles played by various individuals in designing and implementing that curriculum as a community of designers. Third, we will attempt to narrate the process as it unfolded in a series of adjustments rather than as a positive and smooth progression. Finally, we will close with a discussion of the challenges and reservations we faced as we worked to develop and sustain technology integration in our teacher education courses.

PROGRAM CONTEXT AND CURRICULUM

The project described herein focuses on a senior-level methods course in teacher education at MSU, "Teaching English to Diverse Learners."

At Michigan State, teacher candidates in English begin a 4-semester sequence during the fall semester of their senior year that culminates in a yearlong, fifth-year internship. During the first semester of this sequence, learners participate in an English education seminar twice a week, a practice laboratory once per week, and a field practicum in which they are placed with a mentor teacher in a public middle or high school. Drawing on features of case-method instruction in teacher education (Lundeberg, Levin, & Harrington, 1999; Shulman, 1992), Lesson Study (Lewis, 2002; Lewis & Tsuchida, 1998; Stigler & Hiebert, 1999), self-study techniques (Ball & Cohen, 1999; Zeichner & Noffke, 2001), and cognitive flexibility theory (Spiro & Jehng; 1992; Spiro, Feltovich, & Coulson, 1996) in conjunction with video technology, the laboratory section of this course was designed to help preservice teachers learn to operate flexibly in classroom environments through experience with multiple representations of teaching.

In the teaching labs, students practiced designing and implementing segments of lessons that emphasized techniques of explanation and discussion. These activities represent high priority techniques in an English teacher's instructional repertoire (National Council of Teachers of English, 1996). The format of the laboratory enabled students to see and analyze multiple examples of these key strategies from various perspectives in an array of contexts (lessons designed for middle and high school settings, or in urban, suburban, or rural contexts that might effect the presentation of content and draw on culturally specific schema and literacy practices). In lab sessions (12-14 students per lab section), each student was digitally recorded teaching five 10-15 minute minilessons during the fall semester. These videos were used by the students in a variety of ways as texts for further study throughout the course. As a culminating performance assessment, students used their videos and the artifacts they had produced along with them (lesson plans, notes, handouts, etc.) to create a portfolio and represent their progress in learning to teach across the fall semester.

In total, each student engaged in the process of analyzing his/her own and peers' teaching episodes approximately 15 times during the semester, participating either as a discussion leader or a peer discussant. The iterative process was intended to help students internalize both the methods and the vocabulary (provided in a set of analytic categories) that facilitate independent study and professional development beyond their program of preservice preparation.

When we first became aware of the community of designers project at Michigan State, we viewed it as an opportunity to develop ways of supporting preservice teachers as they used their video records from the teaching laboratories to develop "usable knowledge" and learn "in and from practice" (Ball & Cohen, 1999) as they engaged in their pedagogical methods courses. In attempting to do so, we viewed the context of teaching laboratories provided in our English education program as a key to establishing a coherent program where students could "build connections among various areas of knowledge and skill, but where loose ends remain[ed], inviting a reweaving of beliefs and ties to the unknown" (Buchman & Floden, 1990, p. 8). Our belief was that the joint use of digital video and teaching laboratories, with an eye to the eventual use of video in classroom field placements, could maintain the integrity of teaching sufficiently without overwhelming preservice learners with the tasks of the actual classroom environment. Labs such as these are relatively rare in teacher education (Berliner, 1985; Howey, 1996), and we sought to use technology to make this brand of laboratory learning more practicable.

As we discussed the design of a viable curriculum for utilizing video technology, our primary concern was to provide a structured environment and process wherein students would have the freedom to explore issues and problems they found in their own practice and in the practices of their peers in a critical but friendly learning community. This concern was reflective of principles articulated by Mishra and Koehler in the introduction to this text: "teachers' ability to use technology must be closely connected to their ability to teach," and technology should be viewed as a medium for expression, communication, inquiry, and construction that can help teachers solve problems (this volume, p. 9). Our belief and intention was that, by learning how to use video to study their own teaching in laboratory settings, our students would develop a culture of inquiry that would continue as they moved into professional contexts, allowing them to pursue professional development and lifelong learning on their own and also allowing them to teach other professionals how to engage in productive self-study as they moved on to create new communities of practice.

In order to develop a sound curriculum, we began our work by attempting to understand how laboratory contexts and video technology can be used in learning to teach. In the next section, we explore some of the issues involved with creating a coherent laboratory curriculum that facilitates such learning.

TECHNOLOGY AND LEARNING TO TEACH

In essence, a well-conceived teaching laboratory allows students to observe complex phenomena and practice in a controlled context where they can analyze events and interactions from multiple perspectives. A common criticism of teaching labs is that they tend to be artificial environments that provoke inauthentic responses on the part of both the teacher and the peer "students" who participate in them; however, Metcalf (1993) turns this perception on its head, finding that labs in teacher education contexts actually provide a quality of experience that cannot be duplicated in field experiences. According to Metcalf's study,

> Implicit in these results is the importance of *opportunities for limited but guided application of professional practices* and relatively immediate, structured feedback from a small group of peers who witness the teacher's performance. Teacher educators could, perhaps, provide such opportunities in field settings; however, it would be difficult and expensive to do so. (p. 172, emphasis added)

Gliessman (1984) also argues that teaching laboratories such as the kind we attempted to create in our program can affect changes in teaching behavior that are unlikely to occur in any other teacher education setting, including real classrooms.

In addition to the efficacy of laboratory teaching described in the literature, advances in technology have significantly reduced the costs and complications of using video in laboratory settings, making it useful for the representation of cases and the creation of records of practice (Ball & Cohen, 1999; Howey, 1996; Lundeberg et al., 1999). In addition to solving what we viewed as a long-standing technical problem in our program, we saw the emerging popularity of using video records and commentaries in teacher education programs as another motivation for our project. Using video as a text for self-study and assessment, the classroom teacher or preservice candidate can analyze her own and others' practice over time and may use videos to provide evidence of successful teaching. We sought to develop a curriculum that would take advantage of advanced technological applications like this because we saw the use of video as a new competency for teachers in professional development programs like those advocated by the National Board For Professional Teaching Standards (NBPTS). National organizations and their recommendations for teacher assessment reflect the growing use of video as a central artifact in teaching portfolios. Such uses of video reflect a clinical perspective on learning to teach (Howey, 1996), and because teaching must be particularized for unique contexts (Ball & Cohen, 1999), preservice candidates should have as much experience as possible in simulated laboratory contexts (Berliner, 1985; Howey, 1996; Rentel, 1992) as well as real classrooms. Digital video recording should make all of this much simpler to achieve.

Having described the context of our work along with our rationales for integrating technology into that program, we turn now to a description of the design community we formed for our project. In a large and complex program like the one at Michigan State described above, several individuals played significant roles in order to implement and administrate our work. In the next section, we examine those roles and discuss the ways in which each of them played a part.

ROLE PLAYERS

Dr. Koziol, the initiator of our video project, was serving as chair of the teacher education department at MSU at the time—a large program with a history of high national rankings and a reputation for producing high numbers of effective teachers. In previous years, Dr. Koziol had taught versions of "Teaching English to Diverse Learners" and had both designed and implemented earlier versions of the teaching laboratory described above. This laboratory curriculum had been implemented with success at the University of Pittsburgh, where he had formerly served as chair and faculty member, and it was so successfully transplanted into the MSU English education program that many other subject areas in secondary education also adopted the laboratory format. During the course of this project, Dr. Koziol consulted with and advised the graduate instructors employed in our program, and developed a system in which these graduate assistants rotated through an apprenticeship for teaching the senior level methods courses. First year graduate instructors assisted more experienced teachers in the seminar section of the methods course, and took on the responsibility of leading the teaching laboratories, which allowed them to work closely with a smaller group of preservice learners while learning about the structure and rhythms of the English education curriculum. In the first year of this project, Les Burns and Michael J. Riley taught the teaching labs as graduate assistants; in the second year, Jory Brass and Stacy Tate assumed these positions. In both years, an additional instructor was brought in from a local high school to teach additional lab sections—Dee Schnaar. Schnaar had worked with Dr. Koziol for many years in prior versions of the teaching laboratory, and brought a wealth of experience and enthusiasm for the job. Les Burns, as the senior graduate student in this group and assistant to Dr. Koziol, was responsible for coordinating the labs and designing lab syllabi.

Dr. Koziol, as director of the program and originator of the laboratory curriculum, offered considerable expertise and vision. Along with clear pedagogical rationales for the use of lab experiences, Dr. Koziol also provided an experienced eye for the development of usable and useful analytic frameworks important to the use of digital video cases in learning to teach. Strongly advocating the need for a coherent process and a specialized vocabulary for learning to teach, Koziol developed a set of four over-lapping analytic lenses to be used while observing and analyzing video cases: *learner accommodation, craft of teaching, instructional coherence*, and *content representation*. Working with Burns to refine and implement these lenses, Koziol regularly advised instructors regarding the use of video representations, and also regarding the structuring of laboratory activities in order to maintain a reasonable scope for the project. For example, Dr. Koziol developed minilesson formats that focused not on the teaching of whole lessons, but rather focused on particular elements of teaching a lesson, such as giving an explanation or coordinating various types of discussion. These more discrete skill performances continued to provide rich data for preservice learners to use in their videos, and at the same time prevented those students from feeling overwhelmed by the complexity of analyzing an extended teaching event.

Due to his many duties as a department chair Dr. Koziol was not directly involved with the implementation of technology during the project. While enthusiastic and perceptive about the potential uses of technology in teacher education, he maintained the role of "instigator." The job of implementing the technology and curriculum itself fell to his graduate assistant, Les Burns.

Burns, at the start of the project, was a second-year doctoral student in the department of curriculum, teaching, and educational policy. Having spent the previous year as an assistant instructor for "Teaching English to Diverse Learners," Burns was an experienced laboratory teacher interested in learning more about curriculum design and the performative aspects of teaching. When the opportunity appeared to develop a design team as part of the Preparing Tomorrow's Teachers To Use Technology (PT3) program, it was agreed that he would forestall moving into the role of lead course instructor and remain in the lab setting to redesign its curriculum, coordinate the laboratories, administrate the production, and distribution of video technology and artifacts, and act as a liaison with students and course instructors. He was responsible for learning and teaching the necessary technology in addition to these other duties, and because of this he was perhaps best positioned to experience its successes, failures, challenges, and processes most directly.

The lab instructors: Burns, Riley, Brass, Tate, and Schnaar, were each responsible for explaining the curriculum and exploring it with groups of 12-15 students. Once per week, instructors met with students as those learners taught lessons to each other; after each lesson, the lab instructors worked with their groups to practice using the analytic language provided for the course and to model problem-posing, observational strategies, and critical thinking. It was intended that these strategies in the lab itself would be extended into the preservice learners' later observation of their digital videos. In the first year, lab instructors were also responsible for learning to use digital video cameras. This task was found to be only slightly difficult in technical terms, since most of the lab instructors had experience with the kinds of record and playback functions each camera entailed. However, the practical problems of filming students while simultaneously attempting to observe, evaluate, model, and discuss laboratory performances proved to be cumbersome and difficult to balance. The lab instructors were expected to help explain the rationale for using video to preservice learners, give feedback to students regarding their journal reflections about that video footage, and distribute video recordings for students to use.

Midway through the first year of the project, it became necessary to relieve the lab instructors of their camera operating duties in order to allow them to focus on student assessment and feedback. We hired a pair of aides whose job it was to record laboratory performances, produce videos, and distribute them to students. In the first year, undergraduate students Sean Bertolini and Charles Wilson took these positions. Both were hired using grant funds through the Department of Teacher Education, drawing on a university-wide work-study program. In the second year, Charles was replaced by Ramona Fruja, a first year doctoral student with interest in the use of video technology. These individuals came to the job with little experience using digital cameras and technology, and little or no formal experience with classroom teaching in U.S. schools. Burns trained them in the use of the technology—for example explaining how to set up cameras, how to achieve optimal shooting angles, how to operate microphones, when to track the teacher with the camera, when to focus on a student, when/how to shoot footage of visual aides used in a particular lesson, and so on. It was further necessary to train these individuals in the production of digital videos—how to transfer video from DV tapes to computer hard drives, how to convert video files to mpeg formats, and how to burn mpeg files onto CD-ROMS. Finally, these aides developed a system in the second year for organizing individual students' digital tapes and disks, as well as a system for distributing those videodisks so that preservice learners could use them. In the second year of the project, the digital aides were given the additional responsibility of teaching preservice learners how to use video production software in order to produce video teaching portfolios. Many of these tasks and the problems involved with them will be discussed in later sections.

In addition to the individuals listed above, three others helped our design community. Ken Dirkin, at the time a tech-support specialist for the College of Education (and an unofficial folk hero for members of the college who sought to use technology), frequently lent his advice and expertise. He, along with Rick Banghart and Dave Dai in the educational technology department, provided informal consulting and technical assistance. For example, Dirkin often helped Burns learn about optimal processes for producing video on a mass scale. Banghart advised Burns regarding the pros and cons of streaming video versus the use of digital videotapes and CD-ROM disks; Dai was often available to help Burns troubleshoot during class meetings. Although peripheral, these three individuals were crucial to the work of the project.

YEAR ONE: BURNING DISKS AND GETTING BURNED

Prior to the beginning of our project, the English language arts teaching labs utilized VHS videocassette recording technology. When the MSU labs originated in the early 1990s, VHS cameras were considered state of the art. Students at that time were required to bring a blank videocassette tape, and the lab instructor would record each of the students' practice episodes for later study; they came and left with their own tapes each day. By the late 1990's, access to VHS tapes was widespread, and most students even had their own VHS players at home. By and large, this system worked for the purpose of allowing students to review their own performances outside of the classroom setting. However, VHS technology proved awkward when it came to creating the kinds of teaching portfolios that have since come into widespread use. VHS tapes were large, and editing them required bulky, expensive equipment that was not readily available to most people or education programs. If video representations of teaching were to be more practical and useful for teacher assessment, it was necessary to identify some other means of production. By 2002, posting digital videos to the Internet was becoming a more attractive possibility.

From the outset, we hoped to take advantage of the Internet for our project. Our vision involved using digital video cameras to record students in the teaching labs, and then storing those files on an Internet server so that they could be viewed using video streaming technology. If we could do this, we thought, we could eliminate the use of cumbersome VHS tapes and allow students to access their recordings anywhere they could find a computer with Internet access; further, they could use streaming videos conveniently during labs and classes in order to study concrete records of practice at the click of a mouse button. Even better, we could maintain these records indefinitely, providing our program with a centralized library of teaching records. Along with the laboratory videos, it would be possible to link and store lesson plans, supplemental documents like handouts and worksheets, journal entries, analytic reflections, and other texts related to our students' work as they learned to teach. Best of all, we could give students their raw digital tapes so that they could edit the videos and make portfolios focused on the specific skills they had acquired in the program instead of simply presenting their videos uncut, as had been done previously. A Web server dedicated to laboratory videos would benefit research and practice beyond a teacher educator's wildest dreams. Or so we thought.

Our first challenge presented itself quickly. Having no prior experience with storing video on the Web, we consulted Banghart in the department of educational technology. Banghart walked Burns through the wild world of digital streaming, noting the various options and levels of quality, along with describing the necessary equipment and processes that such streaming would require. The bottom line was that digital video takes up a great deal of memory space, and in order to view it easily a user would require a high quality, high-speed, reliable Internet connection. The typical home computer user with a dial-up Internet service would not have easy access, and using streaming video in our classes would require students to use on-campus computers with faster modems. Further, storing the video on a server would be possible, but difficult given the College of Education's limited resources. With approximately 50 students in our program, each of whom would require five separate video episodes and about 75 minutes of total video in a semester, we had a major storage issue on our hands: each student would require nearly 4 gigabytes of average-quality video per semester for permanent storage, not including lesson plans and other supplemental digitized texts related to the videos that we wanted to post.

Unfortunately, that kind of dedicated storage space was simply not available in the College of Education, and there was no room on the existing joint-use servers to allocate for special projects like ours. We could not provide our own server. Banghart advised our team that there were considerable problems with the reliability of streaming video at the time regardless, making remote access, even in our local classrooms, a dicey proposition. In other words, some days it might work perfectly, and other days it might not work well at all, depending on how much Internet traffic was happening at the time of access. Along with the privacy issues involved with storing student video, even on a secure server, our ideal plan had to be set aside and our design team was forced to search for other options.

Seeking alternatives, Burns turned to Ken Dirkin, a technology specialist widely recommended in the college as a knowledgeable and helpful resource for beginners and dabblers. After hearing the goals of our project, Dirkin suggested that the digital videos could be converted into mpeg format, which would greatly reduce the size of each file without costing much in terms of video quality—1 minute of mpeg video at a decent level of resolution takes about 1 megabyte of memory space. Mpeg movies could then be burned onto CD-ROM disks and given to students, who could then replay their videos on any computer with a CD-ROM drive. Needing to get our project underway, Dirkin advised that this process would prove the quickest and most efficient one for our needs, and with that we armed ourselves with some equipment. Using funds from our PT3 grant, we ordered an Apple G4 Titanium computer, recommended to us by several sources as the best computer on the market for working with video. Along with the computer, we were able to order an external readable/writeable CD-ROM drive for use in burning CDs. Finally, we ordered five digital video cameras, a supply of digital videocassette tapes, and a supply of blank CD-ROM disks. With all this, we assumed that we were ready for action.

It should be needless to say that the production of 50-plus 10-15 minute-long mpeg videos each week became an overwhelming task. In the beginning, Burns was the only person available to do this work, and using only one computer made the job difficult to the point of absurdity. Returning to Dirkin for advice and assistance, Burns learned about the availability of an Apple computer lab in the College of Education that was open for most of the day and which provided the equipment necessary for more mass production of the mpeg videos. Dirkin taught Burns how to feed video from the digital cameras into a desktop computer, convert that video into mpeg files, and then burn those files onto the CD-ROM drives that were connected at each workstation in the lab. With ten stations in the room, it was possible to reduce the time needed for production dramatically. In order to allow Burns to work on all stations at once, Dirkin helped him find space on one of the College's servers where the video could be stored temporarily until it was accessed from one of the workstations for burning.

This was an improvement over the impossibility of the previous situation, but the solution proved far from ideal. In order to make a single video, it first had to be fed in real time into a single computer—the only one in the lab with mpeg converting capability. Then, the computer rendered it into an mpeg file. That file was then transferred to the server, and then, using a password, it could be accessed from any of the other workstations in the lab. Finally, using Adaptec Toaster software, Burns had to name each file and burn it onto an individual CD-ROM disk. The process for producing a single video took at least 20 minutes. At 50 per week, due as soon as possible so the students could complete their coursework, production required a minimum of 17 hours from Wednesday to Friday each week. Burns's assistantship contract for the project provided funds for only 10 hours each week, and while he had an additional 10-hour per week appointment related to his teacher education duties, that time was intended for research and administration of the teaching labs themselves.

With no other options, the task fell to Burns to produce the videos anyway.

Other difficulties presented themselves along with the issue of time. Our initial plan had been for each student to use only one disk in order to store all of her videos and text documents. We quickly found that students forgot their disks frequently, or they lost them, or the disks malfunctioned. In addition, the disks simply could not provide the storage capacity necessary for keeping all of one student's files on a single disk. It was necessary to begin producing and keeping track of multiple disks for each student. Additionally, in order to provide the program with its own source of video data and teaching examples, it was necessary to create a separate set of copies of all students' work. As these problems snowballed, the situation became even more difficult.

For the first 2 weeks of production, things went relatively smoothly, aside from the extreme amount of time necessary for physical production. Burns collected the digital videos from the labs after each meeting, and spent the evenings converting the tapes into CD-ROM formats. Unknown to any of us at the time, however, the computer lab Burns had to use was a communal space, not only for the College of Education but also for the entire university. Though it was open until late in the evening, it was an open lab and was often used by other students who had video and Web design projects of their own. There was no guarantee that all workstations would be available for our use at a given time. Further, the lab was often used for teaching classes, and at these times the entire lab was inaccessible to nonclass members. Class sessions often conflicted with the needs of our project and caused significant delays, confusion, and inconvenience.

On more than one occasion, the password provided by the College for use in accessing the server where videos were stored failed to work. At these times, production halted until a technology specialist could be located for help. Since production work had to occur after business hours, any password failure resulted in delays of at least 1 day until employees returned to the building, and depending on whether or not other class activities were scheduled in the lab or not. Sometimes, videos took over one week to produce, leading to extensive delays and frustration.

If this sounds rather awful, it was. Soon, Burns was spending over twice the number of hours he was allotted for the project. To make matters worse, this time was not spent on substantive integration of the technology in teacher education, nor was it spent on research and analyses of student learning data resulting from that integration. The technical processes involved with producing the videos in a form that students could use overwhelmed all other agendas. Something had to give.

It was at this time when Burns and Koziol agreed to hire two student hourly workers who could help record students in the teaching labs burn the videos onto CD-ROM disks. Once these two workers were trained in the care and use of the cameras, and also taught how to make the mpeg disks, conditions improved somewhat. Their presence improved production times, but it did not solve the problems of working in an open computer lab. Reliable access to the server continued to be a problem, and the coordination of students' videos and supplemental texts grew into a major logistical issue. Eventually we decided to leave out the students' written texts and focus on the videos alone. By the end of the first year, we found that our students had learned a great deal from using video to study their own development as teachers. We had also learned more than we wanted to know about the difficulty of producing such videos in our institutional context, and we learned the challenges involved with coordinating that production in ways that made the videos useable for students. But while the videos were indeed used by students in their coursework, and while the use of the videos provided some beginning insights into their learning both for themselves and their course instructors, our ultimate goal of using technology to create teacher assessment portfolios was not addressed at all.

YEAR TWO: ONE STEP FORWARD, TWO STEPS BACK

Our description of the first year is not intended to cast a pall on the use of technology in teacher education. The description serves to illustrate the very real difficulties involved with developing advanced programs of technology integration in educational institutions, places where facilities, equipment, access, and funding are constantly in need of upgrade and expansion. The problems we encountered in the first year are common to most colleges of education, which are rarely housed in facilities that meet their needs, rarely well-funded, perpetually behind the technology curve, and frequently used for mixed purposes in ways that sometimes marginalize the college of education in its own house. Furthermore, our own lack of experience and expertise certainly contributed to the problem; more than anything, we suspect that if we had better understood the technology we were trying to utilize, we would have been much more able to ask the right sorts of questions to the right sorts of people. We continued to see the potential benefits for using this technology in our program, and the gains our students demonstrated in their ability to learn in and from their lab practices were enough to encourage us in applying for a second year of funding.

Having secured another year in which to develop our project, we decided to continue with our basic premises, but also to concentrate more on the goal of helping students create digital portfolios that could represent their learning more dynamically than print-based narrative portfolios.

A major obstacle to achieving this goal in the previous year had been the fact that mpeg format videos could not be edited. As a result, students could not efficiently demonstrate how they viewed their own teaching; they could not single out particular instances of their own teaching and learning in ways that were easy to access, and that limitation both complicated the task and reduced the power of their portfolios. We needed a way for our preservice teachers to access their video, select specific pieces, and perhaps even provide audio narrations or captioning of their work. Ultimately, we wanted our students to be able to make movies about how they saw themselves learning to teach.

In defining this goal, we realized that we did not have the space in our curriculum to spend time training students in the use of complicated video production software. At the time we were trying to make our selection, Michigan State was visited by software developers connected with James Stigler's Lesson Lab video case software products (www.lessonlab.com). We were extremely interested in these kinds of programs, but had concerns about the ways in which these platforms tended to shape students' inquiries in normative and reproductive ways. Because we had already designed and implemented our own set of analytic lenses for students' use, we feared that prepackaged video case software would not meet our needs. Due to scheduling conflicts, we were unable to attend these meetings, and we were forced to strike out on our own. For our purposes, we found that the most user-friendly software available was Apple's iMovie. The program was easy to learn and use, it allowed the user to edit video easily, it included filters that allowed the user to insert effects that could highlight particular video segments, and it allowed the user to insert text and audio narration. iMovie was included at each workstation in the Apple computer lab we used in the first year, and we arranged to reserve this computer lab for two evenings each week so that students could work on their video portfolios after lab meetings. Our lab aides were taught to use iMovie, and were additionally paid to staff the computer lab and assist students. Burns visited each lab, distributed a description of the digital portfolio assignment, and gave students a packet of information about how to use iMovie. These materials were discussed both in the labs and in the students' main seminar classrooms in an attempt to clarify the process and offer students the chance to give their input.

While all of this, initially, appeared to be a positive and straightforward step, many students expressed deep misgivings. Across the methods courses, preservice teachers possessed a wide range of skill levels; some were highly skilled in Web design and other technologies, and they were familiar with video technology, for example. Other students had no experience at all, and still others could access such technologies without being able to develop their own projects using software and hardware. Their comfort levels depended on their levels of prior experience with the technology, and most students were afraid. More importantly, perhaps, students expressed grave concerns about the demands this digital portfolio project placed on them in terms of time and effort. Their methods course was already a 5-credit hour class (most standard university courses are classified at 3-credit hours). This project would require them not only to learn how to use new technologies, but it would also require them to do so outside the parameters of the course schedule and syllabus. In order to complete this assignment, they would have to spend significant time and effort above and beyond the norm. While the students almost universally recognized the potential benefits of making and having a digital portfolio of their learning experiences, they perceived the demands of the project to be unfair even in light of the support our program attempted to provide.

In spite of these concerns, we made the decision to forge ahead. We assumed that once the students had discovered how easy it was to use iMovie, and once they saw what they could do with the technology, that they would become much more comfortable and enthusiastic. We were wrong.

After 3 weeks, our lab assistants reported that only a few students had attended tutorial sessions or learned how to use iMovie. In order for the project to succeed—indeed, in order for the students to keep up with the production of their videos, it was important that they begin immediately working to learn the software and develop their portfolios. As time slipped away, it became clear that most students would not learn to use iMovie in time to work productively with their videos and finish anything useful or educative. Burns met with the students in lab and seminar class meetings again, and students continued to express confusion and frustration about the project. It was agreed that the assignment would have to be revised.

In order to accommodate students who were uncomfortable with the technology or overwhelmed with the time demands, we revised the assignment to include optional formats for the portfolio. Students were encouraged to utilize the iMovie format, but they were also given the options of creating a Web page, working in other video software formats, or creating structured narratives that incorporated specific references to edited video using the analytic lenses we had provided them to frame their discussions. These options, we realized, would alleviate many students' fears about the technology, but we also knew that providing these options would allow students who were already reluctant to use iMovie to defer learning the new technologies we advocated. We decided we had no option but to give students these "outs," and we maintained the hope that some students would seek to learn and use the new technologies anyway. Some did.

A small group of students continued to pursue the iMovie format of the original portfolio assignment. However, the scheduling conflicts in the computer lab that we encountered in the previous year continued to plague us. Although we had reserved regular and specific times for our dedicated use of the Apple lab, its ambiguous status as an open room created much confusion. Students not associated with our classes continued to enter the lab and use workstations, and other classes overlapped with our scheduled times as well. When we tried to investigate and resolve these conflicts, we discovered that no single department, program, or individual in the College of Education exercised authority over the room's uses, nor did anyone know who was supposed to be responsible for the facility. Several groups and individuals, from the assistant dean on down, referred us back and forth among each other, until it became clear that no one knew about this room or claimed the authority to regulate its use. Because of this, those among our students who did show up for instruction were sometimes able to do their work, and sometimes they were not. Having been told there would be regular and open lab times, and that they would have assistance whenever they needed it, our students found that such was not always the case. Frustration led all but one or two to abandon the iMovie version of our portfolio project entirely.

A second problem emerged with the use of iMovie. Unlike mpegs, which took up only one megabyte per minute of memory, 1 minute of iMovie video took up 180 megabytes. Even a short digital portfolio, say 15-minutes long, would take up nearly 3 gigabytes of memory space. Because of this, students could not transfer their working files to storage disks, and were forced to leave their files on the desktops of the computers in the unsecured lab. This went against posted policies in the room, but there was little choice. We created a specially labeled folder on each desktop in order to store students' work, and contacted all known parties associated with the lab to try and ensure that these files would not be trashed in the irregular sweeps of the computer desktops. We again attempted to locate server space where we might store these files remotely, but there was no space available.

Then a third-problem emerged. In the preceding year, a second computer lab had received a full upgrade including computers with improved processors, larger memory caches, and mpeg conversion and s-video hardware at each station. Ken Dirkin advised us that this lab would greatly enhance the speed of our video production, and that the lab should be open for our use. Once again, at the beginning of the semester our work to produce videodisks began relatively smoothly. However, while we were given the impression that the lab was free for our use, other classes began taking the room and using most of the workstations on a regular basis. Our lab assistants were unable to produce videos quickly, systematically, and predictably; as a result, students eager to work with their videos in iMovie had to wait. The situation became extremely frustrating and stressful for everyone who was involved.

Burns revised the digital portfolio assignment at least two more times before the end of the semester, including a revision with only 6 weeks remaining, as it became more apparent that the majority of students would not complete the assignment as it was designed. Some of the problem was the result of students' resistance to learning the technology necessary. Most began working on their projects long after it would have been feasible for them to learn the necessary skills for success with the original assignment. However, it seems likely that their reluctance and late starts were not the only reasons, and, frankly, some of their reluctance was understandable. Already engaged in multiple projects, lab meetings, field placements, and other requirements central to the course, it is no wonder that students did not engage the project willingly—particularly when it appeared to be so chaotically organized. In the midst of it all, we were constantly forced to reduce and revise our goals just to achieve minimal results.

At the end of the semester, every student produced a "digital portfolio." However, most of these consisted of a narrative description and included a CD-ROM of their unedited laboratory teaching videos, which the students referred to as best they could in order to identify particular teaching/learning moments. Several more tech-savvy students produced Web pages that included digital video segments they edited on their own, outside of the college setting. Some of these were of very high quality and demonstrated the value of digital portfolios quite well. In the end, though, only one student produced an iMovie portfolio, and no one was ever able to view it.

Because of the size of the file, the one student who used iMovie found that she could not export her movie from the computer in the open lab where it was produced. It was too large to burn onto a single disk, and far too large to send electronically. With no access to server space, we could not move the file to an accessible remote location. During the week of final examinations, Burns agreed to view the iMovie in the open computer lab.

Upon arrival at the lab, Burns discovered a crew of technology support staff dismantling computers. He was informed that the lab had been scheduled several weeks before to be renovated, and that all computers had been wiped clean of extraneous or unknown files so that they could be given memory upgrades. This renovation of the computer lab had gone on unannounced to general staff, and lab users had not been given the opportunity to rescue any work from the workstations since they were not supposed to store any work on the computers in the first place. The one iMovie produced during this project was lost due to the lack of communications about facility management.

AFTERWARDS

Our story sounds grim and frustrating. In many ways, it was. Yet we also learned a great deal from our experiences, and in spite of the chaos that ensued, our students' engagement with the process of self-study using video did seem to benefit them a great deal. The real question is whether or not that learning and success were worth the cost in terms of time and effort over the 2-year project. Regretfully, the answer is "probably not."

Our project experienced severe limitations on at least four fronts. First, no member of our design team had significant experience with technology. While capable of learning what was necessary, each member was engaged in several full-time jobs simultaneously. As the editors of this volume point out, technology integration cannot be managed outside of a full consideration of its relationship to context, content, and pedagogy. It requires the distributed attention of a knowledgeable team. We would agree with others who have said that the best way to learn about technology is to play with it and "muck around," but productive mucking around requires significant time, space, and support.

Second, certain necessary conditions must be in place if teacher educators are to push the boundaries of what is possible in using technology to train teachers. Technology novices require formal relationships with experts and specialists if they are to succeed. It is possible that the goals of our design project were simply beyond the means of current technology and facilities at the university. Because of our inexperience, we lacked the ability to ask relevant questions about what was possible, we were never aware of who we should address a particular question to, and our advisers were only able to address the questions that we raised. Rather than operating in formal settings specifically arranged to consider the unique problems of our design team, we were placed in a position where it was our responsibility to seek out expert advice in informal settings. While our design community involved extensive collaboration toward developing technological solutions to an authentic problem, it is clear in retrospect that our design team lacked the distributed expertise necessary for capitalizing on technology. In this respect, we argue that while faculty should be trusted and freed to pursue their agendas with technology integration, the inevitable contingencies that arise from the integration of new technology require regular access to experienced technology experts who monitor projects and offer intervention. Our design team would have benefited from a much more focused relationship with such experts.

Third, the scope and vision of our project simply outpaced the physical and administrative capacities of the facilities we were working with in the College of Education. Until it is possible to fully fund and attend to the necessary range of computer labs, server space, and other technical requirements for integrating technology on a large scale into teacher education programs, a project like the one described here is unlikely to succeed beyond a small scale.

Finally, it is extremely difficult to help preservice teachers acquire tool literacy—that is, a basic understanding of computer technology and the ability to perform simple tasks—in the context of a teaching methods course. We agree with Mishra and Koehler that "quality teaching requires developing a nuanced understanding of the complex relationships between technology, content, and pedagogy" (this volume, p. 8). However, the use of new technologies always requires at least some initial focus on tool literacy so that users may understand how the technology intersects with issues of content and pedagogy. Furthermore, we feel it would be inappropriate to dedicate time to such tool literacy tasks when the purpose of such a course is to spend time developing pedagogical skills, theoretical orientations to practice, philosophical understandings, and the many complex dispositions needed simply to function with competence in a school classroom. At the time of our project, the teacher education program provided little or no formal time for instruction in tool literacy, unless students elected to take separate courses dedicated to the subject. Rather, students were (and still are) expected to access resources such as computer centers, writing centers, and library seminars in order to learn what they need about technology. While at least one course in our English education program focuses on the design of Web-based hypermedia compositions, this is not the norm; our program does not consciously teach preservice learners how to use technology so much as it may be said that the program frequently requires learners to perform tasks that require its use. As long as this is the case, and as long as no systematic time, space, and facilities are provided for the integration of technology in teacher education on a large scale, it will continue to be difficult to engage in projects such as the one we attempted.

We recognize that these last statements contradict some of the principles highlighted by Mishra and Koehler. In their introduction, they point out that technology integration requires "a thoughtful interweaving of all three key sources of knowledge—technology, pedagogy and content" (this volume, p. 6). They also note Kent and McNergney's (1999) findings that "teaching instructors how to use specific software and hardware configurations without also showing them how it applies to their own instruction often leads to trial-and-error experimentation by teachers" (this volume, p. 4). While we agree with their argument that teacher educators require methods, values, and goals that lead to a deeper understanding of technology, our experiences suggest that at least some prior familiarity with basic computer literacy is necessary for the development of appropriate and efficacious methods, values, and goals.

By the end of our second year, we learned that another design team had been working on a project that also involved the use of digital video and teaching portfolios. However, their focus was on the design of such tools rather than on their immediate use in classrooms. They had secured the assistance of a technology specialist within the college who went about designing a wholly new and independent platform for converting, editing, and displaying video representations of teaching. In doing so, he employed a newly developed brand of programming that allowed digital video to be stored in a remote location, accessed easily by users, converted into a text code, and inserted into a user-friendly display for the creation of whole movies. These files, moreover, could be stored easily on standard disks because they were text files only—not video files. The video was stored elsewhere, and accessed only in small pieces based on the coded text files of the students' movies. This useful tool came as a result of the other design team's serendipitous meeting with an expert who happened to say, "Don't bother buying a bunch of prepackaged, complicated software. I can build something for you myself that will work better and faster, and it will cost next to nothing." We certainly could have used a fortunate connection like this one when we began our own work.

It is important for us to repeat that our students benefited and learned from the curriculum that we provided for them: a process and a vocabulary for self-study of video teaching cases. But the process was very difficult in administrative terms and in terms of our lived experiences for the duration. The lack of dedicated equipment, facilities, staff, and time seriously impeded our ability to follow through with our work, and the vast majority of these missing elements seemed beyond our control. With adequate facilities and time, along with focused and formalized expert advisors dedicated to design teams, we believe that our experiences mucking around with technology would have been far more productive, and our success in terms of product quality and student learning would have been even more positive than it was.

In the year following our project, Dr. Koziol left MSU. Les Burns advanced in his own studies as a doctoral candidate and was replaced in the English education program by other graduate student instructors. The teaching laboratories were maintained in the following year, and students were still given digital video for use in self-study, but the digital portfolio project was discontinued, as was the use of the analytic lenses we developed over the past 2 years. The sexy beast of technology that nearly ate us alive in the previous year quickly devolved to near extinction. Our final lesson was that maintaining a loving relationship with educational technology proved unattainable in the face of irreconcilable differences.

REFERENCES

Ball, D., & Cohen, D. (1999). Developing practice, developing practitioners: Toward a practice-based theory of professional education. In L. Darling-Hammond & G. Sykes (Eds.), *Teaching as the learning profession: Handbook of policy and practice* (pp. 3-32). San Francisco: Jossey-Bass.

Berliner, D. (1985). Laboratory settings and the study of teacher education. *Journal of Teacher Education, 36*(6), 2-8.

Buchman, M., & Floden, R. E. (1990). *Program coherence in teacher education: A view from the United States.* East Lansing: Michigan State University, The National Center for Research in Teacher Education.

Feiman-Nemser, S., & Buchman, M. (1985). Pitfalls of experience in teacher preparation. *Teachers College Record, 87*(1), 53-65.

Gliessman, D. (1984). Changing teacher performance. In L. G. Katz & J. D. Raths (Eds.), *Advances in teacher education* (pp. 95-111). Norwood, NJ: Ablex.

Howey, K. (1994). Partnerships in the laboratory and clinical preparation of teachers. In M. J. O'Hair & S. J. Odell (Eds.), *Partnerships in Education: Teacher Education Yearbook II* (pp. 77-84). New York: Harcourt Brace.

Howey, K. (1996). Designing coherent and effective teacher education programs. In J. Sikula, T. J. Buttery, & E. Guyton (Eds.), *Handbook of research on teacher education* (pp. 143-170). New York: MacMillan.

Kent, T. W., & McNergney, R. F. (1999). *Will technology really change education? From blackboard to Web.* Thousand Oaks, CA: Corwin Press.

Lewis, C. C. (2002, April). *Lesson study: Teacher-led research on the "swiftly flowing river" of instruction.* Paper presented at the meeting of the American Educational Research Association, New Orleans, LA.

Lewis, C., & Tsuchida, I. (1998, Winter). A lesson is like a swiftly flowing river: Research lessons and the improvement of Japanese education. *American Educator, 12*, 14-17, 50-52.

Lundeberg, M. A., Levin, B. B., & Harrington, H. L. (Eds.). (1999). *Who learns what from cases and how? The research base for teaching and learning with cases.* Mahwah, NJ: Erlbaum.

Metcalf, K. K. (1993). Critical factors in on-campus clinical experiences: Perceptions of preservice teachers. *Teaching Education, 5*(2), 172.

National Council of Teachers of English. (1996) *Guidelines for the preparation of teachers of English language arts.* Urbana, IL: Author.

Rentel, V. M. (1992, May). *Preparing clinical faculty: Research on teacher reasoning.* Paper presented at the conference on faculty development, Washington, DC.

Shulman, J. (Ed.). (1992). *Case methods in teacher education.* New York: Teachers College Press.

Spiro, R. J., & Jehng, J. C. (1992). Cognitive flexibility and hypertext: Theory and technology for the nonlinear and multidimensional traversal of complex subject matter. In D. Nix & R. J. Spiro (Eds.), *Cognition, education, and multimedia: Exploring ideas in high technology* (pp. 163-205). Hillsdale, NJ: Erlbaum.

Spiro, R. J., Feltovich, P. J., & Coulson, R. L. (1996). Two epistemic world-views: Prefigurative schemas and learning in complex domains. *Applied Cognitive Psychology, 10,* 51-61.

Stigler, J. W., & Hiebert, J. (1999). *The teaching gap: Best ideas from the world's teachers for improving education in the classroom.* New York: Summit Books.

Zeichner, K. M., & Noffke, S. E. (2001). Practitioner research. In V. Richardson (Ed.), *Handbook of Research on Teaching* (4th ed., pp. 298-330). Washington, DC: American Educational Research Association.

CHAPTER 5

THE TECHNOLOGY AND LITERACY PROJECT

Crossing Boundaries to Conceptualize the New Literacies

Dorothea Anagnostopoulos, Jory Brass, and Dipendra Subedi

Creativity is merely a plus name for regular activity ... any activity becomes creative when the doer cares about doing it right, or better.

—John Updike

The phrase "new literacies" has emerged in recent literacy research to signify the current unsettling of our conceptions and practices of literacy that has accompanied the rapid expansion of communications technology (Alvermann & Hagood, 2000; Luke & Elkins, 1998; Tyner, 1998). Digital technologies have altered the very nature of the texts that people encounter in their everyday lives. These changes have had significant consequences for how we think about literacy in relation to adolescents. Young people increasingly consume multimodal texts that incorporate graphic arts, music, and cinematic forms as well as print (Kirst, 2000; Kress, 1997; Luke & Elkins, 1998; Negroponte, 1995; New London Group, 1996).

Faculty Development by Design: Integrating Technology in Higher Education, 93–111

These texts open new possibilities for expression at the same time they demand new types of communicative competencies of both consumers and producers.

Though the new literacies are entering schools slowly and unevenly, the National Council of Teachers of English (1996) has acknowledged their importance by including the achievement of literacy in nonprint texts among its core standards for English language arts. At this stage, however, scholars and educators are just beginning to conceptualize what is meant by "new literacies," and to envision what new literacies might look like in secondary English classrooms. Some scholars focus on popular media, while others envision the use and generation of multiple forms of representation, and the design of multimodal, multigenre texts.

The emergent nature of our conceptualizations of new literacies poses several challenges for English educators. First, given the newness of the literacies, it is difficult to determine what skills and knowledge secondary students need to develop in order to become literate consumers and producers of new texts. Second, and related to this, we know little about what skills, knowledge and learning opportunities preservice English teachers need to teach the new literacies. Third, as our tools and conceptions of literacy are changing, traditional notions of literacy as reading and writing printed texts retain their primacy in K-12 schools. As schools are the institutions that credential competency in our society, English educators must prepare teachers who can ensure that their students master both traditional literacies *and* the new literacies that are increasingly important to participating proactively in our information- and technology-rich society. Finally, English educators need to consider the questions of equity tied to the new literacies, and, in particular, how they can best prepare novice English teachers to teach new literacies to students who, because of economic and social inequality, have limited access to the technologies that will enable them to become producers of new texts. All of these challenges make it necessary for English educators not only to rethink how we prepare secondary English teachers, but also to engage in the current work of redefining the nature of literacy, itself.

These changes and challenges were the impetus for our creating the Technology and Literacy Project (TALP). The TALP centered around the design and enactment of a 10-week, after-school workshop in which we, along with Punya Mishra, worked with students at a local high school to create digital videos. In addition to helping the high school students become competent consumers and producers of digital texts, a central goal of the project was to help us develop an understanding of the new literacies from the inside out. Rather than using technology to solve a pedagogical problem, we wanted to understand better what types of literacy practices digital technologies make available to and demand of adolescents in order, ultimately, to inform our own work as English educators and educational researchers.

In this chapter, we describe how we constructed an "inside-out knowledge" of the new literacies through creating and participating in the TALP. The TALP rested upon a design-based approach to learning on several levels. First, we developed a design-based curriculum that engaged students in learning digital technologies through constructing meaningful texts and sharing them with their peers. Through creating and presenting their own videos, the students moved from being consumers of new texts to being producers. The processes of design were also central to our own learning. Creating and teaching the curriculum for the TALP required on-going interactions among ourselves, with our students, with the tools we used and the products we created, and with the social context in which the TALP was embedded.

Through our work in the TALP, we have come to believe that "boundary crossing" is an essential element of a design-based approach to learning. "Boundary crossing" refers to the exchange of expertise that individuals who occupy different institutional positions and who possess different competencies engage in as they seek to solve new problems or understand new phenomena. We believe that boundary crossing is particularly relevant to understanding, teaching, and learning the new literacies. Through our participation in both the creation and implementation of the TALP, we have come view the new literacies as expansive. On the one hand, the literacy demands they place on both consumers and producers are quite high. They require the use of multiple literacy practices and competencies. On the other hand, they also afford a high degree of flexibility and reflexivity. They can incorporate multiple types of texts, genres, and sign systems. This allows producers to juxtapose images, genres, and the literacy practices they entail to create both ambiguity and critique. In short, teaching and learning the new literacies place high demands on teachers and teacher educators. We met these demands by drawing on the different competencies and expertise of our design team members. In addition, digital texts and technologies themselves afford a blurring of the boundaries of genre, styles, and sign systems. In both ways then, boundary crossing became central to our developing an inside-out knowledge of the new literacies.

In the following sections, we describe how we created the TALP through the construction of two design teams—a university-based team who developed and taught the curriculum, and a school-based university team comprised of ourselves and the students we worked with, who enacted, adapted, and transformed the curriculum. We then develop the notion of boundary crossing more fully and illustrate how various acts of boundary crossing centrally mediated our learning and that of our students. By describing these boundary crossings and how they shaped our work and our learning in the TALP, we hope to provide insight both into the new literacies and into one of the key processes of design that enabled us to develop these insights.

THE TECHNOLOGY AND LITERACY PROJECT: A DESIGN-BASED APPROACH TO LEARNING THE NEW LITERACIES

The processes of design, as we will illustrate in this chapter, facilitated our development of the "inside-out" knowledge we believe the new literacies demand of English educators. We understand design to be a complex set of interactions that occur between individuals working together to achieve a set of production goals, between individuals and the tools they use and the products they seek to create, and between individuals and the context in which they work. In our case, we worked together to create and teach a curriculum that engaged high school students in producing digital videos in order both to help students develop competencies in digital literacies and to build our own knowledge and understanding of new literacies. The students, not surprisingly, significantly influenced our work. Over time we came to view them as codesigners as we adjusted the curriculum to their learning needs and interests, and, most importantly, to the literacy practices that they brought to the project. We also had to reshape the curriculum and our teaching both to take advantage of the literacy practices the tools (i.e., the digital video software, the computers and video cameras) made available, and to cope with their limitations, as well. Finally, we negotiated unexpected changes and disruptions in the school schedule, our own schedules, our students' lives, and within the broader social context. Teacher/parent conferences and after-school activities disrupted the project and forced us to extend it a month in order to allow students time to complete their final videos. During this time, students got suspended, joined other after-school activities, and experienced family difficulties, all of which prohibited some students from completing the project. The nation's politics also shaped the project in quite significant ways. We had decided to focus the students' first video assignments around the theme of courage. This theme took on greater significance than we had anticipated when, during our work with the students, President Bush declared and initiated his war on Iraq. The war entered into our discussions with students and, as we discuss below, into their videos, as well. In short, our work and our learning through the TALP was mediated by our interactions with each other and our students, and with our ongoing engagement with the problems and puzzles that arose as we attempted to teach students how to use various digital technologies within a continually shifting immediate and distal social context.

ORIGINS

We designed the TALP as an after-school program for high school students that met from January to May 2003, at Eagleton High School located in a small city in Michigan. (All names of schools, teachers, and students are pseudonyms.) Along with Roberta, an English teacher at Eagleton, and Punya Mishra, we met with 5 to 10 of Roberta's 10th grade students each Wednesday for 2½ hours to view and create digital videos.

The TALP emerged out of a series of conversations and interactions that we had among ourselves and with a local high school teacher and her students. Throughout the 2001-2002 school year, Dorothea and Punya engaged in a series of conversations about digital video-making and its potential to engage adolescents in complex literacy practices. During these conversations, Punya shared his experiences teaching digital videos to practicing teachers, and expressed his desire to explore how he could use these experiences to work with adolescents. Dorothea described her own experiences working with adolescents in Chicago to create videos, and expressed her interest in developing a deeper knowledge of more recent digital technologies and in exploring the potential these new technologies had for literacy teaching and learning. The conversations were thus driven, in part, by our desire to expand our individual knowledge and understanding of digital literacies.

Concurrent with these conversations, Dorothea began working with Roberta. In summer 2001, Roberta had designed a summer school program for students who had failed her freshmen English course at Eagleton. Dorothea secured resources at Michigan State to have Roberta's students hold classes at the university and to use laptop computers from the College of Education. During the summer program, Roberta, Dorothea, and the students began to talk about the students creating videos to represent and critique their experiences of schooling. The students' interest in producing the videos presented an opportunity for Dorothea to develop her own understanding of digital literacies at the same time it posed a new set of problems as Dorothea had limited experiences in and knowledge of teaching digital technologies. In response to both the students' interests and her own learning needs and interests, Dorothea began to talk more earnestly with Punya about developing a program that would both teach the students how to design digital videos and provide her the opportunity to develop an understanding of the new literacies that could inform her work preparing secondary English teachers. On

Punya's advice, in April 2002, Dorothea wrote and secured a Preparing Tomorrow's Teachers for Technology (PT3) grant from the College of Education to create the Technology and Literacy Project.

THE DESIGN TEAM

The design team for the TALP comprised Punya Mishra and all the authors. The team met at the College of Education on a weekly basis throughout the 2002-2003 school year, to design and revise the TALP curriculum, and, in spring semester 2003, to teach each workshop session and analyze the students' work. Each of us came to the project from a different disciplinary and institutional position that responded, in large part, to our different teaching backgrounds, research interests, and experiences with and knowledge of digital technologies. It is easy to divide us into technology and literacy experts, though, as we will describe below, this distinction was blurred throughout the project in a quite generative way. Punya and Dipendra, working in the College's Technology, Culture, and Learning program, brought a deep knowledge of digital technologies and an equally deep interest in understanding how people engage in and learn through the processes of digital design. Though Dorothea and Jory, working in the College's Teacher Education department, shared an interest in understanding how people learn through technology, they had little experience using digital technologies. Rather, they possessed experience and knowledge of literacy instruction and adolescent literacy practices. In our work with adolescents, both of us had engaged students with multiple types of texts, such as music, film and art, though primarily as readers rather than designers. The TALP provided an opportunity, then, for Dorothea and Jory to examine the types of literate practices adolescents engage in as they produce digital texts, and to consider the implication of these practices for preparing secondary English teachers.

Roberta played a pivotal role in the TALP. She allowed us to use her classroom for the sessions and provided us information about the school and the students. During the after-school workshops, Roberta interacted with the students' as they planned, shot, and edited their videos. In addition, she frequently talked with the students about their projects during school hours, helping them to develop their ideas and, for one student, to navigate school authorities when an official stopped the student from videotaping in the school's cafeteria.

Given our central interest in understanding the nature of the literacy practices digital technologies make available and demand from adolescents, we consider the students who participated in the TALP as critical members of the design team. Students participated in the TALP on a purely voluntary basis; they did not earn any school credit for their participation, nor did we pay them. The project began with 10 students who differed in their histories of school achievement, their racial and ethnic identifications, and their experiences and interests in digital technologies. They also had quite different reasons for attending the TALP. Two students were enrolled in the school's new technology program, and had created digital videos at home prior to the TALP. These two boys enrolled to learn about new types of digital editing and technologies. Most of the other students were relatively unexperienced in using digital technologies. While some of them owned video cameras, neither they nor their families owned digital cameras or video software. These students wanted access to digital technologies and to our knowledge in order to create their own videos. Two students wanted access to the digital cameras but did not want to actually use the computer technologies. Interestingly, these two girls held some of the most interesting conversations about video aesthetics and representation. In particular, they talked between themselves and with us about how different camera angles and shots conveyed particular messages about the people whom they videotaped. These conversations led to interesting and important discussions about the ethics of video making that were quite thoughtful. Finally, two of the students attended the program to hang out with their friends, with Roberta, and with us. These students tended not to use the technology, though they did participate verbally in planning for, producing, and discussing the videos.

At its base, then, the TALP actually consisted of two overlapping design teams each comprised of people with different competencies and expertise, and with different learning goals. At times, we constituted the university-based design team. A significant amount of our work and interactions with each other occurred in and through the university. We were driven, in large part, by a desire to gain a better understanding of how students learn and engage with digital literacies to inform our work preparing preservice and in-service teachers. At other times, when we worked with the students and Roberta in their classroom we constituted, with them, a school-based design team. Learning and development, thus, occurred in these two overlapping design communities. These communities further had a highly reciprocal relationship. The university-based design team created the curriculum, materials, and instructional tools and practices that the school-based team variously took up, negotiated, and adapted in the process of producing the students' digital videos. These adaptations and negotiations then fed into the university-based design team members revising the curriculum and their instructional approaches.

THE CURRICULUM

Over the course of fall 2002, we created the curriculum for the TALP. The curriculum reflects a design-based approach that we believe is essential to teaching and learning the new literacies, for teacher educators and for high school students, alike. Digital literacies, like other new literacies, are highly interactive. A design-based approach takes advantage of this interactivity as it engages students in developing digital competencies through learning how to use various technological tools in the context of constructing multimodal texts that seek to convey the students' own ideas, beliefs, arguments, and perspectives. Students learn through using techniques, such as selecting camera angles, editing with special effects, and applying transitions between clips, how digital tools can both position viewers to read digital texts in particular ways and can shape the very ideas and expressions producers are trying to convey. A design-based approach also helps us, as teachers and teacher educators, to understand how students learn and engage with new literacies. As we helped the students to produce different types of digital texts, we could observe how they made sense of and with new literacy practices. In particular, we were able to observe the ways in which students used different digital tools to construct their "message" or "big-idea" to influence their audience and to identify the difficulties they encountered as they attempted to use these tools.

We structured the TALP around several minidesign projects that culminated in the students creating their own digital videos. These minidesign projects helped students to develop skills through hands-on-experiences using digital technologies that they could carry through to their final projects. Throughout the minidesign projects and the construction of the final videos, we sought to engage students in the activities of design with minimal instruction in the digital technologies. We provide "just in time" technical assistance upon request by students or as we deemed necessary.

We created the miniprojects both to introduce ideas and technological tools, and to foster discussion around critical design issues. The minidesign projects introduced students to different aspects of digital technologies, including the use of video cameras, importing images to the computer, and editing. Within each project, we emphasized that meaning making, aesthetics, and questions of representation drive students' video productions. For example, we planned the first two sessions around students using digital cameras to create still pictures of ordinary objects that represented some aspects of their own identities, and then moved to students experimenting with camera angles, color, and cropping to make familiar found objects, like soda bottles, books and school desks, unfamiliar. In both cases, students learned how to use digital cameras, how to import the pictures to the computer and how to use the digital editing tools in the context of saying something about themselves. They also gained an awareness of how the use of different camera angles and different framing and cropping decisions fundamentally shaped the images they produced and could, thus, influence how people read the texts they created.

The next two sessions engaged students in making two short videos about courage. The goal of these two mini projects was to encourage students to think more carefully about how to use digital technologies to express their ideas about a given concept. The first project involved the students creating a video of the poem, "The Ballad of Birmingham," which describes a young African American girl's death in the bombing of an African American church in Birmingham, Alabama by White supremacists that occurred during the 1950s civil rights movement. After reading the poem as a group, talking about its imagery and structure, and relating it to the different ideas about courage that we had generated, students broke into three groups and transposed the poem into a video. After this, students created a video to express their own views of courage. We followed each of these mini projects by group discussions and reviews of the student videos. We intended these discussions to help students learn to accept feedback and to understand that a designed object can be read and interpreted in many ways. The curriculum culminated in the creation of student-generated digital videos.

In addition to an emphasis on learning digital technologies through constructing meaningful texts, we also incorporated several viewing sessions into the curriculum that required students to make their texts public. At the end of each minidesign project, we set aside time for students to present their digital texts to their peers whom we encouraged to provide critical feedback and pose probing questions. Admittedly, getting students to engage in this type of critique was a challenge that we did not always meet. These discussions did, however, engage students in considering critical issues about how their construction of particular images, their use of particular musical and print texts, and their use of various pacing, framing, and cropping tools both conveyed and shaped their messages and ideas. As such, we believe that the discussions represent an essential tool that students can use to become more critical consumers and producers of digital texts. As students examined each other's videos and asked about why their peers made particular composition decisions and selected particular camera angles, music tracts, and framing devices, they developed a better sense of both how producers construct digital texts to influence viewers, and how the digital technologies, themselves, shape the messages and ideas producers seek to convey. Because such discussion fosters a dialogue between producers and consumers of digital texts, and between producers and the texts themselves, we believe that they are a key part of a design-based approach to new literacy teaching and learning.

BOUNDARY CROSSING AND DESIGN

In its origin, approach and content, the TALP entailed a series of boundary crossings (Engestrom, Engestrom, & Karkkainen, 1995). Through our participation in the TALP and our on-going analysis of the students' work, we have come to view these boundary crossings as a central component of the design processes through which both the university and the school-based teams learned. Engestrom et al. (1995) conceptualize boundary crossings as the horizontal exchange of expertise that generates new understandings. More specifically, they define boundary crossing as the process of knowledge production that occurs as people from different positions within or across organizations transport the tools, language, and rules of social interaction from one domain into a new domain. As new technologies become available to shape and reshape the work of different institutions, individuals are increasingly called upon to enter new institutional domains and/or to wrestle with new tools, practices, and problems. As a result, individuals encounter the different practices that others bring with them and must work collectively with others to transpose these practices into new ways of knowing and acting. Because people are entering into new and undefined domains that challenge their claims to expertise, boundary crossing necessitates a shift from a vertical notion of expertise in which knowledge is viewed as distributed hierarchically among people who possess different levels of skill and competency, to horizontal notions that view knowledge as distributed across actors who are competent in different types of practices, and with whom individuals must negotiate the use of multiple tools and patterns of interaction.

Engestrom et al. (1995) identify two types of tools, or *boundary objects*, that facilitate boundary crossing. The first are representational and include shared external depictions of a problem or domain, such as those that may be embedded in flow charts or written standards for performance, and shared mental models that become internalized through the process of collective knowledge construction. The second set of tools is dialogic and includes argumentation and dialogue. These tools serve as boundary objects as they facilitate the airing of multiple perspectives that can disrupt established practices and expose differences between people in ways that either force people to examine and recommit to their established practices or that serve as an impetus for the creation of new ones.

HORIZONTAL EXPERTISE:
NEGOTIATING AND CONTESTING CONCEPTIONS OF LITERACY

One of the most important processes that occurred among the university-based design team during the TALP was the exchange and contestation of the competing notions of literacy that we brought to the project. As we planned the curriculum, taught the workshop sessions, and reflected on student work and on our own participation in the project, we asserted and negotiated these different notions. Significantly, while we incorporated the various conceptions of literacy into the TALP curriculum, we never actually resolved our differences into a shared model. We contend, however, that our different conceptions of literacy served as boundary objects. Throughout our interactions we refined our own understandings and became more aware of their potential and their limitations.

In an early meeting, Punya defined literacy as the ability to subvert signs, and went on to explain that by subversion he meant the "creative (re)construction of rules and/or conventions." In addition, Punya brought with this definition an emphasis on aesthetics and the sensual engagement with texts. While Punya's emphasis on subversion resonated with the understandings of literacy that Dorothea and Jory held, in many ways Punya's definition of literacy also stood in opposition to that held by Dorothea and Jory. Grounded in literacy studies, literary theory, and critical discourse analysis, Dorothea and Jory viewed literacy as the use and manipulation of different sign and symbol systems grounded in and about complex social relations. While Punya's notion of literacy highlighted the individual actor's use and response to signs situated outside of the actor, our notion of literacy highlighted the ontological nature of literacy practices, as well as their signatory purposes and consequences. That is, Dorothea and Jory understood literacy as social practices that are both reflective and constitutive of particular social identities and relations. Because at any one time or place, multiple types of literate practices exist to both define and be used in a particular social context, individuals can variously take up, negotiate, transform, or resist particular signs and symbols. Individuals, however, are also always socially positioned by the signs and symbols they use or do not use within a given social setting. In short, Dorothea and Jory's view of literacy requires taking into account the relationship between particular types of literate practices and the social identities and relations they both reflect and make possible. It requires a dual focus on the individuals and the structure of social relations that literacy practices mediate. The most important division among members of the university-based design team thus had little to do with our different levels of technological expertise and knowledge, and more to do with our competing visions of literacy.

The differences in our visions of literacy surfaced frequently through-out our planning and implementing of the TALP. For example, during one meeting Jory showed a number of digital videos created by adoles-cents that he found from various Web sites. Our intention was to identify videos that we could use as models of adolescents' critical inquiries into their social worlds. As we watched the videos, Jory and Dorothea read them to identify how the students challenged common ideas about what it meant to be consumers, to be teenagers, and to be Americans. In contrast, Punya and Dipendra talked about issues of camera angles, pacing and rhythm, and the videos' "force" or impact on the viewer's sensibilities. As we viewed the digital texts together, then, we exchanged our different conceptions of literacy around a joint problem, understanding how ado-lescents constructed digital texts and how we could use such texts to help our own students do the same.

Such exchanges helped us to articulate, clarify, and defend our differ-ent, and in some ways competing notions of literacy. The final videos that the students created, and how they talked about these projects, reflect our differing conceptions. One set of students were centrally concerned with "saying something." As they worked to film and edit their videos, they brought up questions about what "messages" they were sending in regards to given social issue, such as gay and lesbian rights or dropping out of school, that they wanted to address in their videos. It was among these students that questions of power and of ethics explicitly surfaced. These students grappled with their power as video makers to ascribe particular social identities to the people, usually other students in the school, whom they filmed. In both their desire to convey a "message" about a social issue they viewed as important, and their discussions of the ethics of video representation, these students began to engage with questions of power and meaning that are at the heart of the critical notion of literacy that Dorothea and Jory held.

In contrast, one of the students explicitly rejected this view and took up Punya's focus on aesthetics. This student, Lonnie, created a video that pictured students eating in the school cafeteria and that incorporated a song that Lonnie found among his father's music albums. Though Lonnie imposed the question, "Do you know what you're children are eating?" over the initial image, he rejected any attempts to articulate a "message" or a social critique. During one workshop session, Dorothea told Lonnie about numerous Internet Web sites where he could find information and statistics about adolescent food consumption and food-related health problems. Lonnie dismissed Dorothea's suggestions, arguing that he did not want to include statistics in his video because "everyone else was using them." Lonnie focused, instead, on issues of timing and humor, and was more concerned with the look of the video than with its power to critique the social practices he filmed.

THE OPEN EXCHANGE OF EXPERTISE: DECONSTRUCTING THE TEACHER/STUDENT RELATIONSHIP THROUGH THE NEW LITERACIES

If the TALP served as a site on which we exchanged our different types of expertise and contested our competing notions of literacy, it also served as a site on which the traditional teacher/student relationship was constantly open to negotiation and deconstruction. Though we acted as "the teachers" throughout the project, designing, refining, and enacting the curriculum described above, all members of the design team, including the students, moved into and out of the roles of "teachers" and "learners" throughout the project. As each week of the project emphasized different technological tools, social arrangements, purposes, and communicative practices, the nature of our participation and contributions to large and small group activities changed with each workshop. The collaborative culture of the TALP provided for an open exchange of expertise among partners rather than between "experts" and "novices" or between "teachers" and "students."

In part, the after-school nature of the TALP allowed for a flexibility of activities and of participation that would have been constrained by the regulation of time, space, and interaction that structure the "regular" school day. At the same time, as we engaged in the TALP and talked about and examined the design processes the students engaged in and the products they created, we have come to believe that both the digital technologies and our design-based approach contributed to this flexibility in significant ways. The example of how Jose (pseudonym) created his video illustrates how digital videos allow adolescents to incorporate multiple types of texts that draw on the knowledge of their social lives and youth cultures in ways that position teachers as partners in, and, sometimes marginal to, production processes. The story of the making of Jose's video also points to the quite complex literacy demands that new, multimodal texts place upon both adolescents and their teachers.

CREATING #1

Jose's final video, titled "#1," centered on questions of what constitutes success for young people. The multimedia text incorporated music, printed words, and film and print images, and drew upon a variety of texts from Jose's home worlds, including downloaded lyrics from the rap-per *Nellie*, images from urban culture magazines, including *Vibe* and *The Source*, wall calendars of luxury automobiles, and hand-held video of stu-dent fashions that Jose and another boy, Tim, filmed at the school. Jose imposed printed questions that asked, "What does it mean to be number one?", "What is success?" and "What is courage?" over these images throughout the text.

The video's focus on success and youth culture initially arose from a conversation Jose had with two other boys in the project. During this con-versation, which occurred immediately after Dorothea and Punya had described the final video project to the whole group, the boys talked about hip hop fashion and athletic wear, and their importance to students' social relationships within the school. Dorothea, Roberta, and Punya entered into the boy's conversation at different points to prompt them to identify an idea or concept around which they wanted to organize their video. In particular, Dorothea, Roberta, and Punya each picked up on the consumer orientation of the boys' talk to encourage them to make a video that would critique materialism. In response, as they talked, Jose and the other boys began to outline a video that would focus on the numerous decisions they made each morning about what to wear, and that would articulate the social nature and consequences of these decisions. More specifically, they talked about videotaping Jose selecting clothes, shoes, and jewelry in his room at home, and that would include a voice over of what he was thinking about as he made each decision. The boys also talked about videotaping a shopping excursion to a local store that sold the athletic wear popular among students in the school.

Over the course of the next 3 weeks, Jose and one of the boys, Tim, began to videotape students at the school, focusing in on the brand names of the shoes and shirts the students wore. Throughout this, Dipen-dra addressed the boy's questions about editing their video clips with the computer software, and showed them how to locate information on the computer to help them work independently, as well. Also during this time, Jory invited Heather, a student from the English methods course he was teaching at Michigan State, to observe the project. Heather was inter-ested in the use of multimedia texts in secondary English classrooms. As a 20-year old, she brought with her knowledge of popular youth culture that we did not possess. Heather spent much of her time with Jory talking to Jose about the nature of the images he was videotaping. In particular, she and Jory talked with him about how he wanted to place the different images in relationship to one another, and what he wanted to "say" with the images and with how he filmed, edited, and sequenced them. Partly in response to these conversations, Jose began to incorporate images of rap-pers, clothes and jewelry, and advertisements from the sports and hip hop magazines and posters he had in his room at home. He also decided to import into the video a popular rap in which the rapper identifies the attitude and social practices that distinguish him from other rappers and that make him "number one." In the final session of the project, during which students presented their final videos, Jose filmed and incorporated a picture of an American flag into the last frame of his video, and typed a final question that asked what the relationship between "being number one" and "real courage" was.

In creating his video, Jose drew upon his local knowledge of adolescents' multiple social worlds, both in and outside of school, and the relationship among them. The film clips that Jose and Tim shot at the school reflected their sophisticated knowledge of how their peers positioned themselves within the school through their "gear," and the status credentials the students' fashion choices afforded them in their in-school social world. It also reflected Jose's experiences with multiple types of visual texts, and his knowledge of and engagement in a popular youth culture that existed outside of school and yet, as the video indicated, permeated it as well. Indeed, the video took much of its shape only after Jose incorporated the hip hop lyrics and popular cultural images from his own adolescent literacies—listening to rap music, browsing hip hop and fashion magazines, and consuming sports images and statistics. Jose thus drew upon his knowledge of and competence in a highly diverse set of literacy practices that constituted a body of expertise that we did not possess.

At the same time, Jose's focus on materialism and, ultimately, on questioning its relationship to courage indicates that he also drew on the conceptual tools we brought to the project and our own expertise in concept-based literacy instruction. As we noted above, two of the minidesign projects involved students in creating videos centered on their notions of courage. During the first of these miniprojects, Dorothea facilitated a whole group discussion in which all members of the school-based design team, university participants as well as high school students, constructed a joint definition of courage centered on taking risks and making sacrifices for the betterment of others, and defending or promoting one's beliefs, values, and freedoms. The definition, which remained relatively abstract and quite open, served as a mental model that enabled Jose to critique aspects of the youth culture in which he participated. Jose drew on the concept and the group's open definition of it by naming it in the final question he posed in the video. By representing courage with an image of the American flag at a time when the United States had recently invaded Iraq, Jose inflected the group's definition of courage by incorporating the idea of patriotism into it. While Jose's use of the flag in the context of his video and in the historical context in which he created it was unsettling to us, Jose's use of the concept illustrated how the group's definition of courage served as a boundary object that enabled Jose to incorporate the tools that we brought to the TALP into his video in ways that ultimately enabled him to critique both the definition of the concept that we brought to the project and the social practices and values of the youth culture in which he participated.

CONSTRUCTING NEW UNDERSTANDINGS OF THE NEW LITERACIES THROUGH THE TALP

As a highly informal and collaborative project, the TALP deconstructed the simple dichotomies of teacher-student and literacy expert-technology expert. Through engaging in an open exchange of expertise and in argumentation, the TALP allowed us to gain a richer understanding of the New Literacies and the learning opportunities they provide and demand of adolescents. In particular, through working alongside the students as they created digital videos, and negotiating the competing notions of literacy we brought to the project, we came to view the new literacies as *expansive literacies*.

The new literacies can be understood as expansive literacies in several ways. First, consuming and producing digital texts, as our story of Jose's video production suggests, involve developing and using knowledge of multiple sign systems (i.e., music, film, photography, and print), genres, texts, and literate practices, and learning how to make sense of how these systems, genres, texts, and practices interact with and inflect one another within a single text. Students and teachers, alike, need to become competent in identifying the multiple genres merged into digital texts, and in interpreting, critiquing and, we argue, manipulating the hybrid images and genres that the texts embed and make possible. In short, we have come to understand the highly complex literacy demands that new texts hold for both students and teachers.

Related to this complexity, the new literacies are expansive in that they allow adolescents to draw on the symbolic tools and resources associated with the multiple social worlds, including but extending beyond the school, in which they engage. We saw how Jose was able to incorporate images and music that signified the youth and popular cultures in which he engaged. He also drew on a highly nationalistic identity, as represented by the image of the American flag, as well. Recent literacy research highlights how students often negotiate the more "official" school worlds through appropriating the more familiar symbolic tools, such as the stories, genres, and language play, that they bring into classrooms from their out-of-school lives (Dyson, 1993; Gutierrez, Rymes, & Larson, 1995). In particular, popular culture often provides students with their preferred symbolic tools to make sense of school writing and reappropriate these symbolic resources to meet their own social purposes and to position themselves among their classmates as effective users of language, whether the schools' official curriculum acknowledges these tools or not (Dyson, 1993). Our participation in the TALP suggests that the new literacies may provide students opportunities to directly engage their multiple, unschooled literacy practices in school and to provide them an avenue to draw upon these practices to become competent in both the "old" and "new" literacies.

Participating in the project also reinforced to us the importance of preparing teachers who can engage students in being critical consumers and producers of new texts and literacy practices. The new literacies allow for a reflexivity that can engender adolescents' critical engagement with questions about the relationship between texts and literacy practices, on the one hand, and social relations and power on the other. We saw how filming their peers raised for the adolescents we worked with, questions of power and ethics inherent in producing texts. Students had to consider what it meant for them to position their peers as particular types of subjects, and what it meant for their relationships with their peers and, thus, their own social identities. Further, as Jose's video suggests, digital technologies offered students the opportunities to incorporate the literacy practices of their particular youth cultures and to critique those practices and the identities and values they embed. Engaging students with multimodal, digital texts thus offers teachers the possibility of building on and developing this reflexivity.

At the same time, the multimodal nature of the new literacies leaves both consumers and producers open to being taken by issues of image and aesthetics. This was most evident in the TALP when Lonnie renounced any efforts on our part to have him think more critically about the social aspects of his video. He was taken up with the idea of the images themselves. Interestingly, Lonnie told us that several students he filmed were concerned about their image being used in his video, though he refused to engage with the ethical and social implications of these concerns and his role in prompting them. Jose's final video reveals, too, the power of images in the new literacies. Jose's video was replete with multiple images of popular youth culture, but drew much of its force, both critical and aesthetic, from juxtaposing the image of the American flag with the pop culture images to create a highly ambiguous text. We argue that this ambiguity opens up possibilities for engaging Jose in an examination of the multiple messages that the image of the American flag conveyed, and how those messages related to the particular historical context in which Jose created the video and to the images of masculinity and success of the youth and popular culture that Jose also incorporated into the video. In short, while incorporating new literacies into the classroom may create opportunities for adolescents to engage the out-of-school practices and expertise they possess and to position teachers as colearners, we also believe that they increase teachers' responsibility for providing students the conceptual tools to engage in investigating the multiple meanings these practices convey, as well as developing and building upon them.

Our participation in the TALP has made us aware of the complex literacy practices that consuming and producing "new" texts allow for and demand of adolescents. As we think about how to draw upon the TALP to inform our work with preservice English teachers, it is clear that the depth of subject matter knowledge that teaching the new literacies require of teachers surpasses that of conventional print literacies. As we noted above, reading and designing multimodal texts requires understanding the structure of different types of sign systems and being able to construct new understandings of how these different systems interact with each other within a single text. At the very least, the new literacies will require rethinking the types of texts and literacy practices that we engage our preservice teachers with as they move through their college career, and will ultimately, we think, require us to broaden our notions of what constitutes the "subject matter" of English, itself.

Finally, our participation in the TALP illustrates the value of a design-based approach to both student learning and to our learning, as teacher educators, as well. Preparing teachers to teach the new literacies poses considerable problems and puzzles for teacher educators, not the least being that many of us have only minimal knowledge of and engagement with such literacies. Working in design teams that consisted of individuals with different competencies and from different parts of our own college as well as those based in different institutions provided the expertise we needed to engage with these highly complex literacies. Much as the design-based approach enabled the adolescents we worked with to learn how to use new technologies to construct meaningful digital texts, the design-based approach to our own professional development as teacher educators helped us to gain a better understanding of what teaching the new literacies demands of and affords teachers and teacher educators.

REFERENCES

Alvermann, D., & Hagood, M. (2000). Critical media literacy: Research, theory, and practice in "New Times." *Journal of Educational Research, 93*, 193-205.

Dyson, A. H. (1993). *Social worlds of children learning to write in urban primary schools.* New York: Teachers College Press.

Engestrom, Y., Engestrom, R., & Karkkainen, M. (1995). Polycontextuality and boundary crossing in expert cognition: Learning and problem solving in complex work activities. *Learning and Instruction, 5*, 319-336.

Gutierrez, K., Rymes, B., & Larson, J. (1995). Script, counterscript, and underlife in classrooms: James Brown vs. Brown vs. Board of Education. *Harvard Educational Review, 65*, 445-471.

International Reading Association & National Council of Teachers of English. (1996). *Standards for the English language arts*. Newark, DE and Urbana, IL: Authors.

Kirst, W. (2000). Beginning to create the new literacy classroom: What does the new literacy look like? *Journal of Adolescent and Adult Literacy, 43*, 710-718.

Kress, G. (1997). *Before uniting: Rethinking the paths to literacy*. London: Routledge.

Luke, A., & Elkins, J. (1998). Reinventing literacy in "new times." *Journal of Adolescent and Adult Literacy, 42*, 4-7.

Negroponte, N. (1995). *Being digital*. New York: Knopf.

New London Group. (1996). A pedagogy of multiliteracies: Designing social futures. *Harvard Education Review, 66*, 60-92.

Tyner, K. (1998). Literacy in a *digital* world: Teaching and learning in the *Age* of information. Mahwah, NJ: Erlbaum.

CHAPTER 6

MAPS & MORE

Engaging Maps and Social Science Data as Narratives About the World

Avner Segall and Bettie Landauer-Menchik

The map is not the territory.
—Alfred Korzybski

INTRODUCTION

In this chapter we explore the design of *Maps & More,*[1] a technology-rich pedagogical environment intended to facilitate the exploration of maps and social science data as socially constructed narratives that need to be actively read. The goal of the *Maps & More* project was to develop a Web-based series of curricular modules for teachers, student teachers, and students that facilitate a critical engagement with maps, charts, and graphs across the curricula of middle school. *Maps & More* invites users to think about, with, and through a variety of maps and social science data presentation formats to consider the political, economic, and social implications

Faculty Development by Design: Integrating Technology in Higher Education, 113–130
Copyright © 2007 by Information Age Publishing
All rights of reproduction in any form reserved.

113

of these formats to name, construct, and depict our geographic and social imagination.

As we planned and worked on this project, our intent was therefore not to simply integrate content, pedagogy, and technology. Instead, and assuming, as we did, that pedagogy is a technology, that technology is always already pedagogical, and that content not only informs those it engages about the world but also positions them, pedagogically, to think about and act in the world in some ways rather than others, we hoped to bring the content, pedagogy, and technology together through an exploration of how each is already embedded in, underlies, and makes the other possible. With this in mind, and believing that the pedagogical nature of a Web-based platform can, under certain circumstances, invite particular kinds of teaching and learning, our initial intent was to create a Web-based curriculum. By "curriculum" we do not mean a prepackaged and fixed course of learning but rather one that merely provides direction in the form of possibilities, openings that still require teachers to think through and construct a learning sequence that best addresses the specific needs of their particular classrooms. That is, within this specifically designed Web-based environment, teachers would not be asked to simply execute a predetermined curriculum designed by others (us), but where they would create their own curriculum through a process of selection that requires construction, where learning would transcend the linearity of students producing knowledge only for the teacher, and where thinking would be made explicit and be shared and scrutinized publicly as students and teachers worked together to explore the world and one's learning of it through new and different lenses.

The dominant rhetoric around technology has tended to advance the idea that, through its affordances, technology forces certain kinds of pedagogical approaches, mostly ones emphasizing student-centered open-ended curricula. While we believe there is some truth in that, we contend that it is not the technology in and of itself that generates pedagogy but rather the pedagogical nature of technology that invites particular kinds of teaching and learning and, if used appropriately, helps make them possible. Thus, while we hoped the nature of an open-ended Web-based format would help foster classroom pedagogies, we did not envision the technology as their creator. In other words, and as will be explained later on, a technology-rich, Web-based environment was not meant to generate teachers' pedagogy but to help realize what we and the teachers participating in this project already conceived of as both pedagogically possible and desirable.

With much of this project being a negotiation between the desirable and the possible (with the university-based team focusing mostly on the desirable and the teachers constantly keeping the possible front and center), the end result of this project bears only slight resemblance to the one we envisioned at the outset. Like most ambitious projects that begin with a grand scheme, we hoped to accomplish much more than we eventually did. Somewhere along the road, as our vision met the reality and needs of classroom teachers, project goals were redefined, objectives reconsidered, scope reduced. In many ways, then, this chapter is a story about that transformation, what was won and lost in that process, and what, beyond this particular project, might be learned from it about balancing varying assumptions and divergent goals when designing technology-rich learning environments for K-12 education.

We begin the chapter by elaborating on our initial approach to the design of this project and how it coincided with what and how we hoped to promote as teachers and students explore maps and social science data through a series of activities. We then move to explain why and how our end product (a CD-ROM rather than a Web-based platform), while maintaining most of the pedagogical and content issues we initially hoped to address, tends to use technology in the service of content and pedagogy, thus "hiding" its pedagogical nature rather than (as we initially hoped) make it apparent and open to critical investigation. In doing so, we explore and examine the transformation of our project/product, how and why that transformation occurred, how it impacted our thinking and the design of our product, and what we learned in the process about the role and uses of technology in education, about what its infusion makes im/possible not only for those for whom the product was intended but also for us as a community of designers working on this project. We conclude with some observations of lessons currently being learned, not from the process of designing *Maps & More* but, rather, from its use in university teacher education classrooms as well as in social studies classrooms in public schools.

DEFINING THE "PROBLEM": CONCEIVING *MAPS & MORE*

We came to this project primarily as social studies educators. While we have both engaged technology in teaching (and in the preparation of teachers) prior to this project, our main purpose in this project was to develop a technology-rich learning environment—a "curriculum"—that addresses an authentic pedagogical problem underlying existing K-12 social studies education. The problem is best summarized as an unquestioned acceptance of maps, charts, and graphs as natural (and neutral) depictions of the world as it *really* is. Put otherwise, the problem could be defined as the lack of a critical engagement with those texts as socially constructed narratives that not only promote particular understandings about the world but also position those engaging them to think about and be and act in that world in some ways rather than others. Our definition of this as a "problem" emanates from our particular understandings—based in critical pedagogy and cultural studies—about the purposes of social education. Rather than seeing social studies education—or, for that matter, education in general—primarily as the preparation of students to actively participate in the political, social, economic, and cultural domains as they are, we believe social education should help students engage those domains critically by imagining otherwise as they challenge the knowledge, knowing and ways of being offered by those domains as well as what and who they advantage, gloss over, silence, and render invisible.

Underlying our thinking about this project is another important element borrowed from critical pedagogy—its definition of pedagogy—which helped us engage the relationship between content, pedagogy, and technology in a specific way. While not diminishing pedagogy's concern with 'what's to be done?' in classrooms, pedagogy, claim Giroux and Simon (1988), is something more than "the integration of curriculum content, classroom strategies and techniques, a time and space for the practice of those strategies and techniques, and evaluation purposes and methods." Rather, they propose, pedagogy refers to any "attempt to influence how and what knowledge and identities are produced within and among particular sets of social relations" (p. 12). As such, Simon (1992) adds, pedagogy is a process "through which we are encouraged to know, to form a particular way of ordering the world, giving and making sense of it" (p. 56). The practice of pedagogy, according to Simon, is an attempt to influence experience and subjectivity. As a mode of organizing and regulating symbolic productive practices, pedagogy attempts to "influence the way meanings are recognized, understood, accepted, negotiated, challenged, and/or refused" (p. 59). Broadly conceived, then, pedagogy is inherent in any message, contained in any form of action, structure, or text that organizes someone's experience as well as organizes that someone to experience the world in particular ways (Segall, 2004).

Holding that broad view of pedagogy in mind at the outset of the project, we did not regard content, pedagogy (in its traditional, confined fashion), and technology as separable entities, each occupying a separate node on a triangle to be brought together—hopefully, integrated—through our project. Rather, and assuming, as we did, that pedagogy is a technology and that technology and content are inherently pedagogical, we viewed the three as always already embedded in, underlying, and making the other possible (Koehler, Mishra, Hershey, & Peruski, 2004; Mishra & Koehler, submitted). Technology, then, was not intended simply as a means to service content and pedagogy (again, in its limited sense) but as an equal partner in constructing knowledge, knowing, and experience. Indeed, we viewed the entire project as a pedagogical device (Bernstein, 1996).

This project, as we will explain in more detail later on, not only centered on this broad notion of pedagogy but also intended to be inherently antipedagogical (Felman, 1982) in nature. [By antipedagogical we do not mean that our project attempted to somehow transcend its pedagogical imperative. As described above, that effort would be impossible.] Rather, what we take "anti" to imply is that we hoped our project would be oppositional to existing pedagogy in K-12 social education. We envisioned the oppositional nature of this project in two ways: first, as challenging the kind of knowledge presented in social studies classrooms with regards to maps and visual representations of social science data; and, second, as challenging the "delivery system" in which learning those—indeed, most any—texts are currently engaged in social studies classrooms. To anticipate, we hoped that the content used in our project—a series of maps charts and graphs and, more importantly, the questions asked of them and the activities surrounding that questioning—would provide an alternative to existing ways of engaging those texts and allow for critical conversations around that engagement that would encourage students to explore them as stories about the world that need to be critically examined. One of the primary purposes of social studies education is to enable students to become critical readers of the multiple kinds of texts they encounter both inside and outside of school (This is true with regard to K-12 students as it is to prospective social studies teachers while learning to teach). Both the ability and inclination to read texts critically—questioning their purpose, their underlying assumptions and values, and their mechanisms of persuasion—are fundamental to the critical citizenry we need in a democracy. Consequently, teachers of social studies have long focused on teaching students how to read print materials (and, increasingly, also the moving image) in ways that question them rather than simply taking the information provided by them as given. Text formats traditionally escaping such scrutiny, in K-12 schools as well as in disciplinary courses offered at the university, are maps and visual representations of social science data (e.g., charts and graphs). While similar theoretical understandings that call for a critical engagement with texts underpin this project's engagement with maps as well as with charts and graphs on the other (with each, as we explained earlier, constituting a separate space in our "curriculum"), we will, for lack of space, restrict our explanation in this chapter to the issue of maps while inviting readers to draw similar conclusions regarding the various manifestations of charts and graphs.

As staples in social education, maps are, more often than not, still regarded as unproblematic texts, transparent windows to the world. Like all texts, however, maps are not found in nature; people create them. Although such a statement may be self-evident, its implications are often overlooked in many social studies classrooms. The crisp and precise appearance of maps lends them an air of scientific authenticity (Wright, 1977, p. 8), diminishing their created nature—them being stories told by mapmakers. While maps are often considered as simply telling things as they are, maps are not merely witnesses, silently recording what would otherwise take place without them. Instead, they are committed participants, driving the very acts of identifying and naming, bounding and inventorying that which they pretend to no more than observe (Wood, 1992, p. 79). Indeed, as Kaiser and Wood (2001) explain, every map tells a story that serves a purpose and advances an interest (p. 4). Using language and symbol, icon and image, mapmakers, to borrow from Hall (1981), produce representations of the world, images, descriptions, explanations, and frames for understanding of the world: what it is and what it can and should be. They do so through what and who they include and exclude and by where that or those included are positioned within the map, rendering some aspects of the world significant while ignoring and marginalizing others. The traditional perception of a map as a mirror, a graphic representation is thus untenable (Harley, 1990, p. 3). Mapmakers must choose *what* to show and *how* to show it, and, by extension, what not to show. Indeed, as Wood (1992) points out, a map is a *show*, a representation, and the mapmaker a creator rather than reflector. While what is shown is no doubt real, all maps, inevitably and unavoidably, embody their authors' perspectives, assumptions, and biases, offering a *selective* view of reality (Monmonier, 1991, p. 1).

Engaging maps for the narratives they are is often hindered, however, since maps, by the very nature of their mode of presentation, actively work to deny the existence of signification. Most prominent in enabling this "denial" is the map's lack of an apparent author. In fact, Wood (1992) explains, the map is powerful precisely to the extent that its author remains absent. For it is only to the extent that the author escapes notice that the world the map struggles to bring into being can be taken *for* the world. With the disappearance of the author, we no longer see the map as something *arranged* for us. "Soon enough, it is the world, it is real, it is *reality*" (p. 70). The absence of an author has a double, interrelated effect on our perceptions of and interaction with maps. It implies the map is unmediated, a facsimile of the real rather than a perspective on it. When no author is made to stand behind or claim responsibility for that which is depicted, readers' ability to converse with the map—to talk back to it, to

challenge or dispute its claims or its underlying assumptions and values—
is diminished: When something purports to come from nowhere, to be
created by no one, how could it be disputed? To whom might our disputa-
tions be addressed?

A critical engagement with maps is hindered in other ways as well. As
products of our educational system, we have all learned to argue with
words much more than with icons and images—the language with which
maps convey the world to us. More, those icons and images remain
unquestioned because they fit seamlessly with the sign system of other cultural artifacts—road signs, logos, pictures on cereal boxes, patterns on
wrapping paper, picture books, posters, and billboards—that we have
learned to accept from childhood. Thus, while we may need to learn how
to use maps, such learning comes easy for maps and the symbols they use
are congruent with the larger system of signs underlying our culture
(Wood, 1992, pp. 143–144). No map symbol, Wood (1992) explains,
"stands up and says, 'Hi, I'm a lock,' or 'We're a marsh,' anymore than
words of an essay bother to explain *themselves* to the reader." And no matter how many readers are convinced that pictograms of lighthouses and
mountains explain themselves, or that blue naturally represents water,
those

> Signs are *not* signs for, dissolve into marks for, those who don't know the
> code.... [Rather,] each of these *signs* is a perfectly conventional way of saying
> what is said ("lighthouse," "mountain," "water")—which is why the map
> seems so transparent, so easy to read. (p. 99)

Maps, however, not only fit into our existing cultural understandings,
they also reproduce them through their promotion of particular cultural assumptions and biases. Most map projections (at least the ones
we are familiar with in the West) display a European and Western bias,
splitting Asia in half in order to put Europe and the Americas front and
center (Levstik, 1985). That Europe and the Americas should be at the
center of the map, or that zero meridian should be the one running
through Greenwich is, of course, not because they actually are. Instead,
they are a reflection of the role of Europeans in the development of car-
tography and consequently their power to position themselves in the
center and thus as *central* (Black, 1997, p. 37). The implications of neu-
tralizing those forms of depiction, of ignoring them are grave for when
students are made to believe they stand at the center of their world,
they tend to understand—indeed, learn to divide—the world and its
people (Willinsky, 1998) in ways that reflect that particular perception,
with all the dangers of superiority and domination that go along with it.

DESIGNING A CURRICULUM TO ENGAGE MAPS AS STORIES ABOUT THE WORLD

The intent behind the curriculum culminating from this project was to disturb the existing taken-for-granted nature of map-work in social studies classrooms (especially, in middle school classrooms where students first engage world maps in a serious manner), encouraging teachers and students to explore maps and map-making for the explicit, implicit, and null claims to knowledge they make and the understandings they help produce. Our hope was that, having engaged *Maps & More*, teachers and students will look differently at maps—not only those provided within this project but any map they encounter in the future. In that sense, we hoped the project will be not only be informative within its own boundaries but would be generative (Perkins, 1992), helping to transform map-work and the learning derived from it throughout social education (and, hopefully, beyond).

To help teachers and students think more deeply *with* and *about* maps, we needed to make maps and map-making problematic, for as long as the two are taken as neutral, we believed, they will remain unquestioned, beyond discussion. While the limited space of this chapter does not allow us to describe the curriculum inviting teachers and students to consider maps in that fashion, it might be useful to introduce some of the guiding questions posed across that curriculum that help ensure such an examination takes place. These questions, ones not often addressed in the social studies classroom, help make maps problematic by connecting them to the political, cultural, social, and economic spheres that gave rise to them as well as to those they help produce. That is, such questions, adapted from Werner (2000), help students explore the assumptions maps make, the interests they serve, and the worldviews they promote. While this list is by no means exhaustive, we believe it provides a good place to start a critical engagement with maps and of reading the world constructed by them: What is this map depicting and what story is it attempting to tell through that depiction? What is your reaction to this portrayal? In what ways and how does this map serve to perpetuate or challenge existing political and/or social goals, issues, and interests? What might this map imply about the assumptions, commitments, and values of its maker as well as those of its intended readers? What might the map tell us about prevailing social attitudes and power relations at the time and place the map was produced? What and whose interests does it advance and/or marginalize? What position (i.e., powerful or powerless, insider or outsider) does the map invite you, its reader, to assume and how does it accomplish that positioning (what textual devices or conventions does it recruit)? What alternative depictions might be possible? That is, what (or who) could be included that is currently missing or how what is/are presented could be displayed otherwise to make the map more acceptable (and to whom)?

By posing these questions and through the design of the activities in which they are embedded, our intent was for teachers and students not only to recognize that maps are authored, "made," but also for their contingent and conditional nature to be revealed, and for things represented to become open to discussion and debate (Wood, 1992, p. 19). Indeed, the educative value of studying maps is quite different, if one begins with the conviction that maps give meaning to the world rather than find meaning in it. Exploring maps in a manner that is aware of their construction, students are made to consider that between the world and the map is a process of selection and interpretation, both of which are shaped by the values, assumptions, and perspectives of a particular mapmaker. This allows students to use maps to ask different questions about knowledge, about our relationship to the world, as well as about the nature of map-making as a way to narrate and appropriate it.

Approaching maps in that fashion, it should be emphasized, is not, in any way, intended to either deny or diminish the value of maps and their making; it simply attempts to return both to the social and political contexts in which they have (and from which they derive their) meaning— meaning not without controversy but in controversy (Black, 1997, p. 168). When maps are considered as narratives, as serving a purpose and promoting an interest, we can afford to no longer think of them in "either/ or" terms—as true or false, accurate or inaccurate, objective or subjective (Harley, 1988, p. 278). Rather, we can begin to explore *all* maps for the messages they convey, for the assumptions they embody, and for the values they promote since all maps, by definition, are highly selective and necessarily biased (Monmonier, 1995, p. 297).

To best encourage teachers and students to think differently not only *about* but also *with* and *through* maps, we wanted to achieve two interrelated pedagogical objectives. The first pertained to the "content" of this curriculum, the other to its design. As for content, and in order to facilitate students' interrogation of maps rather than the acceptance of them, we wanted to incorporate a variety of maps (historical and contemporary, conventional and unconventional, from the center of our culture and the periphery) and map formats (political maps, physical maps, cartograms, pictorial maps) in our project. Many of the maps we envisioned are untraditional in nature. That is, maps that students have probably not encountered beforehand, ones that do not fit well into and onto students' already established expectations of maps. To achieve our goals of disturbing existing map-work, however, such maps, we believed, must be used in conjunction with traditional maps with which students are already familiar. For it is only by comparing different maps, by letting the "strange" speak to and question the "ordinary" that the interests, perspectives, and world views underlying maps and our definition of some of them as "ordinary" and others as "strange" can come to light. The importance of multiple perspectives in social studies education (Banks, 1997) is equally applicable while working with maps (and thus, to our project). Where only one view is given, it is not only hard to imagine alternatives; it is also difficult to question the given.

With regard to designing a curriculum that might incorporate the above-mentioned sensibilities, we struggled with the issue of *structure*. While we understood that any curriculum must have some structure to guide learning in a particular direction, we did not want it to be over-structured in ways that would inhibit teachers thinking as they engaged *Maps & More*. That is, we wanted to provide teachers with a variety of Web-based resources comprising the kinds of maps they might need, resources from which they would have to choose maps as they constructed a curriculum to best suit their particular goals and students. It is in the process of designing one's curriculum, we felt, that teachers' thinking is activated as they make choices and decide among alternatives with a particular purpose, audience, and learning context in mind. This, we believed, would constitute a departure from the more traditional units "given" to teachers that, by and large, require them to follow someone else's directions and (mostly hidden) thought processes. We wanted teachers, especially in an age of "accountability" and pacing guides that have taken curricular decisions out of the hands of teachers, to be creators of their curriculum rather than simply implementers of ours.

Ambitious as we were, we hoped for more. We also wanted *Maps & More* to break with the prevailing delivery system of knowledge production in classrooms. This did not entail asking teachers to fully give up control, but rather having students gain more control with regard to their learning—if not with regard to what they were asked to do then regarding *how* they were asked to do so and, more importantly, how knowledge production was to be shared and discussed. Rather than have students complete assignments designed for the eyes of the teacher alone (as is most often the case), we wanted the process of students' thinking as they engage *Maps & More* to be open, public, and exposed to others—not in order to be criticized but to be critiqued, a process that pushes one's thinking productively rather than shutting it down. Making students' thinking public within the classroom community, would also allow the teacher to engage, not intervene, with students' work in-the-making instead of only grading its final—"for-the-teacher"—version. Both of these substantive pedagogical issues (that is, teachers selecting their own materials and students sharing their knowledge-in-the-making with others) we felt would best be accomplished by using (in our case, creating) a sophisticated Web-based platform upon which to construct our curriculum.

This is how the initial university-based design team conceptualized the project in its early—grant-writing—phases. Two other constituents, however, were soon to join us: Gayathri Santhana, our programmer; and a group of four middle school teachers we invited to be part of this project.[2] It was important to get both on board as soon as possible in order for them to become part of the thinking behind the design of *Maps & More* rather than only its executors. This was especially the case with teachers. We wanted *Maps & More* to be created *with* teachers rather than simply *for* them and thus wanted teachers to be involved as soon as we received our funding and were "ready to go." We contacted our teachers immediately after our project was accepted as part of the larger MSU The Preparing Tomorrow's Teachers for Technology (PT3) grant and conducted our first meeting with them within a month into our project (October, 2001).

This first meeting with teachers, in which we introduced our thinking to that point regarding the project and requested their reaction, was pivotal in the design of *Maps & More*. Several things became immediately apparent to us. First, and in many ways as we anticipated, we learned that much of the theoretical underpinnings of our project—the ideas presented earlier on in this chapter as to how and why maps ought to be considered and engaged as socially constructed narratives about the world and its people—were mostly unfamiliar to teachers. Thus, we believed an extensive professional component for teachers needed to accompany this project (see next section). Following an explanation by the four teachers as to how each had, thus far, been using maps in their classrooms, it also became apparent that our initial hunch that teachers need help in this area was on target for none of the teachers participating in this first meeting had engaged maps critically with students. Rather maps were, by and large, used as unproblematic depictions of the world that need to be "mined" for information about it. We further learned that the incongruence between our vision of how to engage maps and the kind of practice teachers described did not pose a problem for our participating teachers. Quite the opposite was true. Following an explanation by the university team of the goals of the project, teachers were excited about the possibilities such a project might open up for more meaningful and generative map-work in social studies classrooms.

Although teachers were enthusiastic about the potential of this project to help students think more deeply with and about maps, they voiced several reservations concerning our conceptual design for the project and its platform. Teachers raised two issues in particular. The first, and we would argue most substantial for us at that time, was, to put it mildly, their lack of excitement about our intent to design a Web-based curriculum, one they claimed would render the project unoperational in their own (and many other) classrooms. They pointed to the fact that none of the classrooms in which they teach have enough computers with Web access to accommodate our intended platform. In fact, none of the four teachers had more than a few (in three cases no more than two) computers in their rooms, and in all of those classrooms only one computer (the one operated by the teacher) had access to the Web. While all teach in schools that have a computer lab that can accommodate an entire class and provide Web access, none believed that reserving such a lab (often the only one in school) for an extended period of time for each of their classes would be feasible.

Teachers also raised other issues significant to the initial stages of design. One of those pertained to the desired length of the project's curriculum. In the current culture of accountability in schools, where so much time and effort is required of teachers to prepare students for state-mandated high-stakes standardized testing, they claimed, teachers could not afford to spend more than two weeks engaging students with such a project, important as it may be (in that sense, they realized it would be easier to justify to administrators and parents using the section of *Maps & More* that deals with charts and graphs since the latter are used in most of the prompts students are provided with on those state-mandated tests). The last issue teachers raised was that in order for a curriculum to be well received by teachers—indeed, for them to be willing to use it in classrooms—it needed to be less open-ended than we envisioned. Specifically, they felt the idea of providing teachers only with a template and asking them to select their own maps and, in that sense, design their own curriculum would be problematic for them and would probably be so for other teachers as well, not only since teachers are not accustomed to designing their own curriculum in an age of accountability and standardized testing but also for the more pragmatic reason that most teachers—and they brought themselves as examples—are not yet able to download a map from the Web onto their computers (we have indeed also found that to be the case with many of the student teachers who engaged the first, Web-based version of *Maps & More*). Instead, and in line with the kind of curriculum they have seen handed down to them in the past, they asked for a more prescribed curriculum where most, if not all, of the choices were already made for teachers by the external designers of that curriculum.

We went straight back to the drawing board following that meeting. We realized we needed to rethink a variety of elements of this project if we wanted it to be used by teachers rather than remain a white elephant full of bells and whistles that continues to lie, unused, on the shelf. We wanted to first address the two issues teachers raised most forcefully: the lack of accessible technology in classrooms and the desire for a more directed/

directing curriculum. In a sense, a response to the former already provided a response for the latter. While we kept the concerns of the four teachers participating in this project with regard to technology in mind, we also anticipated that technology would become more prevalent in classrooms and wanted to design a curriculum that could accommodate a variety of levels of accessibility to technology rather than take the current situation (the lack of computers with Web access) as a long term given. We therefore opted for a CD-ROM format for the project. This, we felt, would achieve several goals. First, it could address the need of various learning contexts. Teachers with Web access computers could use the links provided in the CD-ROM and access the resources in that manner. Other teachers, for example, who have access to computers but not to the Web could use the images of maps stored on the CD-ROM, either by projecting them on a screen for students to engage, or by printing a hard copy of those maps and having students engage them in groups without any technology. For teachers who have multiple computers in their room but no Web access, we designed a separate CD-ROM for students that included activities for working with those maps, allowing students to open Word as they work through those activities and, if technology provides, to also e-mail their work to other students or post it on Blackboard via other means.

The more constricted nature of a CD-ROM also meant that our curriculum would have to be more directional. In that sense, the change of technology also worked to accommodate the teachers' other strongly voiced concern: their desire for a more directed and linear curriculum. But while we agreed to give up the idea of a loosely structured curriculum in order to create this more prescriptive curriculum, we did not want the kind of thinking we hoped to maintain as teachers engaged in the project to disappear by only "telling" teachers what to do in classrooms. To that end, we wanted to ensure that what teachers were provided included an elaboration of the thinking informing each section of the curriculum and the kind of thinking it hoped to generate and why (and why the particular ways suggested might help move students toward such thinking). When we presented a sample of the first lesson of the curriculum written in that fashion during our second meeting with the teachers, they were not very pleased with what they saw. They did not like the long narrative form in which it was presented, one with an extensive explanation of the rationale for that lesson and the theoretical frameworks underlying it. Nor did they appreciate the narrative form of the remainder of the lesson. Instead, and in accordance with other curricula handed to them in the past, teachers wanted less of an emphasis on the "why" part of the lesson. They also wanted the remainder of the lesson—that which dealt with the "how"—to be presented in the form of laconic, bulleted directions. Though we agreed that some of the theoretical lenses for the first lesson might be best engaged by teachers before they teach this lesson, that is, in the Professional Development section of the CD-ROM, we were not ready to let go of the format—of narrating the activity in ways that would make the thinking behind it, or the one it hoped to generate, explicit. We felt that in order to break with how maps are currently engaged in classrooms, it is not enough to include new and different content (maps). Rather, we also need to find a new way to narrate that curriculum, one that does not fit well into and onto teachers' expectations of curriculum just as the maps we present in the project do not fit well into and onto students' understanding of maps. It would be hard to change how teachers come to the project, we argued, if teachers are not made to engage their teaching and their thinking about what underlies that teaching differently.

In subsequent meetings, teachers requested that the project be more explicit about possible connections between the curriculum of *Maps & More* and the remainder of the social studies curriculum. In other words, how can what teachers and students learned here be translated into other curricular engagements in social education beyond and after this project ends. They also asked for specific resources (especially maps) that could be used differently while teaching the "regular" curriculum. Both issues were addressed. We chose to "resolve" the first issue by actually having the teachers participating in our project design units in their respective areas that illustrate to teachers how understandings underlying *Maps & More* can be used in the remainder of the curriculum (this part of the project is soon to be added). We addressed teachers' desire for resources by creating a section, "Resources," in the CD-ROM that directs teachers to a wide variety of maps and other resources that offer enrichments to the regular middle school curriculum.[3]

CONCLUSION AND LESSONS LEARNED BEYOND DESIGN

While we have learned some important lessons in, from, and through the process of designing *Maps & More* we are still very much at the beginning of our learning as to what it can make both possible and impossible when actually used in social studies classrooms. Much of what we learned (or were made to learn) pertains to our initial assumptions about the availability of technology in schools, about teachers' skills in using technology, and about their dispositions to utilize those skills in the service of such a project. In all three areas, we assumed much more than teachers were able or willing to do. Further, we soon found out that the infrastructure needed for the kind of technology we hoped to incorporate was not available in the schools to support our envisioned project. We also learned that in order for a curriculum to be readily adopted by teachers it has to speak the language and format of existing curricula and that the more one deviates from the lexicon and grammar of what teachers are comfortable with, the less they will be inclined to adopt it. Following Derrida (1979), we learned that it is much easier for teachers to accept subversive representations that questions the substance of existing knowledge as long as those come in language, form, and pedagogical packaging that do not question the overarching mechanisms, codes, and conventions of *how* knowledge is constructed, mediated, and learned in public school classrooms. Form, then, as we have shown, and regardless of the technology accompanying it, is (and serves as) a technology in and of itself—one that is very much part of what determines teachers' inclination as to whether and how technology (in its traditional sense as hardware and/or software) will be incorporated in pedagogical environments. We also learned that, while technology is touted as the enabler of certain pedagogies, it is clear to us that technology does not come with any such imperatives or that certain pedagogies require particular technologies to make them possible. As our project shows, technology can be used, manipulated, designed, repurposed to fit multiple agendas often without compromising the intent for which it was created—in our case, the promoting of particular ways of thinking and being in classrooms.

More than anything (or, more accurately, in the process of learning that "anything"), we learned that for technology, indeed, for any pedagogical tool to be effective in classrooms, it needs to be developed *with* rather than simply *for* teachers. While we came to this project with this in mind (hence our invitation to teachers to join the project almost from its inception), we do not believe we were fully cognizant of how important it was to prevent it from becoming yet another white elephant, a glitzy, innovative technology project that simply collects dust on our office shelves. Bringing teachers on board so early on required us to change some fundamental aspects of the project, but what resulted was something useful to teachers, something they might actually use with students in their classrooms.

Where we are only beginning to learn is with regard to the use of *Maps & More* in classrooms. That is, for how our curriculum is actually used by teachers and students. The only section of the curriculum that has been piloted in schools is the one dealing with charts and graphs. Still, several lessons can be learned. First, students enthusiastically participated in manipulating data in different ways and experimenting with different methods to display their results. We also found students to be excellent critics of textualized data—be it their fellow students' charts and graphs or those provided in the curriculum presented to them. Exposed to a number of different types of graphs, students became more adept not only at interpreting information from graphs but also at exploring the political and social agendas those graphs attempt to promote. In other words, students were more ready and inclined than we had initially anticipated to become "theorists," whereby theory is not considered "an abstract apparatus of mastery, but an inquiry into the grids of social intelligibility produced by the discursive activities of a culture" (Zavarzadeh & Morton, 1994, p. 53).

Our learning as to what teachers might bring to their engagement with *Maps & More* will be part of that study. We have nevertheless already begun to explore that issue through our interactions with student teachers, specifically with interns taking the first author's TE 802 and TE 804 class, Reflection and Inquiry in Teaching Practice–Social Studies, where they both "do" the curriculum designed by us for middle school students and then think about it and its implication as teachers. While many find the map section of *Maps & More* described in this chapter intriguing, innovative, and are excited for the potential it opens up for map engagement in social studies classrooms, there are always several students in each class who actively resist the implications of these activities or implicating themselves in the knowledge generated as their result. Student teachers engaging *Maps & More* have claimed that the unconventional maps used (i.e., the McArthur projection that puts Australia at the top) "gives [them] a headache," that they "don't want to deal with this," or "that it raises questions too difficult to entertain." Even with some of the student teachers who think that troubling high school students' thinking about maps is important, frustration is often voiced when issues of power, positionality, and voice emanating from our curriculum hit too close to home—e.g., to their own schooling, to their teaching, or to the traditionally "American" ways of constructing and dividing the world. While students are comfortable dealing with critical issues inherent in maps and map-making at a theoretical level, that is, one that is removed from their own ways of thinking about and living in the world, things often turn contentious when their own assumptions about the world begin to be questioned publicly. What we have seen is a form of ignorance that Felman (1982) explains is not as much a lack of knowledge but an active refusal of it and of its implication. Thus, while many students, having mastered the culture of schooling through so many years of classroom experience are able to give us—the author—the "right" responses, even enthusiasm, it is often evident that even having gone through *Maps & More*, student teachers (and we suspect practicing teachers as well) are, very often, not ready to allow their own underlying beliefs about the world to get shattered sufficiently enough to want to do something beyond the activities provided by *Maps & More*, using it as a stepping stone to question other maps, narratives, and representations beyond the immediacy of the curriculum we provide.

NOTES

1. The university-based design team for *Maps & More*, the only one to incorporate faculty outside of education, included Avner Segall, assistant professor in the Department of Teacher Education and a former social studies teacher; Bettie Landauer-Menchik, a former social studies teacher, now a demographer, who trains school administrators how to use social science data at the Education Policy Center at MSU; and Mark Wilson, an associate professor of urban planning, who has created online courses and studied technology use for the promotion of geographic understanding (Mark left the project after 1 year). Our project also included four Michigan middle school social studies teachers who also serve as mentor teachers in our university's teacher education program. Gayathri Santhana, a graduate student from engineering was our programmer. Her task, beyond initial design was to continuously recreate the project, attempting to transform our constantly evolving ideas into a workable reality. In those tasks, she was aided by Punya Mishra who also provided insights as the design team was conceptualizing the project.

2. The four Michigan area teachers were Dorcas Lanz (Otto Middle School, Lansing), Linda Dow and Scott Shattuck (Mason Middle School, Mason) and Randy Lloyd (Holt Junior High, Holt). Dorcas and Randy teach in urban schools while Linda and Scott teach in a suburban school. Scott teaches Grade 8 American history, Linda and Dorcas teach Grade 7 world cultures, and Randy teaches an integrated humanities courses. We chose these particular teachers, all of which have been working with our teacher preparation program in social studies, since we wanted to bring as diverse views as possible, conveying perspectives of a wide range of teaching contexts and subject areas.

3. Six to eight maps of each continent displaying minerals, agricultural uses, geological features, and land use were included. One section provides links to cultural resources for each region. These include personal narratives of modern day explorers in Africa and Asia from National Geographic and BBC voice archives. Other resources focus on the role of religion and its impact on culture. Resources are available to supplement both the world geography curriculum and the American history curriculum commonly taught in Michigan schools.

REFERENCES

Banks, J. A. (1997). *Educating citizens in a multicultural society.* New York: Teachers College Press.

Bernstein, B. (1996). *Pedagogy, symbolic control and identity: Theory, research, critique.* London: Taylor & Francis.

Black, J. (1997). *Maps and politics.* Chicago: Chicago University Press.

Derrida, J. (1979). Living on: Border lines. In H. Bloom, P. de Man, J. Derrida, G. Hartman, & J. H. Miller (Eds.), *Deconstruction and criticism* (pp. 75–176). New York: Continuum.

Felman, S. (1982). Psychoanalysis and education: Teaching terminable and interminable. In B. Johnson (Ed.), *The pedagogical imperative*. Yale French Studies, *63*, 21-44.

Giroux, H. A., & Simon, R. I. (1988). Schooling, popular culture, and a pedagogy of possibility. *Journal of Education, 170* (1), 9–26.

Hall, S. (1981). The whites of their eyes: Racist ideologies and the media. In G. Bridges & R. Brunt (Eds.), *Silver linings: Some strategies for the eighties* (pp. 28-52). London: Lawrence & Wishart.

Harley, J. B. (1988). Maps, knowledge, and power. In D. Cosgrove & S. Daniels (Eds.), *The iconography of landscapes: Essays on the symbolic representation, design, and use of past environments* (pp. 277-312). Cambridge, England: Cambridge University Press.

Harley, J. B. (1990). Texts and contexts in the interpretation of early maps. In D. Buisseret (Ed.), *From sea charts to satellite images: Interpreting North American history through maps* (pp. 3-15). Chicago: University of Chicago Press.

Kaiser, W., & Wood, D. (2001). *Seeing through maps: The power of image to shape our world view.* Amherst, MA: ODT.

Koehler, M. J., Mishra, P., Hershey, K., & Peruski, L. (2004). With a little help from your students: A new model for faculty development and online course design. *Journal of Technology and Teacher Education, 12*(1), 25-55.

Levstik, L. (1985). Literary geography and mapping. *Social Education, 49*(1), 38-43.

Monmonier, M. (1991). *How to lie with maps.* Chicago: University of Chicago Press.

Monmonier, M. (1995). *Drawing the line: Tales of maps and cartocontroversy.* New York: Henry Holt.

Mishra, P., & Koehler, M. J. (submitted). *Technological Pedagogical Content Knowledge: A framework for integrating technology in teacher education.* Manuscript submitted for publication.

Perkins, D. (1992). *Smart schools: Better thinking and learning for every child.* New York: The Free Press.

Segall, A. (2004). Revisiting pedagogical content knowledge: The pedagogy of content/the content of pedagogy. *Teaching and Teacher Education, 20*(5), 489-503.

Simon, R. I. (1992). *Teaching against the grain: Texts for a pedagogy of possibility.* New York: Bergin & Garvey.

Werner, W. (2000). Reading authorship into texts. *Theory & Research in Social Education, 28*(2), 193-219.

Willinsky, J. (1998). *Learning to divide the world: Education at empire's end.* Minneapolis: University of Minnesota Press.

Wood, D. (1992). *The power of maps.* New York & London: Guilford Press.

Wright, J. (1977). Map makers are human: Comments on the subjective in maps. In L. Guelke (Ed.), *The nature of cartographic communication.* Toronto, Canada: Toronto University Press.

Zavarzadeh, M., & Morton, D. (1994). *Theory as resistance: Politics and culture after (post)structuralism.* New York: Guilford Press.

CHAPTER 7

COLLABORATIVE DEVELOPMENT OF TECHNOLOGY-BASED SOCIAL STUDIES MATERIALS

Timothy H. Little

Always design a thing by considering it in its next larger context:
a chair in a room, a room in a house, a house in an environment,
an environment in a city plan.

—*Eliel Saarinen*

The focus of this chapter is on the remarkable and largely unpredictable tale of a group of high school and university teachers who initially came together simply to create a new social studies course for a high school. Several years later, this same group had evolved into a close-knit team that revolutionized and technologized the pedagogy sequence for secondary social studies teachers in training at Michigan State University (MSU).

Faculty Development by Design: Integrating Technology in Higher Education, 131–145
Copyright © 2007 by Information Age Publishing
All rights of reproduction in any form reserved.

THE DISCONNECT BETWEEN TRADITIONAL SOCIAL STUDIES CURRICULA AND CONTEMPORARY SOCIETAL DEMANDS

Social Studies textbooks have traditionally purveyed static knowledge to generations of Americans. Unfortunately, while a knowledge base of cultural and historic information is clearly still necessary in the year 2003, it is no longer, in and of itself, sufficient. To train teachers to singularly disseminate static textbook knowledge in a day when national and state tests call upon school students to reason and to demonstrate proficiency in higher order thinking skills is to prepare teachers for social studies classrooms which are doomed to failure.

A RATIONALE FOR MICROCOMPUTER USE IN SOCIAL STUDIES

Why should social studies teachers exchange the familiar and the comfortable for new, strange, and potentially embarrassing modes and topics of instruction? We can offer at least three reasons. (See also, Berson, Lee, & Stuckart, 2001; Crocco, 2001; Friedman & Hicks, 2006; and Whitworth & Berson, 2003).

Systematic Thinking

The teaching of critical thinking skills has long been given lip service in the social studies. Teaching youngsters how to think rather than focusing on what to think is an appealing instructional goal, and one that has been voiced frequently by social studies educators. But, has practice matched pronouncement? To what extent do social studies courses systematically teach students systems for reasoning to a conclusion? Clearly, one can infer from these rhetorical questions that we believe social studies educators have all too often promised more than is commonly delivered. Therefore, our goal was to acquaint students with systems of reasoning to a logical conclusion in social matters.

One way to accomplish this is with the microcomputer. For example, running tool programs such as databases or surfing the Internet to extract and/or organize social science data calls for students to apply categorizing skills drawn from Boolean algebra. Cost/benefit decision-making templates installed on spreadsheet programs permits students to make multi-criterion complex policy decisions. By their very nature, such programs call for systematic thought on the part of the user. While not judging or guaranteeing the quality of the logical thought produced, the use of microcomputers can prove to be a powerful catalyst to systematic thinking on the part of students enrolled in social studies classes. Viewed in this context, microcomputers in social studies classes represent a powerful means to a frequently shortchanged end.

National and State Social Studies Objectives

Prominent among standardized national and state objectives, are numerous intellectual process objectives. Gathering data, organizing data, inferring, and reasoning systematically to a decision: these and numerous other intellectual targets are all too rarely part of the typical social studies basal text. Lacking significant support from the textbooks, social studies teachers should be happy to learn that numerous educational microcomputer programs available to them place process objectives at the core of their raison d'etre.

Providing a Social Science Laboratory

For too long, the social studies teacher has looked with envy at the science teacher whose instruction is enhanced by access to a science laboratory, be it real or electronic. With the advent of sophisticated microcomputer programs and simulations, social studies instructors can make it possible for students to test their ideas against social science models of reality.

The microcomputer has promise for the teacher as a capacitating device that permits the instructor to develop dimensions of social studies frequently slighted as difficult to teach with traditional methods.

PREPARING TEACHERS IN TRAINING TO UTILIZE THE DYNAMIC CAPABILITIES OF TECHNOLOGY BASED LEARNING TO COMPENSATE FOR TEXTBOOK LIMITATIONS

We have identified some concrete measures which, if taken, can (1) hasten the implementation of technology-based instruction within both university and public school social studies classrooms, and (2) provide us with the means to the end of producing social studies teachers who will be capable of preparing lessons that lead to socially constructed knowledge and at the same time promote skills-based reasoning (Berson, Mason, Heinecke, & Coutts, 2001; Mason, Berson, Diem, Hicks, & Lee, 2000). Specifically, these measures revolve around the following goal cluster:

Goal 1. Maximize the likelihood that teacher candidates will regularly experience, analyze, and plan technology-based instruction as learners in our university pedagogy classes.

Goal 2. Make a concerted effort to collaboratively develop, with selected cooperating teachers, social studies instructional materials that will be commonly used in the College of Education's social studies courses and in secondary school classrooms in which our students are placed as seniors.

Goal 3. Build into the overall social studies teacher education curriculum during the senior year, specific episodes of teaching, which require that our students develop, present, and be evaluated upon their proficiency with electronic instruction. The broad goals delineated above came into being as a result of collaborative work between Michigan State University faculty/staff and selected teachers from Holt High School, in Holt, Michigan. The process by which this group came to be and derived the above cited goals serves as the focus of the next segment of this narrative.

UNINTENDED OUTCOMES: CREATION OF A NEW HIGH SCHOOL COURSE OFFERING CULMINATES IN THE DEVELOPMENT OF A TECHNOLOGY-BASED PEDAGOGY COURSE FOR SOCIAL STUDIES TEACHERS IN TRAINING

The origin of the MSU social studies technology team began innocuously, with no initial relationship to technology or to the teacher-training classroom. A committee composed of Holt High School social studies faculty and administrators decided in 1990 that a senior high school course in global studies would be an important and valuable addition to the curriculum. A University faculty member was invited to participate in the team that was to design the course. As various models of instruction were discussed, what appeared to be a most intractable problem surfaced. Specifically, "forefront" global issues came and went from semester to semester at such a pace that concern was expressed regarding the long term value and utility of the course content. This Gordian knot was severed when the design team opted to treat generic systematic reasoning skills as the core of the course, with frequently changing "hot topics" serving as the "data" to be subjected to systematic analysis.

The primary emphasis of the course, then, was for students to acquire systematic thinking skills, to realize that a reasoned decision is better than an emotional one, to develop a personal stake in making the most rational decisions possible, and to see that free societies depend on rational citizens who make informed choices in the voting booth. The original planning group also decided that global studies would be resource based, with readings from a variety of print and visual sources, as opposed to textbook driven.

As the faculty committee tussled with translating the conception of the course into teachable reality, we began thinking about what "tools" would help us reach our goals. Traditionally, textbooks have played a major role in providing the "tool base" for courses, but the teachers had specifically opted not to rely exclusively on textbooks. The planning group knew what it wanted to present to students, but had not identified a specific vehicle for delivering this content. In other words, we had a general instructional message, but no medium for delivering it.

ENTER TECHNOLOGY

After a brief flirtation with both transparency and HyperCard versions of prototype teaching units, we settled upon PowerPoint as our teaching vehicle and set to work. Our fascination with HyperCard as the software chassis upon which to fabricate our lessons was largely a matter of "what was hot" when we began to work and the fact that it permitted us to write nonlinear instructional materials. When we opted to move on to PowerPoint for reasons of simplicity of use and market share, we did so with regret that we were trading off the wonderful flexibility of random access, which had been a hallmark of HyperCard. It would be several years before we learned a way to regain that capability from within PowerPoint.

Phase I: First Steps

The initial set of generic PowerPoint units in social studies was designed to present the "barebones" reasoning model to students. Three clusters of thinking skills were identified as components of the core reasoning curriculum model. Therefore, three freestanding PowerPoint units were created and we usually presented them in a serial sequence to students [alternate ways to frame an issue, analyzing data, and making a systematic multivariate decision].

Phase II: Creation of Generic Templates for
Teacher-Designed PowerPoint Units

After the Phase I generic reasoning skills units were created and utilized in the global studies classes, enthusiasm was generated to create a second generation of topical PowerPoint units which called upon students to further apply and practice the generic skills learned in the round one units. At the same time, the systematic reasoning model began to see use in other social studies classes at Holt High School.

New Phase II PowerPoint units were developed which placed an emphasis upon melding the systematic reasoning skills within instructional units treating traditional social studies topics. From these prototype units, a set of templates for the design of subsequent technology-based instructional modules eventually emerged. Limitations of space preclude us from including a detailed set of instructions for development of each of the models to be described.

Below is a brief list of topics / templates for PowerPoint social studies units generated in Phase II of the curriculum development effort.

Skill Cluster #1: Alternate Ways to Frame an Issue

- Teaching Alternate Views of a Cultural Symbol: Topical Example-Columbus
- The Concept of a Continuum of Attitudes Toward a Social Studies Subject: Topical Example—"War"

Skill Cluster #2: Analyzing Data

- Case Studies in Assessing Alternate Types of Social Science Evidence: Topical Example—Anastasia—Did one of the Russian Czar's Daughters Survive the Russian Revolution?
- Simulating an Institution at Work: Topical Example—The Federal Trade Commission as a Judge of Truthful Advertising
- Testing Alternative Causal Hypotheses—Topical Example—The Internment of Japanese Americans During World War II

Skill Cluster #3: Making Systematic Decisions

- The Tendency of Criteria for Making Decisions to Change Over Time: Topical Example—Product Liability Laws in America
- Cultural Norms and Decision Making: Topical Example—Designing a Public Health Policy During the Influenza Epidemic of 1918

MEANWHILE BACK AT THE COLLEGE OF EDUCATION

Early in our push to prepare our teachers in training to use technology in their instruction, we opted to teach them to use off the shelf software to teach generic social studies thinking skills.

Teacher candidates were introduced to social studies lesson formats utilizing low complexity software (Works/Inspiration). Subsequent teacher-made units included such topics as: "Using the Atom Bomb to End WWII," which utilized a decision-making spreadsheet. Three other lessons utilized database software. They were titled: "The Riddle of Amelia Earhart's Disappearance," "Lincoln's Volunteers: Who Were They," and "Gunfighters in the Old West: Did the Hollywood Profile Fit the Facts?" These units were intellectually attractive; however, they initially tended to exist in isolation, largely outside of the collective effort that was transpiring around the projects emerging at Holt High School.

While the high school PowerPoint units were originally inspired by thoughts of a high school audience of consumers, their utility as generic model lessons for use with university social studies teachers in training remained a question. Furthermore, the lure of being able to introduce teacher trainees to technology-based lessons on campus, and then have those trainees use these units in their field placements, watched over by teachers who were intimately familiar with the lessons, was irresistible.

As the semesters passed by, we eventually arrived at a point by which all instruction at the College over the two semester social studies pedagogy sequence was delivered via PowerPoint. Nested within that PowerPoint teacher-training curriculum at MSU were a number of teaching units originally developed for use at Holt. Thus, our teachers in training were exposed to hypermedia instruction twice weekly for an academic year and encouraged to use that format in the construction of their own lessons for use in the field. Furthermore, they were also encouraged to utilize the Internet as an integral source of data of all kinds for inclusion within their original technology-based lessons.

Phase III: Yet Another Generation of Hypermedia Model Lessons

MSU Professors Yong Zhao and Punya Mishra brought to the attention of the Holt team the existence of the The Preparing Tomorrow's Teachers for Technology (PT3) grant program. With support from both the Professional Development School initiative and the PT3 technology grant programs, Phase three of our technology based curriculum project consisted of inviting Holt social studies teachers to create yet another layer of hypermedia teaching units keyed to their own particular topical interests. The team leader also benefited greatly from participating in a semester long faculty development seminar taught by Professors Zhao and Mishra, which focused upon instructional design. Intellectually and fiscally enriched by the PT3 grant, specifications for the new hypermedia units stipulated that teaching materials had to possess several features. First, they had to be built around one of the social studies technology (SST) teaching models created during year one of the social studies project. Second, they had to be keyed to one or more of the state of Michigan/National Council for the Social Studies content standards. Third, they had to be designed to capitalize upon the capabilities of the Internet as a research tool. Fourth, they had to be built around the generic systematic reasoning skills clusters developed earlier: Framing/Analyzing/Decision Making. Finally, they had to be suitable for us as lesson plan templates with MSU College of Education teacher training classes.

Given these specifications, eight original dual use PowerPoint units were developed as the outcome of our Phase III effort. These units are to be employed in both Holt High School classrooms and on the MSU campus in senior level pedagogy courses.

ANALYSIS OF VARIOUS ROLES OFPARTICIPANTS: THE EVOLUTION OF A TECHNOLOGY-BASED SOCIAL STUDIES CURRICULUM DEVELOPMENT TEAM

To date the MSU/Holt High School social studies staff has met many objectives. For example, we created a new global studies course; we incorporated a new systematic reasoning strand into the curriculum across courses/grades; and, we generated several new PowerPoint-based instructional units keyed to systematic reasoning skills. To take account of state standards, we analyzed and matched the Michigan Educational Assessment Program (MEAP) Social Studies Content Standards to new hypermedia instructional units, as well as moving major portions of the curriculum from paper/pencil to hypermedia. In order to achieve ongoing assessment of the program, we implemented a case study based assessment instrument that utilizes a pretest/posttest model. Finally, in addition to being invited presenters at more than a dozen national social studies conferences, we also generated, cowrote. and sold out a book describing the new curriculum development process.

The Composition of the Development Teams

Professor Tim Little has served as the social studies project director since its inception. The cadre of cooperating teachers was formed around nine Holt High School social studies teachers who worked on the project during the first year of its operation and who stayed on throughout the project. Among these nine we included the social studies department chairman, who has been teaching a section of the College of Education secondary social studies methods class, and a social studies teacher/media specialist who has taught the social studies lab section at MSU. A social studies graduate student with a technology background was employed as the senior level TA for 2001-2002. In addition, we have made contact with some 35+ teachers from around the state who have expressed interest in our work.

Underlying our collaborative team effort was PT3 faculty including Drs. Yong Zhao, Punya Mishra, Matt Koehler, and Rick Banghart. Their help was particularly vital during the design of some of the Phase III prototype units, which led to the creation of a set of templates for use by our teacher and graduate student participants from the MSU College of Education.

Crucial to the creation of our array of new social studies lessons were funds provided by the PT3 Grant which were utilized to subsidize the work of our public school teachers as they set about the task of creating original technology based lessons using the templates created during year one of the social studies project.

Given the fact that the MSU portion of the team was operating on a MAC platform while Holt High Sschool was PC based, grant funds enabled the MSU team to obtain some MAC laptops early on for demonstration teaching purposes.

Over the past several years, the MSU/Holt Technology Social Studies Development Team has been most productive. In the course of this collaborative effort, we took time to reflect upon the forces that catalyzed us to engage in such an ongoing and intensive effort.

Staff Training

Importantly, the project director enrolled in a graduate seminar conducted at MSU by the College of Education that focused on the creation and functioning of communities of technology designers. Much was learned in that course about the process by which a team of instructional technology staff can be assembled and set about the task of building a long-term curriculum design effort.

Due to limitations of both time and place, two distinct and mutually exclusive collaborative design teams came to exist. While the original cadre based at Holt High School continued on with its social studies technology developmental agenda, a second group formed on the MSU campus composed of members of the graduate technology seminar. In sharp contrast to the Holt group, which was composed entirely of social studies teachers, the seminar team was made up of persons whose primary interest was educational technology. Only one member of the on-campus team had any background in social studies. Led by Professor Little, this team pushed the limits of PowerPoint as an authoring tool. Using the creation of a "test bed" social studies unit on "Revolutions Over Time," the seminar team explored different authoring techniques. For example, we embedded segments of Hollywood film within an up and running PowerPoint teaching unit. Given adequate compression, such a seamless interface would allow teaching unit developers to present data for analysis to students, which was crafted with high production values. Such a process would, of course, require that permissions be obtained. After much time and experimentation, it was determined that, for the moment, compression and memory limitations of machines precluded such ready encapsulation. Our PowerPoint units continued to rely upon either VHS or CD-ROMs for our upscale data presentations.

In another exploration, the team hyperlinked PowerPoint frames so that students could navigate our units with random access capabilities. As noted above, one of the reasons we were hesitant to abandon our earliest experiments with HyperCard lay in the fact that it did not limit us to a linear presentation protocol. After some investigations, our team discovered a then little known feature of PowerPoint identified in the user's manual as "the hidden slide." It turns out that this capability, touted in the Microsoft manual as useful in meetings to avoid treating "a question you don't want to address unless specifically asked," actually could be employed to create a fully branching instructional program.

As new authoring techniques were discovered and tested by the MSU collaborative development team, they were hastily carried back to the Holt High School social studies curriculum development team. Thus, persons who had a fast learning curve for technological matters carried out the experimentation, and the results of this group's investigations were transmitted to the Holt team whose "fast track" was social studies content.

Training sessions were held on site at Holt High School for the participating teachers and graduate students for a period of approximately 3 years on a monthly basis. In those seminars, matters ranging from topics to be developed as systematic reasoning units to who was to present at national conferences were discussed and settled.

Catalysts to Achievement

At any given time our "team leader" has ranged from an MSU professor to senior year interns. Over time we have identified a bevy of support catalysts to our team's efforts and our catalysts have included (a) creation of an initial group identity, (b) social and professional relationships, (c) intermediate production goals, (d) outside funding, and, (e) building across teacher generations.

Creation of a group identity. Team members transcended professional boundaries and formed a unified group identity as professionals interested in improving social studies education with the infusion of technology, as indicated in this quote by one of the team members.

> I caught myself realizing that ... I was thinking about it as a member of the ... (social studies) team. I think one of the things we've done ... is we've created this third thing.... It's not university-based norms, it's not school-based norms; it's our group's own set of norms about what we're doing and why we're doing it and I find myself looking at the world ... from a ... (team) point of view. (Social Studies Team member.)

Social and professional relationships. The team has presented its work at several national, regional, and state conferences. On those occasions, we have made a pointed effort to always schedule group social activities. These activities support our professional relationships and cement our group identity.

Intermediate production goals. We have carefully arranged our schedules to ensure that we have built into our major projects, publications with deadlines, refereed presentations, and all manner of "pit stops" which collectively preclude our putting off work until final due dates. Such intermediate goals and reinforcements have given us an ongoing sense of purpose and movement.

Outside funding. While some of our fiscal support has come out of team participant pockets, we have been fortunate to have written proposals to, and been funded by, the following organizations over the years: Holt High School, The MSU Professional Development School Project, and the PT3 grant.

Building across teacher generations. Over the decade that our team has been in operation, we have carefully worked to involve each new wave of teachers who join the MSU/Holt High School senior level social studies staffs. Thus, over the years the teams have consisted of several "layers" of team members. The founding team was the original global studies group. The second generation was comprised of other members of the department who joined the team after the initial year of the project, as well as

MSU doctoral students. The third generation included new hires at Holt High School, and the fourth generation included MSU interns.

DISTRACTIONS AND FRUSTRATIONS

Our development team continues to be a work in progress. In fact, as we complete this chapter, team members are leaving to present two new microbased units at yet another national conference. This chapter may leave one with the impression that the process of infusing technology into social studies education to improve teaching and learning has been a relatively smooth one. On the contrary, as in any creative endeavor and exploration into new territory, the team faced several distractions and frustrations, mainly related to software and hardware.

Software

At last count, we have singly and collectively generated more than 200 discrete PowerPoint instructional units. That volume of production represents a massive investment of professorial and teacher time. Yet, just last week new versions of software were installed in our classroom computers that do not recognize earlier versions of PowerPoint. Responding to this software upgrade will sidetrack us for several weeks. However, this is not the first time we have encountered this problem. While we fully understand the need to stay abreast of the latest in software, the need to repeatedly divert talent and energies to reworking existing PowerPoint presentations clearly cuts into our overall ability to generate new materials.

Hardware

Paralleling the software problems described above, we have encountered problems with noncompatible hardware as well. While our earliest PowerPoint programs would fit on a floppy disk, later graphics and branching heavy programs were developed and stored on zip drives due to increased memory requirements. The latest computer upgrades in classrooms now favor CD-ROMs. Again, while there is no resisting progress, the need to repeatedly transfer and retransfer data coupled with the need to reformat after the programs are transferred can diminish the intellectual ardor of even the most devoted technophile. Reworking one program to upgrade it to run on new software or hardware is not that difficult. However, completing the rework process on 200 programs is another matter entirely and it conflicts with any economy of scale arguments that might be made to encourage teachers to plunge ahead with development projects of their own. Hi-speed Internet exchange and download capabilities would seem to represent a possible way to ameliorate this problem in the future. However, as of this writing, the problem remains.

Implications and Some Hard Lessons Learned

If our long-range goal is to entice "mainstream social studies teachers" to embrace the new technology, we feel the distractions and frustrations described above represent a serious impediment to achieving that goal. It would seem that for "mainstream teachers" to invest the intellectual time to develop technology teaching units in social studies or to learn how to utilize "off the shelf" materials, at least two conditions have to be met. First, the teachers must be convinced that the technology-based units will produce effective learning on the part of the students. Our informal pre/posttest data on our own PowerPoint units would seem to suggest that the above criterion for teacher acceptance of technology could be met in social studies. Second, the additional time invested by the teacher in either creating social studies units or mastering the use of off the shelf units will provide the teacher with additional satisfaction in their teaching roles.

Let us say teachers have the choice between arriving at class with a sheaf of tattered lecture notes written years ago, and investing many new advance hours in creating and mastering technology-based instruction which may or may not be useable at class time due to software and hardware problems. How many typical teachers can be expected to enthusiastically opt for the latter course of action? We fear that, all too often, the former choice will prevail.

FINAL REFLECTIONS ON THE PROCESS

At the microlevel, we are in the midst of determining whether or not to encapsulate our hypermedia units developed to date on a series of CDs for distribution within Michigan and nationally. Our most recent focus has been on the proposed creation of three online hypermedia graduate courses in social studies philosophy, teaching methods, and alternate models of assessment. Sample units to be utilized in the online environment have been developed and are in the process of field-testing as we go to press.

At the macrolevel, we have come to believe that generic software which calls upon students to exercise and to apply systematic reasoning skills to social studies topics will tend to remain our center of developmental attention. Tool programs such as databases and decision-making templates ensconced within spreadsheets call forth student application of logical and systematic streams of thought. Presentation programs, such as PowerPoint and Inspiration, become ready instruments by which students can teach themselves to socially construct and order knowledge. We see both types of learning as vital to the creation of logical decision-making citizens who will, in the future, effect the direction of our Democratic system.

Finally, our experience with a design team clearly underscores the old adage that "the whole is more than the sum of its parts." Without the intense and creative interaction of team members, the group's most recent instructional units would not exude the intellectual sophistication, which they do. Indeed, some of our most intellectually fulfilling and stimulating hours have been spent in staff meetings, a format not frequently noted in the literature for its motivational punch. The creation of our design team has also provided us with the critical mass to push for substantive curricular change. Specifically, moving from an emphasis upon the transmission of static social knowledge to an emphasis upon knowledge generation by the students themselves with technology as the catalyst for this paradigm shift.

ACKNOWLEDGMENTS

A special thank you goes out to the Holt social studies staff at large for their creative energies and to Ms. Mary deWolf and Mr. Jerry Gillett for their continuing efforts to help Michigan State University improve its teacher training program through the use of instructional technology.

REFERENCES

Berson, M. J., Mason C. L., Hienecke, W. F., & Coutts, C. B. (2001). Technology innovation: An examination of beliefs and practices of social studies methods faculty. *The International Social Studies Forum, 1*(2), 89-105.

Berson, M., Lee, J., & Stuckart, D. (2001). Promise and the practice of computer technologies in the social studies: A critical analysis. In W. E. Stanley (Ed.), *Critical issues in social studies research for the 21st century*. Greenwich: CT: Information Age Publishing.

Crocco, M. (2001). Leveraging constructivist learning in the social studies classroom: A response to Mason, Berson, Diem, Hicks, Lee, and Dralle. *Contemporary Issues in Technology and Teacher Education, 1*(3). Retrieved September 25, 2004, from http://www.citejournal.org/vol1/iss3/currentissues/socialstudies/article2.htm

Friedman, A. M., & Hicks, D. (2006). The state of the field: Technology, social studies, and teacher education. *Contemporary Issues in Technology and Teacher Education 6*(2). Retrieved July 21, 2006, from http://www.citejournal.org/vol6/iss2/socialstudies/article1.cfm

Mason, C. L., Berson, M. J., Diem, R., Hicks, D., & Lee, J. (2000). Guidelines for using technology to prepare social studies teachers. *Contemporary Issues in Technology and Teacher Education, 1*, 1-13.

Whitworth, S. A., & Berson, M. J. (2003). Computer technology in the social studies: An examination of effectiveness literature (1996-2001). *Contemporary Issues in Technology and Teacher Education, 2*(4). Retrieved September 27, 2004, from http://www.citejournal.org/vol2/iss4/socialstudies/article1.cfm

CHAPTER 8

DESIGN AS PROFESSIONAL DEVELOPMENT

The Inner and Outer Journeys of Learning to Develop Online Learning

John M. Dirkx

The lyf so sort, the craft so long to lerne.
—Geoffrey Chaucer

The graduate students I teach aspire to work in various contexts of higher and adult education, and represent a wide range of practitioners, from teachers and program planners to administrators and counselors. For the most part, these students have not undertaken formal academic preparation in education. Our program in higher and adult education, like many around the country, emphasizes history, foundations, policy, theory, and research. The study of such a curriculum can be theoretically exciting and challenging, causing students to reflect on and possibly reframe many implicit assumptions they hold about education. It can be a valuable

Faculty Development by Design: Integrating Technology in Higher Education, 147–165
Copyright © 2007 by Information Age Publishing
All rights of reproduction in any form reserved.

approach to developing future faculty in these areas. Because of their theoretical orientation, however, these approaches risk not speaking directly to the practice contexts in which most of our students work or will work. This is particularly true for a course in adult learning that I have taught for many years. Often a core component of programs in adult education, as well as many higher education programs, such a course often focuses on a systematic review of research and theory on the sociocultural contexts for adult learning, participation and motivation, individual differences in adult learning, and various theoretical approaches to understanding how adults learn (Merriam & Caffarella, 1999). In other words, they are heavy on research and theory and light on practical application.

In the project described here, I explore how we might ground the study of theory-oriented courses more closely within the practice contexts of our students, while at the same time preserving academic rigor and fostering awareness among our learners as reflective practitioners. In the redesign of this course, I sought a more solid grounding within a constructivist epistemological framework (Mahoney, 1991; Steffe & Gale, 1995), as well as in key principles for fostering adult learning and change (Brookfield, 1986; Jarvis, 1992; Merriam & Caffarella, 1999; Tennant & Pogson, 1995; Vella, 2002). For reasons that I discuss further in the next section, I also wanted to explore how online technology might address the unique issues created by trying to locate a highly theoretical course within the world of educational practice, given the particular kinds of students in our program and their needs and interests. In this chapter, I further elaborate on the nature of the design issues posed by this problem, the processes used to address the problem, the community context in which this problem was approached, and lessons learned about the role of technology in addressing these kinds of curricular and pedagogical issues.

CONSIDERATIONS OF DESIGN

It is challenging within current face-to-face settings and contexts to design and implement graduate-level and professional development activities that reflect constructivist, adult-learning principles. A casual walk through any conference hotel hosting a professional development event might reveal any number of sessions in which adults are seated close together at rows of tables, eyes fixed on a large PowerPoint slide projected on the white screen at the front of the room, and all listening to the "expert" who is talking from the slide or worse, reading from a text or manual. Despite everything we know about how adults learn and the limitations of the "update" model of continuing education (Nowlen, 1988), transmission methods of delivery stubbornly persist in many professional development and higher education programs, suggesting the difficulty in such settings of incorporating active, reflective, and constructivist approaches. Although this scene may be less apparent in graduate programs of education, because of their heavy emphasis on research and theory these programs often still suffer from the theory to practice disconnect so readily apparent in the update model of continuing professional education. In spite of attempts to incorporate active, reflective learning strategies, students in these programs are often left wondering how the material they are studying relates to the problems they typically encounter in practice.

As a scholar and practitioner of adult learning, with strong interests in the professional development of educational practitioners, I entered this project with a desire to learn how I could ground the curriculum and my teaching more fully within contexts that were meaningful and relevant to the learners' life experiences. In short, I wanted to more effectively incorporate into my teaching what we know about how adults learn. For this reason, I turned to problem-based learning as an instructional strategy.

Problem-based learning (PBL) represents one approach that has been used to address these concerns (Evenson & Hmelo, 2000; Savi-Baden, 2000). According to Savin-Baden (2000), PBL refers to the idea of learning specific content and skills by solving or managing real world, practice problems. Additionally, she argues it also stresses "an approach to learning through which many students have been enabled to understand their own situations and frameworks so that they are able to perceive how they learn" (p. 2), and how they see themselves as future or current professionals. In PBL, students learn how to address complex, ill-structured practice problems by using and applying appropriate subject matter as resources to frame the problems and develop solutions to these problems. They also learn about themselves as emerging and seasoned practitioners. In essence, PBL represents an approach that honors key elements or principles of adult learning and one that relies on an essentially constructivist epistemology to frame the process of teaching and learning.

Although its use is fairly widespread in medical education (Barrows & Tamblyn, 1980) and other health professions, PBL has enjoyed a somewhat slower adoption within more mainstream areas of educational practice, such as higher education (Bridges & Hallinger, 1995; Savin-Baden, 2000; Wilkerson & Gijselaers, 1996) and experiential learning (Boud & Feletti, 1991). PBL demands close, collaborative working relationships among small groups of learners. In medical education and some other professions that have successfully used PBL, meeting this demand is not particularly problematic because students are often full-time and fully immersed within their professional practice contexts. Graduate study in education, however, as well as formal continuing professional education programs, often involve participants on a part-time and limited basis, and usually in physical settings quite removed from their practice environments. Many graduate students in education are employed full-time and their courses meet once a week or in weekend formats 4 to 6 times per term. These constraints pose considerable difficulties for the design of collaborative, face-to-face environments necessary to make PBL work effectively. Such issues may partially account for the limited use of PBL within these latter educational programs.

Given the physical and time constraints of our traditional course structures in graduate and continuing professional education, I wanted to explore the possibilities that online environments offered for addressing these goals. Online technology is emerging as a major delivery system across a wide spectrum of educational programs. Because of its "anytime, anywhere" quality, online programs provide access and opportunities for many groups and individuals who otherwise may not have been able to participate in formal learning programs. In particular, online technology is rapidly becoming a major component of professional development for educators. Driven, in part, by the so-called knowledge explosion, professional development programs are scrambling to provide educational practitioners with the means and access to staying abreast of their respective fields.

Online technology also offers the possibility of overcoming difficult constraints to effective implementation of PBL for educational practitioners. Its "anywhere, anytime" quality allows learners to work with one another within their own time frames, continuously over long periods of time, while remaining closely connected to their particular practice contexts. Its potential promise of addressing these limitations is evident in a small but growing body of literature in using PBL online (Roberts, 2003).

Yet, the problem remains of how to design, develop, and implement learning experiences that address the real-world contexts of educational practitioners within a virtual environment, while at the same time as a practitioner myself learning to use online technology in my teaching. PBL relies on extensive collaborative group work, from defining the problem to conducting the inquiry, to completing the final group product. Design of the instructional environment needs to provide opportunities for participants to continuously negotiate the meaning of assigned problems or cases and how they relate or do not relate to their various life contexts. This process of negotiation involves identifying, naming, and giving voice to the differences that mediate this sense-making process, and learning to work across these differences in a collaborative manner to address the problem or case at hand (Dirkx & Smith, 2003a, 2003b). In addition, learners need to engage in extensive reflection and analysis of their individual and group behaviors. These issues, then, led to my involvement in this Preparing Tomorrow's Teachers for Technology (PT3) project as a form of professional development and as a means to address the difficult issues presented by redesigning a graduate level course in adult learning as a problem-based learning experience within an online environment.

THE PROCESS OF SEEKING A TECHNOLOGY SOLUTION

To get started, I joined a community of other faculty members and graduate students in a formal classroom-based experience to study the design and development of online educational environments. This course, a PT3 project, was intended as a faculty development experience for those interested in designing courses to be taught online. The goals and professional development challenges of this PT3 project were multiple. Although I had previous experience with other forms of distance education, such as two-way video, and with online augmentations of face-to-face courses, I had never designed or taught a course completely online. Furthermore, this project was conducted within the context of a team approach to professional development and instructional design. As a team, we had to learn more about PBL and how it might be used within a graduate course in education while at the same time learning to design and develop educative experiences within online environments. We needed to create contexts that were perceived by the learners as real-world. Strategies and structures were required that would facilitate the students' collaborative, working relationships.

All of these tasks had to be addressed within a medium and a culture that seems to valorize individualized, self-directed study. The process to address this pedagogical problem presented several learning projects for our team: (a) curriculum, (b) teaching and learning; (c) technology; and, (d) group process. From the outset the goal for our team was to design a course built around or within the principles of problem-based learning (Bridges & Hallinger, 1995). We explored online technology to see what it might contribute to the overall design and implementation of this approach to teaching. The task was to design an instructional environment that facilitated and furthered skills of critical inquiry, problem solving, and group processing, as well as learning the appropriate content. While the content was important, however, emphasis was not to be on transmission and mastery of a body of content but on the problem posing and solving process. This perspective challenged us to "walk the talk" of social constructivist approaches to education (Steffe & Gale, 1995) and principles of adult learning (Merriam & Caffarella, 1999).

Furthermore, we wanted to use technology to address existing problems or limitations with PBL in face-to-face environments. While I had some experience with PBL in medical education, most of my team had little experience with this instructional approach, what it was, how it worked, or what were its instructional design requirements. As a team we had to learn more about PBL, the various contexts in which it has been applied, and its different forms and interpretations. PBL demands a radical shift in several areas of our thinking about teaching and learning: the locations of power and authority in the learning environment; the fostering of relationships and patterns of communication conducive to group inquiry; and, individual disclosure, challenge, and support (Boud & Feletti, 1991). PBL is more about learning to learn than learning a particular content area.

When approaching the technological design to address these issues, our group members had to be on the same page with regard to these ideas. Because many of us were products of 16 or more years of educational enculturation into ways of learning not consistent with PBL, we struggled with our own beliefs, meaning perspectives, and paradigms of teaching and learning. This process involved considerable unlearning and relearning. We learned as we went along, learning from each other.

Collectively, our group represented impressive skill and knowledge about technology. This knowledge, however, was not equitably or even normally distributed among our members. While most of the members had at least some knowledge about Web design, most had little or no knowledge of the use of technology in instructional design. I had knowledge of neither. Again, as a group we were faced with the challenge of learning about the instructional design uses of technology by doing it. Being embedded in the broader community of the faculty development class provided us with additional resources to help address the myriad of questions and problems that arose in the design process. While our actual texts seemed only nominally helpful, we made considerable use of the instructors, and others in our broader group.

Finally, this work was done within the context of a group. As I indicated earlier, we learned from each other, but we also struggled to develop the group processes and interactions necessary to effectively use the group as a source and facilitator of our learning. The curricular, pedagogical, and technological challenges all had to be addressed, in one way or another, as a group. As with any group, we faced similar practical and process issues: planning a timetable of work; who can do what; how to make assignments; when to meet; and, the process issues was extensive. As individuals, we had varying relationships with and knowledge of each other coming into the group. Differing levels of knowledge and skill sometimes were interpreted and used as forms of power. Personal and interpersonal issues quickly emerged and presented challenges to moving forward with the work. We struggled with individual schedules and conflicts with other commitments. The quality and quantity of work varied from member to member. Differences of opinion, style, and work habits presented numerous challenges for moving our project along. Tensions continually surfaced between our individual goals for the project and the evolving goals of the group.

At some level, we knew we were engaging in the very curricular and instructional process we were trying to create. We also realized that we were "walking the talk." In learning to design and develop PBL in an online environment, we were actually engaging in PBL ourselves. As with any work team, our dynamics and processes were a central feature of our life and work together. We sought to honor individual expressions within their own right, while at the same time building a quality group product. As an instructor and group leader, I also struggled with my own authority. I was continuously conscious of the fact that I was a professor and my group members were students. By that I mean I was always mindful of the need for the experience to be more than a "make-work" experience for them, but one that they found to be challenging and meaningful. I wanted this experience to be truly educative for the group members, so I was not at all reluctant to authorize individual members. Yet, I was deeply invested in the curricular vision with which I started the project and seeking actualization of this vision within our collective work was not always entirely compatible with my desire to authorize individual members of the group.

The demands of the task, however, often overshadowed our ability to stop and reflect on this process and what we were learning from it about one another, the technology, the process, and ourselves. Like the teams we use in our own instructional processes, we fell victim to the bias of seeing the work of the group in terms of the specific tasks needed for the group's ultimate product. We shied away from or even vigorously avoided the socioemotional dynamics, conflicts, and paradoxes of the group (Smith & Berg, 1987), and the intense and deeply meaningful learning that can result from consciously and reflectively attending to these dynamics (Boyd, 1991). In retrospect, I believe we could have been more mindful and self-reflective about our group process. This aspect of the experience is something I would encourage others to build into similar projects upfront. The intersection of the work, the dynamics of individual members and the group, and the culture of the broader community in which our group was embedded provide rich opportunities for faculty and students to develop deeper understandings into themselves as teachers and learners (West, 2001). I learned a great deal about the complexities of using teams within learning contexts. This appreciation has helped me better understand the challenges and struggles the teams in the classes that I teach face in their work together.

ROLES OF PARTICIPANTS IN THE COMMUNITY

The effort to redesign my course in adult learning required the involvement of numerous individuals, offices, and structures within the university. One of the major learning outcomes for me in developing this project was the realization of the critical and central role that organizational structures and various institutional communities play in getting something like this off the ground. This professional development experience was also linked with the development and implementation of a college-wide online master's program, in which most of the departments in the College were planning to offer an area of concentration. Courses developed in this experience and participating faculty were expected to be involved in this online program. As a member of the Department of Educational Administration, my course was intended to be part of a concentration within this new program in K-12 and postsecondary educational leadership. Its presence within this new curriculum, however, reflected the involvement of our program faculty and departmental curriculum committee, as well as the online program's curriculum committee.

This experience of the role of communities in creating online learning environments (Palloff & Pratt, 1999) debunks the myth of this experience as a lonely, solitary effort of individual instructors or learners. It takes a whole university to develop an effective online course. The faculty development course in which I enrolled was cotaught by two of the College's faculty with considerable experience in educational technology, and who were involved in the PT3 grant. The course was supported and strongly encouraged by the dean of the College of Education, as well as university administration, which provided an overarching organizational framework for our online developmental efforts, as well as technological and financial support to individual faculty members. It was also partially supported financially through the PT3 grant, and we met as a large group once a week in a state-of-the-art technologically equipped classroom. In this space, we had access to technology that few of us even recognized, let alone understood at the beginning of our time together. As we struggled through this experience, the Virtual University staff was made available to us for technological advice and support. Library staff members were available to assist us in integrating library resources into our instructional designs. Our instructors identified these resources early in the course and repeatedly stressed their availability throughout the semester-long experience.

My showing up for class on our first night together reflected the cumulative and collective efforts of many individuals, groups, and structures within our university. The design and development of the course that I would eventually teach online, however, evolved from a small group of graduate students who were also enrolled in this faculty development experience and who worked with me throughout the semester to help realize my vision for this course. Each of the six professors in the faculty development course was asked to briefly describe their goals and intentions for the course they wished to develop. Based on these descriptions, the graduate students were self-selected, with some encouragement from the course leaders to achieve approximately equal numbers, into one of six groups that formed around these professor-led course design efforts. All but one of the individuals who volunteered for my group was also a student in our program's doctoral program. Although none of these students had taught online before, they all, in different ways, brought to the experience considerable knowledge of the technology. They knew little about my subject matter or about problem-based learning, but they all could create at least some semblance of a Web page.

Given the fact that books like *HTML for Dummies* was written for people like me, the composition of my group was serendipitous. Each of them took an interest in different aspects of the course design and development. One person was interested in the group dynamics aspects of problem-based learning and how we might facilitate the collaborative learning required by this teaching strategy. Another was interested in graphics and the use of flash technology. A third member was drawn to issues of page layout and design. All were interested in the medium and its use for instructional purposes. I knew virtually nothing about any of these interest areas, but I brought to the group a vision for the course, based on my understandings of the promise and possibilities, as well as the potential issues represented by problem-based learning. As we struggled to define our goals and direction and settled into the work, these interests formed a basis for the group's division of labor.

Although our group was also part of the broader community of the class, much of our work was done within the context of the small group. The value of being part of a larger community was manifest in various ways. Perhaps most importantly, however, was the role of this larger community in creating a broader narrative context for our own evolving journeys and stories. Through our meetings together, we drew on one another's successes and struggles, compared notes, and occasionally used each other as resources. Being able to think about and talk through within this larger context the questions and issues arising in our developmental work helped me deepen my understanding of the bigger picture as well as the technical details of our work. While we were actually in the work, it felt at times that the broader community might actually be holding us up. In retrospect, however, I now recognize the tension that developed between our small group and the larger community as a healthy one that I have seen repeatedly manifest in my own online teaching. While we could have as a larger community addressed some of these tensions in a more explicit manner, each community finds its own way within its own context. We learn from these experiences, and we move on.

The single most important aspect of this work for my small group was the realization that they were involved in something new, something that had not been done before to any great extent. It was not just or maybe not even primarily the technology that provided this spark of enthusiasm. Rather, it was the challenge of designing a new learning experience, one that few have attempted in graduate education, and using the technology to help realize the philosophical and pedagogical goals that were at the heart of our project. As we worked with the theoretical framework for the course and online technology, we all began to appreciate the powerful intersection of these two parts of the learning experience. Our work demonstrated that PBL was not only possible within but seemed particularly well suited to an online environment.

OUR ONLINE, PROBLEM-BASED LEARNING DESIGN

Of course, my professional development about designing constructivist and contextual learning experiences within online environments is continuous and ongoing. Before I consider these issues and my reflections on this process, however, I will provide a brief description of the product that resulted from our team's work.

The core of our initial design consisted of four ill-structured practice problems that many, if not most, of our students would confront as practitioners in one form or another. For the most part, these problems were derived from my own experience of over 14 years as a professor, researcher, and educational consultant. In identifying and developing these case scenarios, I relied extensively on my interactions with practitioner groups. Although no single problem is based entirely on a particular experience, each problem represents a composite of what others and I have learned about the particular issues involved. For example, one of the problems reflected the difficulty that many teachers in community college settings have with retaining students in their individual courses. This problem reflects the broader issues within the fields of higher and adult education of participation and motivation to learn. Another problem focused on developing professional development programs that effectively incorporate what we know about how adults learn.

Because the primary instructional strategy was to be PBL, our course design placed considerable emphasis on process and structure, and less on providing specific content. We sought to design an experience that would deeply involve the students in the appropriate content and promote some level of mastery of that content, while at the same time fostering their skill in learning to learn and their abilities to work reflectively and collaboratively within a team environment. For this reason, we emphasized the need for a clear and explicit structure to the course and within each lesson. We knew we needed to provide sufficient information related to the problems so that the participants could readily enter into the required work with at least some conceptual framework or structure. To accomplish this need, we relied heavily on prior work on PBL done within face-to-face educational leadership programs (Bridges & Hallinger, 1995). This work provided a general conceptual structure that we adapted for use within our online problem units, representing a kind of guide to the intellectual territory that students could follow in addressing the issues raised within any given problem scenario.

We also stressed the importance of navigation within the site. To the extent possible, we wanted our participants to be able to easily move from one page to another and back again. We wanted to be sure they always knew where they were within the site and the particular unit, and that they could easily get back to where they started within any given work session. For this reason, our pages were extensively hyperlinked with one another, a point that I will address in the section on final reflections.

Within this design, students would be working extensively with one another. For this reason, we had to attend to the structures and processes for interpersonal and group interactions. We relied on both asynchronous and synchronous interactions. Class wide discussion boards were created to promote interaction and sharing among all members of the class. In addition, class wide chat rooms were created, allowing small groups of students from the class as a whole to interact directly with the instructor and with one another. This same structure was also recreated within each team. Only team members could access their own team discussion boards and chat rooms. Students were encouraged to interact online through the class Web site, instead of by e-mail, face-to-face meetings, or telephone, but were not discouraged from using these forms of interaction.

The problems that made up the core of the curriculum were bracketed with reflective experiences at the beginning and end of the course. As a team, we knew that few students would have had experiences with a PBL teaching strategy. In addition, although many may have participated in group learning, we also assumed that very few had ever been involved in the intensive, semester-long group experiences we were building into the course. Finally, we also knew that PBL would require extensive use of outside resources, such as the Internet and searching online databases. For this reason, we structured into the beginning of the course a 2-week orientation period during which we sought to introduce the participants to the fundamentals of PBL, group process and dynamics, and the use of external resources in an online environment. Separate sections within the orientation period were devoted to each of these areas, but we set up online learning experiences and activities to give students an opportunity to experience and practice all of these areas within any single topic.

The concluding lesson for the course consisted of an individual capstone experience intended to help each student reflect on and synthesize what they had learned from both the content in the course as well as the processes of problem-based and collaborative learning. In these experiences, they were essentially asked to reflect on what they learned from the research and theory on adult learning, about learning in and through an online group environment, and what they learned about themselves in this process.

In between these bookend experiences, of course, were the problem units. Each unit ranged in length from 3 to 5 weeks. The problems were sequenced to be increasingly complicated and messy, and to draw whenever possible on what was learned in the preceding problem units. For each problem, each team was expected to analyze the problem, develop a strategy for researching the problem, and then develop a written group product that addressed what they considered to be the key issues of the problem scenario. These products were group authored and every member of the group would receive the same grade. At the conclusion of each problem unit, we built in debriefing exercises in which team members were asked to collectively reflect on and assess their work together, what went well, what they needed to work on in the next unit, and what they were learning about adult learning through the process. In addition to these group debriefings, each participant was also to reflect on their individual experience with the problem and their team and to write a two to three page reflection paper describing what they had learned from the process.

Finally, each participant was to maintain a learning journal off-line, making at least a weekly journal reflecting on their experiences with both the content and the process of their learning. These journals were to be private and maintained in a manner in which the student felt most comfortable. These journals were not intended to be read by the instructor but only examined after the course was completed.

HOW MULTIPLE ITERATIONS OF
THE COURSE HAVE INFLUENCED ITS DESIGN

At the time of this writing, I have implemented the online version of this course annually for the last 3 years, and am preparing to teach it again shortly. I am sure my fellow group members will recognize much of their work and contributions in the current design. As a result of teaching the course now three times, much has also changed. I have learned as much or more from actually implementing the course than from participating in the overall design process. In between the second and third iterations of the course, we switched to a new online platform, insuring that my learning (as well as my frustrations) would continue.

So what have I learned from these experiences and how have they influenced and shaped both my approach to design as well as my teaching? Given the need for an orientation and a capstone experience, four problems proved to be too many to include within the remaining 11 weeks of the semester. About midway through the first offering of the redesigned course, it became apparent to me that I had underestimated the amount of time teams would require to process each problem, develop a research plan, and come together to construct the team product. This added time had more to do with conflicts in team schedules and their struggle to align their schedules and online communication patterns so they were effectively addressing the tasks at hand. As a result, I eliminated one of the problems and stayed with a three-problem structure for the subsequent two iterations.

Because of the limited number of problems, a tension developed between providing problem scenarios with a manageable scope but yet broad enough to encompass the appropriate research and theory. Although I have made some adjustments in problem scope in the last two offerings of the class, I continue to struggle with this issue. The online technology serves to both expedite the research process but also to create a sense of unlimited possibilities for team members, further exacerbating the problem of scope.

As I indicated earlier, our team structured each problem unit so that participants could easily move around the Web site, using hyperlinks within each unit. I quickly discovered, however, that such structure proved to be more confusing than helpful. The multiple choices created by these hyperlinks made it difficult for the learners to develop a clear structure or schematic map of the site. With the second iteration, I reduced the number of these links. In the third iteration, in which we switched to an Angel platform, these links were mostly eliminated. As one of my students helpfully pointed out, Angel structures a Web site like the chapters and pages of a book. With this realization, we could more effectively implement the needed revisions for this new platform. The result was a Web site with more levels and a more linear structure, but one which students seemed to find their way around more easily.

Another area that has undergone substantial revision in the course is the use of chat rooms. Prior to my first online offering, I had no experience with chat room technology. Several years ago, my children exposed me in a limited way to "instant messaging" (IM), but, after briefly experimenting with IM, I largely abandoned it as a means of online communication. At first, I planned to go online daily in class-wide chat rooms. After a couple sessions of 10 to 12 class members signing on at once, I realized I needed to change this approach. I then arbitrarily assigned students to three to four chat rooms of about one hour in length and this structured remained through the course of the first semester. I also occasionally signed on or was invited into team chat rooms as well. My use of class wide chat rooms was less frequent in the second iteration and, in the third iteration, it was not used at all.

While I initially began using them as a kind of open forum, I now realize that, to be effective, these experiences need to be more focused and structured. The lack of direction and focus contributed to reduced participation among students over time. I think they were expecting something of an online lecture and, when they did not receive it, realized they could more effectively spend their time doing other things. On the other hand, discussion was often frustrating because there were often two or more different conversations going on, and it was difficult for students to keep up with the interactions. However, the chat rooms did provide a means for students to talk and interact with others who were not members of their team, a major goal for the chat rooms.

Chat room communication demands that learners develop a new way of thinking while they talk, to envision dialogue in an alternative form. Unlike face-to-face interactions or even asynchronous online discussions, chat room discussions frequently involve holding at least a couple different lines of conversations in consciousness at the same time. At first, chat room discussions feel fragmented, choppy, disconnected, and almost chaotic. Our experiences have taught us that chat rooms work well under certain kinds of goals and circumstances. For example, scheduling meetings and planning the work of the group probably occurs best within a chat room environment, where the immediacy of communication allows decisions to be made quickly and easily. Using group time to get know each other better and building group climate through informal visiting or chatting seems also ideally suited to chat room discussions. Extensive exploration of theoretical issues or development of an argument for a particular approach to the problem being studied is probably not suitable for chat room environments. This form of interaction requires fairly extensive individual contributions, as well as more reflection and thought than is possible within the chat room environment.

In the first three iterations, I also made little or no use of audio or video streaming. As I began to incorporate PowerPoint into the problem units, however, it became apparent that use of at least an audio component would add to the overall pedagogical value and interest of the information components of each unit. For this reason, I am planning to integrate short segments of streaming audio in the next iteration of the course.

The collaborative approach to teaching has, perhaps, been the most provocative and instructive aspect of my online experiences so far. Online collaboration shares many of the characteristics, trials, and tribulations of the group process within face-to-face settings. It quickly became apparent that the tensions and dynamics of online groups are as powerful as those with classroom groups, but their presence is more difficult to discern in virtual environments. Many of these issues revolve around the tension between the individual and the group and questions of accountability. Much of what I have learned about the group process has resulted from a formal research study of this course and I will now explore these issues in somewhat more detail.

INTERPERSONAL INTERACTIONS AND GROUP DYNAMICS IN VIRTUAL ENVIRONMENTS

My work in this course has now become the focus of an ongoing research project examining the nature of problem-based, collaborative learning in online environments (Dirkx & Smith, 2003a, Smith, 2003). Through this research, we are studying the PBL process and the dynamics of collaborative learning within online environments. I have used this research to help inform my online pedagogical approach, an example of how research and pedagogy have come together within the context of this new technology for teaching.

For example, the research revealed considerably more about the struggles, dynamics, and processes in which the problem-based learning teams were engaged than was apparent in their online presence. It was only through the in-depth interviews of team members and analysis of their reflective papers, class journals, and archived chat material that I became aware of how much of the teams' work was deeply embedded in differences and emotional conflicts. Much of this conflict revolves around the group's need to attend to individual voices while at the same time speaking as a whole through group decisions and the final product (Dirkx & Smith, 2003a, 2003b). Authorizing the group risks deauthorizing the individual, while authorizing individual members risks deauthorizing the group as a whole (Smith & Berg, 1987). PBL groups runs the risk of getting stuck within this paradoxical cycle of emotion.

I now see a critical need to learn how to attend as an online facilitator to this potential stuckness. One of the most significant technological challenges that I currently face is to develop a means of more effectively facilitating group process. The instructor can play a role in helping team members name and work through the powerful emotions and dynamics that threaten to swamp them individually and collectively. This task, however, presents intriguing technological challenges to both how this can be structured and the ways in which these interventions might be accomplished.

One of the ways to develop a better sense of these issues in an ongoing manner is to require students to turn in their class journals on a periodic basis. This strategy, however, runs counter to my avowed use of journals, which is to provide learners with a space in which to talk with themselves about what they are experiencing and feeling in the class. I have indicated to participants that I would be willing to review their journals on a regular basis, if they so choose. However, only a couple have taken up my offer. Such a strategy also creates a significant increase in the amount of time and work an instructor has to commit to online learning. I have quickly learned that teaching online is already immensely time consuming.

I now wonder the extent to which the online technology serves to mask and conceal these profound differences and emotional struggles within the teams. While the teams in my third iteration of the course are, in many ways different, midway through the course, there was little online evidence of these struggles. This question represents a point of departure for both reflecting on my online pedagogy as well as for further research. In face-to-face groups, the dynamics of the group become quickly apparent, and I am used to interpreting and intervening on the socioemotional level within instructional groups. In some way, we need to explore how this can and should be done within online collaborative groups. This issue remains an open question for me in my use of online technology in problem-based learning.

Another observation I made through this research from the first offering of the course was the weak voice of theory within the online environment. As I observed and participated in team and class-wide discussion boards and chat rooms, I was struck by the lack of reference to the research and literature. The team members seemed caught up in the technical processes of the group's tasks and negotiating the technological issues presented by this environment. Through these early observations, I have learned that I need to consciously assist class participants, through the use of appropriately placed questions, to connect their observations, speculations, and interpretations back to the theory. I found the online technology actually enhances my ability to grasp each person's ability to do this, and to provide individual, team, and class-wide interventions when needed. In iterations two and three, I have been more active in the team and class-wide discussion boards, reading drafts of their team papers, providing feedback anchored in our readings, and asking questions intended to drive them back to the texts for further clarification, support, or elaboration of their claims. This issue reminds me that I am the representative of the scholarly community (Bruffee, 1999), and it is my responsibility to ensure that the scholarship of this community has a voice within the context of the teams' work.

In addition, the use of PBL online has also surfaced several other aspects of the environment that influence the overall process of inquiry and learning. For example, the use of asynchronous communication can both contribute to and retard group development. It can provide a means of helping group members move closer together but also to keep them at a distance. By responding to and taking up the issues within one another's discussion board posts, members signal to each other they are listening and that they value one another's voice. Such responsive online communication serves to enhance an overall sense of community and cohesiveness within the teams. Conversely, ignoring a fellow team member's posts, not logging on for extended periods of time, or allowing several days to pass before responding to a team member can raise questions about one's involvement and commitment to the team (Smith, 2003). In subsequent iterations of this course, I am more explicit about the need for members to log on consistently and frequently, the importance of them to actively respond to one another's posts, if nothing more than a few words of acknowledgment. Our ongoing research will help determine if such an approach has been effective but my subjective sense, being immersed currently in the process, that team members are more responsive and timely in their interactions with each other. Few, if any students in my current course, are not logging on at least once a day.

Interestingly, technologically mediated PBL seems to foster or offer opportunities for learning to be more contemplative and introspective, to learn more about one's self and others. As I indicated in the previous sections, numerous opportunities present themselves in the course of this experience in which there is a dynamic intersection of the self of the learner, the content, and the context. PBL's focus is learning about one's self as a learner and a person (Savi-Baden, 2000), and it is clear from our work and research that such opportunities are clearly made evident through this environment. At times, the computer seemed to become personified and the focus of team member's anger or rage at the process or fellow group members, something that was only evident through interviews or the journals (Smith, 2003). The role of the computer in online learning in eliciting or drawing out aspects of the self for reflection, represents an exciting area for future research. Because I believe that a major challenge for professional development is the fostering of a critical self-understanding and self-awareness, this last issue becomes a fascinating perspective with which to approach the idea of faculty development.

CONCLUSION

My involvement in this PT3 project has been one of the most challenging but interesting professional development experiences of my career. Although I am deeply committed to understanding teaching and learning from a depth perspective, I never imagined that a technological, online environment might provide a rich context for furthering our understanding of the powerful emotional dynamics and processes that often threaten to side-track both teachers and learners. In fact, I feared such an environment seemed almost antithetical to the realization of what makes us most human. While there remains the question of whether these environments do mask or mute group dynamics, there is little doubt in my mind of potential for this medium to foster learning about self as well as content, problem-solving, and lifelong learning skills. Filtered through the lens of technology, however, PBL methods raise additional questions about curriculum, teaching and learning, and facilitating group work in this process. We continue to work with these questions in our ongoing research and teaching.

REFERENCES

Barrows, H. S., & Tamblyn, R. M. (1980). *Problem-based learning*. New York: Springer.

Boud, D., & Feletti, G. (1991). *The challenge of problem-based learning*. New York: St. Martin.

Boyd, R. D. (1991). *Personal transformation in small groups: A Jungian perspective*. London: Routledge.

Bridges, E. M., & Hallinger, P. (1995). *Implementing problem-based learning in leadership development*. Eugene: University of Oregon.

Brookfield, S. D. (1986). *Understanding and facilitating adult learning*. San Francisco: Jossey-Bass.

Bruffee, K. A. (1999). *Collaborative Learning: Higher Education, Interdependence, and the Authority of Knowledge* (2nd ed.). Baltimore, MA: The John Hopkins University Press.

Dirkx, J. M., & Smith, R. O. (2003a). Thinking out of a bowl of spaghetti: Learn-ing to learn in online collaborative groups. In T. S. Roberts (Ed.), *Online col-laborative learning: Theory and practice* (pp. 132-159). Hershey, PA: Idea Group.

Dirkx, J. M., & Smith, R. O. (2003b). "Doesn't anyone just lecture anymore?" Adult learners' love/hate relationship with online small group work. In D. Flowers, M. Lee, A. Jalipa, E. Lopex, A. Schelstrate, & V. Sheared (Eds.), *AERC 2003 Proceedings: The 44th annual adult education research conference* (pp. 109-114). San Francisco: State University.

Evenson, D. H., & Hmelo, C. E. (Eds.). (2000). *Problem-based learning: A research perspective on learning interactions*. Mahwah, NJ: Erlbaum.

Jarvis, P. (1992). *Paradoxes of learning: On becoming an individual in society*. San Fran-cisco: Jossey-Bass.

Mahoney, M. (1991). *Human change processes: The scientific foundations of psychother-apy*. New York: Basic Books.

Merriam, S. B., & Caffarella, R. S. (1999). *Learning in adulthood* (2nd ed.). San Francisco: Jossey-Bass.

Nowlen, P. M. (1988). *A new approach to continuing education for business and the pro-fessions*. Old Tappan, NJ: Macmillan.

Palloff, R. M., & Pratt, K. (1999). *Building learning communities in cyberspace: Effec-tive strategies for the online classroom*. San Francisco: Jossey-Bass.

Roberts, T. S. (Ed.). (2003). *Online collaborative learning: Theory and practice*. Her-shey, PA: Idea Group.

Savi-Baden, M. (Ed.). (2000). *Problem-based learning in higher education: Untold sto-ries*. Buckingham, England: Society for Research in Higher Education and Open University Press.

Smith, K. K., & Berg, D. N. (1987). *Paradoxes of group life: Understanding conflict, paralysis, and movement in group dynamics*. San Francisco: New Lexington Press.

Smith, R. O. (2003). *The struggle for voice: student experiences in collaborative online groups*. Unpublished dissertation, East Lansing, Michigan State University.

Steffe, L. P., & Gale, J. (Eds.). (1995). *Constructivism in education*. Hillsdale, NJ: Erlbaum.

Tennant, M. C., & Pogson, P. (1995). *Learning and change in the adult years: A devel-opmental perspective*. San Francisco: Jossey-Bass.

Vella, J. (2002). *Learning to listen, learning to teach: The power of dialogue in educating adults* (Rev. ed.). San Francisco: Jossey-Bass.

West, L. (2001). *Doctors on the edge: General practitioners, health and learning in the inner-city*. London: Free Association Press.

Wilkerson, L., & Gijselaers, W. H. (Eds.). (1996, Winter). *Bringing problem-based learning to higher education: Theory and practice*. New Directions for Teaching and Learning, 68. San Francisco: Jossey-Bass.

CHAPTER 9

A FACULTY MEMBER'S JOURNEY IN USING TECHNOLOGY TO ENHANCE LEARNING

Ann E. Austin

Knowledge must come through action;
you can have no test which is not fanciful, save by trial.

—Sophocles

In fall, 1999, I submitted an application to participate in CEP 822, the Professional Development Seminar on Educational Technology at Michigan State University (MSU), the following spring semester. My interest was encouraged by a colleague and a doctoral student who knew about both my curiosity about uses of technology to enhance teaching and learning and my hesitancy regarding my own knowledge in this area. In the proposal that I wrote in November 1999, I offered an analysis of the potential impact and value of my participation. I noted that I take my teaching very seriously, and, that for several years, I had had a growing realization that my low level of knowledge and skill with technology meant that I was not able to take advantage of some of the available

Faculty Development by Design: Integrating Technology in Higher Education, 167–184

resources that would benefit my students and their learning. I noted that I often teach courses on teaching and learning issues in higher education, and I believe these courses should model innovative uses of technology to enhance learning. I hoped that participating in the design course would help me gain the knowledge and skills needed to fulfill these expectations. Furthermore, I hoped to develop a project to facilitate students' progress toward the goals of the course.

Specifically, I argued, since graduates of the Higher, Adult, and Lifelong Education (HALE) Program are likely to become administrators or faculty leaders in universities and colleges (in fact, some HALE students already hold such roles when they enter the program), the HALE program should ensure that their graduate experiences offer examples of effective uses of technology to support learning. At that time, the HALE faculty was engaged in significant curriculum revision to ensure that we offered a strong, innovative program to prepare leaders and scholars in postsecondary education. As part of this process, some of the faculty members discussed how the integration of appropriate technology could help our students to achieve program learning goals. Thus, in addition to strengthening a course that I taught called Proseminar and my own knowledge, I expected that my involvement in the course would have impact: (a) on future higher education leaders and faculty members who are graduate students in the Proseminar by enhancing their learning and by providing them examples of the uses of technology in teaching which could be instructive for institutions where they work; and, (b) on my HALE colleagues, by modeling innovations our faculty might incorporate into our curriculum development work.

In retrospect, my project was modest in comparison to the fully online courses that other colleagues and their design teams have developed in more recent years. However, I participated in the design course in its second iteration and prior to the College's plans for an online degree. Additionally, I was a complete novice regarding technology. Probably, I was the least knowledgeable about the possibilities offered by technology among the faculty members in the Professional Development Course that year. I had no idea of the possibilities or how to conceptualize uses of technology for the project I had in mind. Everything about the class and the project was new to me. Although the project was not the design of an online course, nor was it as advanced as some of the other projects that year, it was a totally new and innovative experience for me.

In this chapter, I describe my experience in the Professional Development course, a learning community that was powerful and fruitful for me, and, I think, beneficial for the students in the course on which I focused my design project. The first section of the chapter presents the "problem" that the course presented and what I wanted to achieve through my

project. I discuss the goals of the HALE Doctoral Proseminar, the pedagogical strategies used to facilitate achievement of the goals, various challenges associated with this course, and the components of the project I
undertook. The second part of the chapter discusses the various communities within which the design of the project was embedded and implications and issues associated with these communities. In the third section, I
explain the process of design and implementation, including various
challenges that arose and how they were handled. Finally, in the last section, I offer some reflections on the experiences and lessons I gained from
participation in the Professional Development Seminar on Education
Technology.

The story I tell in this chapter about my experience in the professional development course illustrates the central theme of this book
concerning technological integration into teaching and learning as a
sociological issue. In the first chapter, Mishra, Koehler, and Zhao
explain that integrating technology into teaching and learning is not a
simple additive task. Rather, it requires attention to organizational cultures, social group norms and processes, and individual interests and
values. Furthermore, effective integration of technology into a course
requires recognizing the interrelationships between pedagogical goals,
content, and technology. That is, technology affects content and pedagogy, and conversely, the pedagogical goals and content of a course—as
well as, I would add, the characteristics of the students—affect what
technologies will be useful.

DESCRIPTION OF THE AUTHENTIC PROBLEM

Doctoral students in the Higher, Adult, and Lifelong Education Program
at Michigan State University enter the program each fall as part of a student cohort of about fifteen or twenty. All students are required to take
five core courses in the field, beginning with a Proseminar. Designed as
the first course for PhD students in Higher, Adult, and Lifelong Education Program, this course has three primary purposes: (1) to increase students' familiarity with history, key concepts, issues, questions,
contemporary concerns, and literatures relevant to scholars and practitioners of higher and adult education; (2) to provide information on the
doctoral process in the Higher, Adult, and Lifelong Education Program
(HALE) that will help doctoral students successfully navigate their programs; and, (3) to help entering doctoral students enhance their abilities
in areas of critical reading, critical thinking and analysis, writing, and
inquiry.

Doctoral students in the HALE program typically bring considerable professional experience, observation, and reflection to the course. Thus, the seminar encourages students to think about the relationships between practice and theory, and to find specific ways to draw from and build on their professional expertise. At the same time, the course urges participants to deepen their knowledge and understanding of scholarly literatures and theoretical perspectives relevant to the study of and practice within postsecondary education. This focus on literature and theory is intended to inform participants' professional practice as well as their ability to work within and contribute to the processes of scholarly inquiry in the field of postsecondary education. The course is also designed to help new doctoral students frame significant questions, which they will seek to address through their study, professional practice, interactions with colleagues and faculty, and ongoing habits of inquiry.

As the teacher of the course, I use several pedagogical strategies to help students achieve the goals of the course. One strategy is to encourage extensive and probing discussion of course readings, which involves discussions in and out of class about readings and relevant topics. I encourage students to read for more than information; I want them to use the readings as the basis for identifying issues and problems of interest and for framing questions that they wish to consider and pursue during their doctoral study. Dialogue among students both within the context of class sessions and during the week between classes is an important part of the course design.

A second pedagogical strategy is to use peer-writing groups as a vehicle through which students engage in the inquiry process, including the steps of developing research questions, writing literature reviews, and considering design choices. Within these writing groups, students deepen their skills in analytical reading of scholarly work and learn to invite and provide peer review and critical feedback. Early in the course, the students and I work together to discuss strategies for providing effective peer review and feedback. We explicitly discuss the value of making one's work public (at least to a group of colleagues willing to be thoughtful and helpful), even when it is not yet fully developed. My intention is to help new doctoral students see their writing as a process rather than only a product, as a means to gain understanding and engage in creative thought processes as well as evidence of the final outcome of sustained work over time. I want students to move from the notion of writing a paper as a task done once and considered complete to the notion of scholarly writing as sustained thinking, effort, collegial critique, and revising that occurs over a period of time.

A third pedagogical strategy—as well as an intended outcome of the Proseminar—is the development of a community of scholars. I urge the doctoral students to recognize that, while scholarly work requires the discipline of quiet, solitary work, it also benefits greatly from the ongoing interchange and critique provided by a community of other serious thinkers. In my experience, new PhD students often anticipate doctoral study as a process of fulfilling a set of requirements, rather than as an experience of entering a community that involves mutual responsibilities to and benefits from interacting over time with others interested in similar problems of scholarship and practice. During the Proseminar, I work strategically to offer a vision of a scholarly community and to explore with the students the responsibilities of being a member of such a community. As the teacher of the Proseminar, I work to forge a community among the new students that is likely to sustain and challenge them over time, a community with the potential to scaffold their experience as developing scholars as they move into later semesters of their doctoral work. Over the years, a number of students have continued regular meetings with the writing groups and small scholarly communities that were first established during the Proseminar as they proceed through their doctoral study—and for some students, the communities have continued even longer.

A particular challenge in establishing writing groups and a sustainable learning community among the students is the geographic distance that separates many of the class participants. Typically, more than half of the students are part-time and reside and work up to several hours driving time from campus. Even those students who are considered full-time and who live in close proximity to campus often work at least halftime in various assistantships and employment positions. Thus, finding opportunities for small groups to meet outside of class poses some logistical challenges that can lead to frustration with the expectation of peer review and discussion, or, at best, simply difficulties for students in scheduling such meetings.

Given these course goals, pedagogical strategies, and particularities of the student group, I proposed a project for the spring, 2000 Professional Development Course that would accomplish the following within the HALE Proseminar:

1. *Create a Web-Based Class Center:*   I envisioned a Web-based Class Center as a location for all relevant course material, including the syllabus, instructions for assignments, and examples of well-prepared papers, as well as the place to facilitate a chat room for ongoing discussions among class members. Such a Class Center, I expected, would strengthen the kind of learning community that I try to nurture in the course.

2. *Strengthen Class Discussions Through Preclass Dialogue:*   I wanted to post questions about weekly readings and ask students to respond at the Web site prior to class sessions. Class discussions then could be used for deeper, higher level conversations around issues that would have already emerged in the pre-conversations.

3. *Provide Support for the Writing Groups:*   As mentioned, the doctoral students in the course are organized into semester-long writing groups composed of three or four people each. Students are taught strategies for providing and benefiting from peer feedback, which they receive as well as the instructor's feedback, on multiple drafts of the writing projects. Also, as mentioned, the geographic distance between students' homes or workplaces sometimes makes it difficult for these groups to meet out of class. Thus, I wanted to learn to use technology that would facilitate the work of these writing groups. As I proposed the project, I was guessing that some kind of Web site could be constructed where writing group members could interact to provide feedback and engage in collaborative work to improve their writing projects.

4. *Provide Links to Web-Based Resources in Higher Education:*   As mentioned, the Proseminar is designed to help students identify key areas of inquiry within higher and adult education. Focusing on several key topical areas, I wanted to facilitate students' abilities to frame important problems in higher education and help them explore related data in Web resources as well as in traditional print materials. I envisioned identifying Web sites sponsored by major organizations in higher education (e.g., the American Association of Higher Education, the Professional and Organizational Development Network) and linking them to a course Web site. Using these links, I expected, students could both become familiar with significant scholarly and professional organizations and their resources, and gather current data to answer questions raised in discussions or in their writing projects.

I believed that a project that addressed these goals would deepen and facilitate the learning experience for the students; and, through the process of meeting these goals, I would expand my understanding and skills regarding the uses of technology to facilitate learning.

THE DESIGN COMMUNITY: PARTICIPANTS, ROLES, AND IMPLICATIONS

The process of developing this project for the Proseminar occurred within a set of communities: the Michigan State University College of Education, the Higher, Adult, and Lifelong Education Program, the Professional Development Course offered in Spring, 2000, the specific design team organized within the context of the Professional Development Course, and ultimately, the Proseminar itself.

MSU's College of Education

The invitation to submit a proposal to participate as a faculty member came to all faculty members from the dean's office. The clear message from the invitation was that the dean encouraged faculty members to consider participating, and that this activity would help both the individual faculty participant and the College as a whole to move forward in terms of exploring appropriate uses of technology in teaching. Faculty participants in 2000 received laptop computers and software appropriate for their projects. While my interest in participating was not motivated by the prospect of receiving this equipment, I appreciated the up-to-date technology and perceived this investment in the faculty participants as a reminder of the importance with which we should take our involvement in this course. I entered the course with enthusiasm to learn all I could, a firm commitment to protect my time for class participation and design group meetings, and appreciation for the space and support created by the dean's office for this kind of significant faculty investment of time and energy into professional development. I note also that the support I received from the dean's office carried over into the following year, when I received some funds to pay for assistance as I implemented the project into my teaching of the Proseminar. This ongoing support in the form of assistance from a technologically savvy doctoral student eased some of my anxiety about implementing the project.

The Higher, Adult, and Lifelong Education Program (HALE)

As a faculty member in the HALE Program, my teaching is done in the context of the program curriculum that the faculty members have designed. Thus, while the HALE faculty group was not directly involved in the project design for the HALE Proseminar that I teach, I consider the HALE faculty as part of the larger community in which I situated my involvement in the Professional Development Course and my efforts to enhance the Proseminar. Indeed, I always consider any changes I make to my courses as influenced by and influencing the broader curriculum of the whole doctoral program. However, the context provided by the HALE Program was particularly significant during the time I took the Professional Development Course, because, as a faculty, we were involved in significant curriculum revision of our doctoral program. In particular, we were establishing a set of five core courses that each entering doctoral cohort would take together. The Proseminar has always been required for entering doctoral students, but I used this process of curriculum revision to rethink aspects of the Proseminar. My participation in the Faculty Development Course occurred at a particularly opportune time in the process of curriculum revision within the HALE doctoral program.

The Professional Development Course

The Professional Development Course played a major role as I pursued my project. As I mentioned earlier, I entered the course with little knowledge about the specific possibilities through which technologies could assist my pedagogical goals. I knew how to use e-mail and how to word process. Beyond that, I had little awareness of possibilities and considerable lack of confidence as someone who could learn and use more varied technological options. The Professional Development Course brought together about five other faculty colleagues and a number of graduate students from across the College. Participation in the course helped me in a number of ways.

First, I appreciated the camaraderie of being with others who also were interested in addressing some of their pedagogical goals through creative uses of technology. From the start, the course was fun in the sense that I felt comfortable, encouraged, and supported. While I perceived right away that most other participants seemed more knowledgeable about technology than myself, the collegiality that characterized the class gatherings did much to diminish my anxiety. The experience of being part of the course brought to mind my initial forays into statistics years earlier as a new doctoral student. I recall that a group of us in the first statistics class all met to go to the computer lab together to support each other in doing our first assignment. In those days when most people did not have desktop computers and laptops did not exist, we gained some confidence from knowing that, if we visited the computer lab as a group, we could ask each other how to turn on the machines and manage computer glitches that we were sure would arise! Some of the same sense of supporting each other, exchanging successes, and helping each other troubleshoot difficulties permeated the

Professional Development Course sessions. My anxiety diminished in the context of supportive and interested colleagues.

Second, the course provided examples of pedagogical possibilities that I could consider. Since I knew little about the possibilities offered by technology that might be relevant to my course, I relished the class sessions when we heard from others about the options they were considering or the solutions that were emerging for their pedagogical goals. I also appreciated the short lectures, presentations, and demonstrations offered each week by the instructors. Some of these presentations were somewhat too advanced for me to grasp. In particular, I felt lost within a few minutes in the session on "HTML language." Nevertheless, I recognized that, while I might not grasp each detail, I could gain an appreciation of key ideas that would broaden my awareness and extend the foundation of prior knowledge on which I could draw as I continued to learn about technology, teaching, and learning. Other sessions, such as on voice-activated word processing and interactive video conferencing, were easier to understand and immediately offered some new possibilities for teaching and research issues I was considering. I found that the new ideas I was encountering not only offered options for my immediate project in the HALE Proseminar, but also pertained to research endeavors and teaching goals in other courses.

Part of my research program focuses on faculty careers and professional development. A third value for me in being part of the Professional Development Course was the opportunity to observe faculty development in action. A truism that I have heard voiced among colleagues who work regularly in faculty development in universities and colleges is that collegial groups are a particularly effective way to help faculty members learn and change. Within such groups, faculty members encounter new ideas even as they receive encouragement and support from their colleagues. While a key faculty value is autonomy, an equally embedded value is collegiality. The Professional Development Course honored and built on both of these values. Each faculty member had the opportunity to work on the particular pedagogical issues he or she had identified as compelling, while also being part of a community that challenged, supported, and offered ideas and feedback. Since I have studied and written about the processes and outcomes of such approaches to faculty development (Austin, 1992, 1998; Sorcinelli & Austin, 1992), I participated in the Professional Development Course not only as a learner and colleague, but partly with a researcher's eye to how participants were experiencing it, what processes worked well and why, and what difficulties, barriers, or challenges arose. My reflections in this chapter partly emerged from those observations.

Instructors/Experts

The instructors of the Professional Development Seminar in spring, 2000, Yong Zhao, Punya Mishra, and Rick Banghart, were essential parts of the design community. I appreciated their formal lectures and presentations, their informal interactions with my design team, and their ongoing interest both in my project and in me as a colleague engaging with new ideas. During the Professional Development Course, I often reflected on how my learning process pertaining to the possibilities of technology compared to my experiences as a graduate student some years earlier learning about the uses and possibilities offered by statistical analysis. For me, using technology and engaging in statistical analysis presented some parallel challenges; each was something I wanted to learn, but each created some anxiety. Additionally, in each area, I found I had to work hard to learn, rather than experiencing the learning as natural and "easy," as I often experienced in other areas of learning. Although I found statistics somewhat challenging, I had pursued statistics courses to a fairly sophisticated level in graduate school. These experiences in statistics courses had given me considerable opportunity to think about the pedagogical implications of teaching and learning in areas where students often feel some anxiety. Thus, as a participant in the Professional Development Course, encountering technology as another area in which I experienced some anxiety, I was observant of the ways in which the course teachers approached their own pedagogical roles and responsibilities.

What I observed was that Yong, Punya, and Rick created an effective balance between challenging learners and supporting them. They introduced thoughtful design possibilities, but did not overwhelm with too many ideas at a time. They explained concepts, ideas, and options in ways that conveyed deep knowledge, but they never used the teaching environment as a place to showcase their own deep technical knowledge in ways that intimidated learners. They acted simultaneously as colleagues who shared similar pedagogical problems and as experts who had good ideas for possible solutions. They knew when to ask questions to draw out the thinking of the course participants, and when to step in to offer an idea or a word of support to counter moments of rising frustration. They were colleagues and teachers at the same time. I especially appreciated their confidence in each course participant, their calm encouragement, and what I perceived as their ongoing commitment to technology not as a stand-alone solution but as a tool to help teachers and students address learning issues in productive and creative ways. Additionally, their willingness to stop for a quick chat in the hall or stop by my office to help with a problem extended the collegiality experienced in the weekly class sessions to learning opportunities on a daily basis. The contribution of each of these colleagues to what I learned and the ultimate project outcome was indispensable. The success of the Professional Development Course owed much to the abilities, knowledge, and collegiality of the three instructors, Punya, Yong, and Rick.

Design Team

The team itself was the immediate context in which my project was developed. One of the distinctive aspects of my experience in the course pertained to the dynamics of my design team; the team provided some excellent ideas and support, but also some challenges that required time, energy, and tact on my part. I had originally applied to participate in the Professional Development Course at the urging of a doctoral student in HALE who knew I was simultaneously interested in learning more about technology as it might support my courses and somewhat intimidated by technology. This student had been a student in some courses I teach, including the Proseminar and a course that addresses teaching in postsecondary education, and she knew I gave considerable thought to pedagogical issues and processes. She suggested that I apply for the course and that she would register as a graduate student, and that we could work together on a project that I would propose. Both she and I looked forward to the opportunity to work together, and we each had important learning goals going into the course.

As the course began, the instructors asked the faculty participants to summarize their project goals, and the graduate student participants were invited to indicate in which design teams they would like to participate. My team came to include a graduate student from another department with interest in postsecondary and adult learning and some working knowledge of technological possibilities that might be relevant to my course, a graduate student in my department who was interested to work with me and who had taken the Proseminar, and the original student who had proposed that I apply as a faculty participant and that she and I work on my proposed project.

Team members each brought interest and expertise. We met during the course hours as well as during additional sessions throughout the week. Early in the process, some tensions within the group became apparent. One student wanted to use the group as an opportunity to pursue a particular technological idea that she had in mind. As time went on, I had the sense that this student wished to be helpful, but was quite interested in using this project as a time to develop certain technical expertise herself. Though I had explained several times early in the team meetings what I hoped to achieve in terms of my pedagogical goals, I found myself needing to reiterate frequently what the goals of the Proseminar were and why I did not need, what I perceived as, an overly sophisticated technological solution. I needed to emphasize often that the pedagogical goals I had set should not be overshadowed by a technical solution. In fact, I was concerned that the technological solution that this student was strongly advocating might actually detract from the learning processes that I hoped my Proseminar students would pursue as developing writers. On the other hand, I felt that this student, who strongly emphasized a particular approach, genuinely believed that what she was offering had usefulness. I appreciated her efforts while also emphasizing the particular goals I was trying to achieve in the Proseminar.

At the same time, I believe the student who had suggested that I apply for the course, and that she and I work together, felt disappointed that the collegial environment which she envisioned did not develop initially. In contrast, some meetings were tense as the different ideas of the other student had to be handled. The third student did his best to offer useful ideas and provide helpful technical input.

I found myself with more tasks and challenges than I had expected. I wanted to interact with the original student in the collegial way we had intended; I knew she was interested in thinking about the pedagogical challenges I was trying to address, and that she had invested considerable time in talking with me about the Proseminar and how technology might help with some of my goals. I wanted to include the third student from another field who seemed genuinely interested in thinking through my pedagogical goals and how technology might help. I wanted to honor the efforts and interests of the other student, but I also needed to ensure that this student's somewhat divergent interests did not frustrate the goals I was trying to achieve in my project. Simultaneously, I was handling my own lack of knowledge about technology and my sense of general anxiety about working on a project where I felt I had virtually no prior knowledge or skills on which to draw.

Thus, the design team experience within the Professional Development Course presented me with some significant and time-consuming challenges, which had to be managed throughout the experience. I benefited greatly from the ideas and technological expertise of the students who worked with me, and I could not have developed the project without their assistance. However, I believe a team that I had selected rather than one that emerged out of the assignments made in the Professional Development Course would have been more productive—and may have required less time to accomplish the project. I recognize, though, that teams often come together for a variety of reasons and often cannot be specifically selected. Thus, my experience probably highlighted challenges that frequently emerge when novice faculty members work with technology consultants.

The Process of Seeking a Technology Solution

Design

Once the team had been identified, we began by reviewing the purposes of the Proseminar and the general goals and ideas I had for the project. The early efforts of the team were to explore possible ways to set up a course Web site. I recall that, early on, I was excited to see an example of a Web site that Punya or Rick (I believe) had developed for another course. Team members looked into and presented a variety of possibilities, including Blackboard. Early team meetings were spent reviewing various Web sites for design ideas. To me, the possibilities seemed a bit overwhelming, but I intuitively also could tell what I thought would be helpful and what might be less useful. Blackboard was not yet used as an official platform available through Michigan State, but we did review the options offered if we were to choose a one-semester trial connection to the Blackboard site. As the first few weeks passed, it became increasingly clear that I wanted the most simple, least cluttered Web site possible. Perhaps because of my own uncertainties about using technology, I did not want a technology solution that would frustrate students who were unfamiliar with technological strategies. At that point in time, many of our graduate students in their 30s, 40s, and 50s had limited exposure to using technology in their classes. I also kept in mind that my experience teaching entering doctoral students over a number of years told me that they often were feeling overwhelmed about the new and demanding expectations of doctoral education. Adding "technology overload" did not seem appropriate or useful.

As team members explored options for a Web site design for the Web-Based Class Center, some tensions emerged around the purposes that we were trying to achieve. As noted above, one team member seemed to be drawn to the high-end possibilities of what technology might offer. Other team members felt somewhat frustrated that this member did not seem responsive to my desire to meet the pedagogical goals in a fairly straightforward and minimally complicated way. At times, I recall, I needed to be fairly firm about my pedagogical goals and my commitment to choosing technology specifically and solely for its likelihood for meeting my goals. Given this emerging tension, team members took on different responsibilities.

The person who had originally urged me to apply for the Professional Development Course assumed the task of researching Web sites of professional associations and other organizations relevant to the fields of higher and adult education. I had envisioned that part of the course Web site would involve links to a number of relevant Web sites of professional organizations. This person's work was very fruitful. While we had expected that she would identify and have to organize and develop links to a number of Web sites, her research led her to the very useful discovery of several Web sites run by major professional organizations that had already located many pertinent Web sites and organized them by topic. She sought and received permission from the institutions hosting those Web sites for us to link their sites to my course site.

Another team member took on the task of overall design of the course Web site. We had determined that Blackboard offered more than I needed and might not be available without high cost for more than one semester. Consequently, we decided to design our own site that would include places for course documents; class communication options for e-mail messages to individuals, the full class, and small groups; spaces for peer writing groups to develop and exchange manuscripts, using WordTracker for providing feedback; a chat room; spaces for student information and photos; and, links to other professional resources and Web sites. The student who took on the task of designing the site worked patiently and steadily, offering me options for layout, color, and style.

The team member who seemed interested in exploring more sophisticated technology possibilities took on a task that she thought would facilitate the writing assignments in the course. She had some ideas about ways to use cyberspace for students to chronicle and save their research ideas and record drafts. While the ideas were very interesting and might work for some classes, they seemed more complicated than I suspected students really needed in my class. Nevertheless, since the student was enthusiastic about the possibilities she was designing, I decided that the best course would be to remain open to see what evolved.

With each person taking on separate roles, the tension in the group was minimized, and I became the link between team members—though the person working on the resource list and the student doing the Web site design coordinated their efforts and often met with me together. By the end of the semester, we had a working Web site that included an excellent resource list and links to a large number of relevant professional associations and bibliographies. The writing template that the third student designed to facilitate writing and research was still underway. This part of the project was ultimately completed the following semester.

Several key aspects of the design process deserve highlighting:

* My ability to articulate what I envisioned for the course was important to the process—even though initially I had no idea how to

make it happen in terms of technological possibilities. The task was a matter of forging links between the pedagogical goals of the course and the technological ideas of the team members. Success required an ongoing effort to keep the team focused on matching the goals and the possibilities.

- Allowing time for brainstorming was a key to developing the project. I needed to be exposed to various options, mainly through listening to team members' ideas and seeing examples of Web sites used for other classes. Team members benefited from the freedom to explore and present possibilities without feeling the need to make quick decisions. Rushing to a solution would not have allowed a variety of ideas to surface. Additionally, my lack of knowledge about possibilities and my nervousness about technology meant we had to move more slowly than teams working with faculty members more experienced with technology.

- I made some discoveries about my own learning process in using technology in my teaching. I am interested in uses of technology in teaching, but I seem to learn the technical strategies more slowly and less spontaneously than what I observe is comfortable for many people. I found that having team members "just show" me possibilities did not always work well. I needed time to try out possible strategies in systematic ways. Our design process had to accommodate time for me to explore and learn these options. The patience exhibited by each of the three team members was an important feature of the support the team provided.

Implementation

I implemented the course Web site in the Proseminar offered in the fall of 2000. The dean's office had provided funding to support a doctoral student (someone with considerable technology knowledge and a previous student in the Proseminar, but not a participant on the design team) to help me with implementation. Through the semester, he helped with various technological glitches (such as student problems in accessing the site) as we mounted and used the Web site. His availability diminished my concerns about any technical problems. We explained the purpose of the Web site to the class as a Course Center, and invited class members to post information about themselves on the site and to use it as a class communication center for scholarly exchange between class sessions. I also explained that we would use the Web site as a way to facilitate the exchange of manuscripts and critical feedback among peer writing group members, and that the site allowed students to collect and post their finished writing for other class members to read.

Since BlackBoard or other Web site course learning centers were not yet used widely at Michigan State at the time, and since the students were new to the doctoral program, none of them had participated previously in a class that had used a Web site for extensive idea exchange and posting of writing. To my surprise, some students resisted the idea of posting their writing, worrying about issues of privacy. In the end, I used the site for communication to students, posting class session notes, and posting course information. Students also made extensive use of the links to other organizations and bibliographic resources. The writing template was offered to the students but was not used extensively. I did not require students to post finished writing products in deference to the concerns and discomfort of some students about this idea. I found that I needed to be flexible, to check in with students, to handle their concerns and questions, and to make adjustments. The implementation was clearly a "process" and negotiation, not a fixed "event." I expect that some of the implementation issues would no longer arise today, since, with so many courses now using Blackboard or Angel as platforms for communication and information exchange, students are well accustomed to these technological aids to their learning.

Further Developments

The technology was changing as the team worked and as we implemented the course Web site. As implementation in the Proseminar proceeded, Blackboard became an official option for MSU faculty members, and, in its MSU version, it seemed a better and easier option than the Web site the team had developed. While I used the course Web site we had designed for just one semester before switching to Blackboard during the next course offering in the fall of 2001, the time spent on the design of the course Web site had long-term effects. By working with the team on the course Web site design, I had lost much of my anxiety about using technology in teaching. I had become more familiar with various terms and processes associated with technology use and comfortable with exploring and experimenting with new options. I had also gained some sense of the ways in which technology could support my pedagogical goals (especially, in the Proseminar, through enhancing communication options and linking course members to an array of Web-based resources). I also felt more confident in my ability to make decisions about technical options as they relate to my pedagogical goals. While I have not yet taught a fully online course, I believe that my experience in the Professional Development Course has made me more comfortable with this possibility.

Reflections

I conclude with a few observations. First, the design process built on and illustrated the value of bringing issues of pedagogical goals, content, and technology into interaction with each other. As conceptualized by the editors of this volume, Technological Pedagogical Content Knowledge involves attention to the pedagogical goals, the content to be learned, and the affordances and constraints of the possible technology to be used—and weaving these components together in making design decisions in an authentic teaching and learning situation.

Prior to my experience in the design course, I had thought deeply about the pedagogical goals and content of the Proseminar, as well as about who the students are. The work within the design team, however, pushed me to articulate my goals more clearly. Furthermore, exploration into technological possibilities opened more content windows for the course. For example, the search to find Web sites to link to the course Web site surfaced information, bibliographies, and professional resources that I had not fully known existed. At the same time, however, I realized that the existence of technological options does not necessarily mean that all possible options should be adopted for a course. Staying true to pedagogical goals sometimes requires resisting the lure of exciting technological possibilities. The particular goals of the Proseminar—as well as the limited technological experience of some of the class members at the time— led me to select technological options that were not too advanced. An effective design process requires the teacher to be vigilant in assessing the likely impacts of choosing particular technological options. As explained by the volume editors in chapter 1, effective teaching and good design require seeing the relationships between pedagogical goals, content, and technological possibilities and developing strategies appropriate to the specific learning situation.

My second observation pertains to the usefulness of a community of designers approach that recognizes, as the editors emphasize, the importance of community, design, products and solutions, and authentic problems. Using "community" as a strategy for promoting faculty growth and learning (including the use of peer feedback and support) has long been recognized as contributing to successful faculty development (see, for example, Austin, 1992, 1998; Cox, 2001; Sanders, Carlson-Dakes, Dettinger, Hajnal, Laedtke, & Squire, 1999; Webb & McEnerny, 1997). My experience with my design team and the larger group of all faculty members, students, and instructors involved in the Professional Development Course illustrates how communities of learners can help faculty members develop technological innovations in their teaching. Even modest projects like mine benefit from having a design team. The ideas, the "moral support," and the creativity stimulated through team conversations were all important for the success of the project. Also, I believe that building faculty development strategies on faculty members' expressed needs tends to lead to success. The design strategy used in the Professional Development Course relies on such a "bottom up" approach successfully.

Establishing communities of support is especially important for finding effective uses for technology in teaching and learning, since so many faculty members, like me, are unsure of themselves in terms of technology. Organizing environments where faculty members and students can come together to learn and share, each drawing on their particular pedagogical or technical expertise, is a good investment if technology, content, and pedagogical goals are to be joined for purposes of improving student learning. As made evident in the examples throughout this book, the successful integration of technology into teaching and learning is, at its core, a sociological process that concerns not only technical details, but also the interactions of individuals within groups engaged in solving challenging problems concerning the relationships among pedagogy, content, and technology.

REFERENCES

Austin, A. E. (Fall, 1992). Supporting the professor as teacher: The Lilly teaching fellows program. *The Review of Higher Education, 16*(1), 85-106.

Austin, A. E. (1998). Collegial conversation as metaphor and strategy for staff development. *South African Journal of Higher Education, 12*(3), 12-18.

Cox, M. D. (2001). Faculty learning communities: Change agents for transforming institutions into learning communities. In D. Lieberman & C. Wehlburg (Eds.), *To improve the academy* (Vol. 19, pp. 69-93). Bolton, MA: Anker and the Professional and Organizational Development Network in Higher Education.

Sanders, K., Carlson-Dakes, C., Dettinger, K., Hajnal, C., Laedtke, M., &, Squire, L. (1999). A new starting point for faculty development in higher education: Creating a collaborative learning environment. In D. DeZure (Ed.), *To improve the academy* (Vol. 16, pp. 117-150). Stillwater, OK: New Forums Press and the Professional and Organizational Development Network in Higher Education.

Sorcinelli, M. D., & Austin, A. E. (Eds.). (1992). *Developing new and junior faculty.* New Directions for Teaching and Learning, 50. San Francisco: Jossey-Bass.

Webb, J., & McEnerny, K. (1997). Implementing peer review programs: A twelve step model. In D. DeZure (Ed.), *To improve the academy* (Vol. 16, pp. 295-316). Stillwater, OK: New Forums Press and the Professional and Organizational Development Network in Higher Education.

CHAPTER 10

INTEGRATING TECHNOLOGY THROUGH COMMUNITY-BASED DESIGN

Martin Oliver

*The real voyage of discovery consists not in
seeking new landscapes but in having new eyes.*

—*Marcel Proust*

STUDIES OF INSTITUTIONAL CURRICULUM CHANGE

Although universities have traditionally seen themselves as autonomous entities, shaped by principles and protected by academic freedom rather than bound to serve the state, the developments of the last few decades have challenged this position. The rise of managerialism and public accountability, the perception of higher education as a market and students as consumers, together with tighter contracts between institutions and the state (either through funding or legislation) have all served to challenge academics' belief that they should be able to teach what they

Faculty Development by Design: Integrating Technology in Higher Education, 185–206
Copyright © 2007 by Information Age Publishing

want and how they want (Barnett, 1994; Henkel, 2000). Increasingly, pedagogy has become a matter of policy and politics, rather than professionalism (Holley & Oliver, 2000).

Change and Resistance in Institutional Development Projects

Although there is a paucity of research investigating these issues in curriculum design practice in Higher Education (Oliver, 2003), it would be a gross oversimplification to suggest that all institutional curriculum change serves such agendas. It is possible to respond to such pressures in a way that reflects individual values and principles rather than requiring conformity to imposed agendas. Walker (2001), for example, describes a project that involved six lecturers across a U.K. institution in a joint endeavour to transform their practice. This project was undertaken to resist the dominant discourses of markets, quality, and effective performance management in order to develop "critical professionalism": practice that demands participants "'talk back' to the marketization of higher education, to assert critical agency for ourselves and our students, and to reclaim the wisdom of our own professional judgements in the face of the 'moral ascendancy' of managerialism" (p. 6).

In part, her project was initiated as a response to "a crisis of professional identity among academics [that has arisen] because there is no serious public debate regarding the values and purposes of higher education" (Walker, 2001, p. 9). It involved a series of action research projects, each addressing locally relevant problems in a way that reflected the values and beliefs of those involved. It involved Walker acting as a "critical companion" to the five other lecturers, a relationship characterized by mutuality, reciprocity, particularity, and grateful care (p. 194). It also led to the development of new forms of working together, focused upon joint endeavors, shared understanding, and the opportunity to develop and elaborate practical theories of learning and teaching; this form of working was described as a learning community.

Importantly, although Walker talks about a learning community and describes this project as a collaborative endeavor, her book focuses on individual accounts, not the communal nature of the work. The sense of wider context—except, perhaps, as something to be resisted—is largely absent from Walker's text. This view of conformance and resistance will be contrasted with other accounts—including those from this book—in the remainder of this chapter.

Academics' Routine Curriculum Design Practices

This absence of context is somewhat strange, since context and community have elsewhere been identified as pivotal to the process of curriculum design (Oliver, 2003). A case study of U.K. academics' curriculum design practice revealed the importance of community, both as a way of gaining ideas and of shaping individuals' identities. This was achieved by identifying oneself with or in opposition to particular disciplinary groups by adopting conventional features (such as key texts), rejecting or reinterpreting established topics (so as to mark the course out as distinctive) and showing a sensitivity to "stepping on toes" by avoiding topics that were identified with someone else.

Inevitably, such processes are highly political, as curriculum researchers such as Millen (1997) have long recognized. At the personal level, relationships with peers within the department and the wider discipline were affected, for example by inheriting a course but having to live alongside its previous owner (and their opinions about how things should be done). At a departmental level, expressions of personal belief (for example, about new forms of teaching) were shaped by or brought into conflict with dominant patterns enforced by the committees that reviewed and approved courses. At a disciplinary level, splits and schisms within the field were reflected in the choice of topics to be included or excluded from the syllabus. The power of government and of professional bodies was felt also through regulatory mechanisms such as external validation or quality assurance.

While political themes are present in Walker's account, what is absent is the way in which engagement in these various communities reshapes the identity both of the lecturer and the community itself. What was clear from this second study was the two-way nature of this process: the communities involved created pressures that individual lecturers could either submit to or resist, but individuals' acts of submission or resistance also served to reinforce or undermine, and hence shape, the identity of the community.

Another contrast between this and Walker's account concerns the process of design. Although Walker's projects all focus upon course redesign, the tone emphasizes creativity, new agendas, and novelty. Within the other case study, "design" as such was considered to be quite rare; instead, there was a constant process of *redesign*, reworking existing practices and materials in response to experiences or student feedback. This situation was complicated by the various ways that participants understood the word "curriculum"—even single individuals used it in multiple ways. It was used to describe a nested set of conceptions, starting from the content (syllabus) and moving to its interrelationship (course structure), the approach to teaching (pedagogy), and the context in which the course was located (the hidden curriculum). In addition, however, participants contrasted this increasingly holistic design with "spaces" in the curriculum, moments for spontaneity and performance that arose from the relationship between tutors and students.

Although this process of redesign was ongoing and was presented as inevitable, it was made visible only by exceptional circumstances such as quality audit or course review, at which point ongoing adaptation—what might be described as the "life" of the course—was formally documented as a change.

These concepts (curriculum as plan and performance, design and redesign, community, identity and learning, project as autobiography) will form part of the structure for the analysis of accounts that follow. Arguably, however, they can only provide a partial analysis—studies of routine curriculum practice cannot capture the distinctive nature of the work presented in this book. For this reason, in the final part of this background section, one final study will be introduced that has explored the interactions between teachers and support staff when designing courses involving new technologies.

Learning Technologists as Agents of Change and Development

While conventional curriculum design practice is rarely researched, there is widespread interest in novel approaches—typically ones that concern the introduction of new technology. Case studies abound, although most focus upon the impact of such new approaches on learning; relatively few document the processes through which technology is introduced or the impact this has on the roles of those involved.

What has recently begun to be documented, however, is the role of support staff within this process of adoption. Within the United States, the tradition of instructional design is well established, drawing on clearly specified principles and processes (e.g., Merrill, 2001). However, a tradition has arisen that has eschewed this formal, industrialized division of labour in favor of a more exploratory, case-based approach. While instructional design focuses on the development of materials, this alternative approach focuses on developing the academics, with materials development being a means to this end. This approach has been documented in the United States, but is well established within the United Kingsom and also arises internationally (Oliver, Sharpe, Duggleby, Jennings, & Kay, 2004), often being associated with roles described as "learning technologists."

Preliminary work has described how learning technologists take up their role (Oliver, 2002). Perhaps most relevant is the community-based way in which they work, acting as brokers, permitting ideas to cross boundaries between communities (Wenger, 1998). This is partly achieved through dissemination, but more significantly by crossing boundaries themselves.

The outputs of such interventions are jointly developed materials; however, it is the *process* that is of primary concern. This involves acting as a broker by undertaking a series of marginal trajectories of "legitimate peripheral participation" (Lave & Wenger, 1991) with different communities. Importantly, this is a two-way process; the learning technologist must learn from the academic (about what learning and teaching practice means to them) just as the academic must learn from the learning technologists (about what they believe it means to use technology well in an educational context).

Learning technologists describe their work as consisting of the following steps:

1. Identifying opportunities for collaboration with discipline-based academics, managers or technical support staff. These often arise as a result of central initiatives, such as a drive for Web-based learning, or external pressures such as quality audit.

2. Providing a meaningful input to the collaboration. (This may initially be in the form of technical advice and support.) This collaboration is then used as an opportunity to learn more about the academic's concerns, values, and working context.

3. Selecting, adapting, and presenting relevant "case lore," expertise, or research material as a way of supporting, challenging, fostering reflection for, or initiating critical discussion with the collaborating academic.

This process of collaboration is described as a form of pedagogy; however, what has not been demonstrated to date is what impact this approach has on the academics involved. Arguably, evidence of this is exactly what the chapters within this book have provided. For this reason, the educational impact of such collaborations and the role played by such individuals will also be used in the analysis of the accounts.

Summary

These three descriptions of learning technologists' work discuss the process of curriculum design from social, cultural, and professional perspectives. In the next section, the issues identified within these sources will be used as an analytical framework to analyze the accounts within this book. This framework will be used to explore the tensions between these different institutionally-based processes and to see how the themes of conformance, design, the role of the community, identity, conceptions of technology, and specialist support played out within this project.

ANALYSIS

Curriculum as Plan and Performance

Given the nature of these projects, it is unsurprising that discussion of curriculum plans were prevalent in the accounts. Various chapters describe what was intended for their programmes, with some authors going further to discuss the hidden curriculum, in the form of political influences on what is taught and how such teaching takes place:

> To help teachers and students think more deeply *with* and *about* maps, we needed to make maps and map-making problematic, for as long as the two are taken as neutral, we believed, they will remain unquestioned, beyond discussion.... These questions ... help make maps and map-making problematic by connecting them to the political, cultural, social, and economic spheres that gave rise to them as well as to those they help produce. (Segall & Landauer-Menchik, chapter 6)

> We saw how filming their peers raised for the adolescents we worked with, questions of power and ethics inherent in producing texts. Students had to consider what it meant for them to position their peers as particular types of subjects, and what it meant for their relationships with their peers. (Anagnostopoulos, Brass, & Subedi, chapter 5)

There is also evidence of planning for "spaces" within the curriculum, reflecting the contrast between spontaneous performance and instructional plans found within the U.K. case study.

> Since variation and choice were designed into our course structure, we could not predict exactly which technologies our students would choose to interact with, or the meaning they would derive from their interactions. (Rosaen & Hobson, chapter 2)

However, what was largely absent from these accounts was a consideration of the "mid-level" design decisions found in the U.K. study, which concerned the interrelationship between modules within a program of study. There is some discussion of this in Little's chapter (7), in terms of

the adoption of PowerPoint across the two-semester social studies pedagogy sequence in the College of Education, but for the most part these
accounts focus on development within, not across, modules. This might
explain the absence of strategic issues, such as consistency across modules, but does raise questions about the way in which projects such as
those funded under The Preparing Tomorrow's Teachers for Technology
(PT3) are integrated into wider institutional practice.

Design and Redesign

The U.K. case study suggested that design was rare, with redesign
being the norm. Even when modules were newly created, previously
taught offerings, other parts of the programme and previous experiences
were all drawn together in a patchwork rather than some formal, abstract
process of design taking place tabula rasa.

Such processes of ongoing design are readily apparent here, illustrat-
ing problems and ongoing debates that cannot easily be solved, only
responded to:

> We are continuing to clarify and refine our guiding conceptual frameworks
> used to organize our course. For example, how might we place technology
> more explicitly within our subject matter framework? Should we treat tech-
> nology as yet a third subject matter that has its own content, process and
> attitude goals? Or does technology become one of the "processes" within
> mathematics and English/language arts? Alternatively, should we expand
> the three types of learning goals in our subject matter framework (content,
> processes and attitude) to include technology as a fourth learning goal?
> (Rosaen & Hobson, chapter 2)

Such redesign typically arose from a consideration of students' experiences:

> Early on we recognized that an obvious corrective to our students' limited
> understandings of children's abilities to respond to literature would be for
> these students to observe literature response activities with real children in
> real classrooms.... However, as novices in classroom practice, our students'
> attention was most often taken up by a range of new experiences (frequently
> involving "managing" children's behavior), as well as by concerns for carry-
> ing out the details of their assignment. Working within that reality, we grad-
> ually came to the conclusion that videotape of thoughtful teachers engaging
> in literature activities in real classrooms would be the best way of providing a
> model for our students and of supporting our efforts to broaden and
> deepen their understandings of literature response. (Apol & Rop, chapter 3)

> To my surprise, some students resisted the idea of posting their writing, worrying about issues of privacy. In the end, I used the site for communication to students, posting class session notes, and posting course information. Students also made extensive use of the links to other organizations and bibliographic resources. The writing template was offered to the students but was not used extensively. I did not require students to post finished writing products in deference to the concerns and discomfort of some students about this idea. (Austin, chapter 9)

This is important, in that it clarifies a gap from the previous work. The previous studies discussed redesign as the consequence of feedback, with design as a separate process based on consideration of abstract "types" This example shows how these processes are intertwined: for the most part, the "types" are based on experience with real individuals; the distinction between design and ongoing course revision is false, since each new "design" is an iterative response to previous experience. Design and redesign are thus intertwined.

The suggestion that such courses arise from one-off formal design processes is clearly an oversimplification; as these accounts show, the process is iterative, responsive, and frequently riddled with unresolvable problems.

Conformance and Resistance

A central theme in the U.K. studies concerned how particular courses conformed to or challenged dominant disciplinary approaches. This was identified as important not only when positioning the course (establishing its "niche market") but also in performing individual identities. For example, Segall and Landauer-Menchik took up a position that challenges the dominant, "naturalised" understanding of maps, creating a radical identity for their course and thus (by association) themselves:

> To anticipate, we hoped that the content used in our project—a series of maps charts and graphs and, more importantly, the questions asked of them and the activities surrounding that questioning—would provide an alternative to existing ways of engaging those texts and allow for critical conversations around that engagement that would encourage students to explore them as stories about the world that need to be critically examined. (chapter 6)

The situation in these accounts, however, is presented in a more complex manner than was seen in the previous studies. Rather than a simple dichotomy between the local and the disciplinary, within these accounts multiple communities are credited with opinions about what curricula "should" achieve. For example, Anagnostopoulos et al. (chapter 5) describe how the course team had to weigh up the beliefs of the instructors of the Professional Development Seminar as well.

> While Punya's emphasis on subversion resonated with the understandings of literacy that Dorothea and Jory held, in many ways Punya's definition of literacy also stood in opposition to that held by Dorothea and Jory.... The most important division among members of the university-based design team thus had little to do with our different levels of technological expertise and knowledge, and more to do with our competing visions of literacy.

Elsewhere, they describe how even within the team, different positions were taken.

> As we planned the curriculum, taught the workshop sessions, and reflected on student work and on our own participation in the project, we asserted and negotiated these different notions (of literacy). Significantly, while we incorporated the various conceptions of literacy into the TALP curriculum, we never actually resolved our differences into a shared model. We contend, however, that our different conceptions of literacy served as boundary objects. Throughout our interactions we refined our own understandings and became more aware of their potential and their limitations.

Importantly, this illustrates that the process of conformance and resistance is more complex than was previously understood. Instead of being just a local-global binary, as suggested by Walker's (2001) study and that of routine curriculum design practice, this example reveals it to be a process of debate and negotiation within and between communities.

Community, Identity, and Learning

It will come as little surprise in a book about communities of designers that much of the text illustrates Wenger's (1998) ideas of learning and creating identities through engagement with particular communities. The value of this as an approach to development is well illustrated within Austin's account (chapter 9):

> Even modest projects like mine benefit from having a design team. The ideas, the "moral support," and the creativity stimulated through team conversations were all important for the success of the project.

However, rather than just use this analysis to endorse the approach, it is possible to explore in greater detail how and why it was useful.

Importantly, one aspect of the learning process is that individuals' understandings are revised as new forms of practice are undertaken. This led Apol and Rop (chapter 3), for example, through an ongoing process of seeking new communities with which to engage. Each time one part of the complex process of developing a technology-rich curriculum was mastered, it became apparent that yet wider understanding of this process was required, meaning that a new community had to be involved.

> Finding or creating a team that could supply all our needs would have been impossible. We had to learn as we went what kinds of partners we needed, and it became frustratingly clear early on that no one or two individuals—no matter how well intentioned or knowledgeable—could possibly "know it all." As we went along, we discovered that we needed many more "team members," a fuller cast of characters than the formal structure of the grant provided. The knowledge we needed to tap into was distributed across a wide circle of people who had a wide range of experiences with technology and who possessed multiple ways of thinking about solutions. In the story of our project, we have come to believe that that is the best—perhaps the only—way that technology learning and development can occur.

Similarly, Anagnostopoulos et al. (chapter 5) describe how individuals with different expertise had to work together, negotiating the differences between the communities each was identified with:

> It is easy to divide us into technology and literacy experts, though, as we will describe below, this distinction was blurred throughout the project in a quite generative way. Punya and Dipendra brought a deep knowledge of digital technologies and an equally deep interest in understanding how people engage in and learn through the processes of digital design. Though Dorothea and Jory shared an interest in understanding how people learn through technology, they had little experience using digital technologies. Rather, they possessed experience and knowledge of literacy instruction and adolescent literacy practices. (chapter 5)

Austin, too, identifies the plurality of communities within which this work engaged her:

> The process of developing this project for the Proseminar occurred within a set of communities: the Michigan State University College of Education, the Higher, Adult, and Lifelong Education Program, the Professional Development Course offered in Spring, 2000, the specific design team organized within the context of the Professional Development Course, and ultimately, the Proseminar itself.

Indeed, much of Austin's account focuses on this process of engagement within communities. It illustrates how the term "community" should not be interpreted as denoting some utopian ideal, but instead as a group that shares common practices and a sense of mutual accountability, even in the face of disagreement and difference:

> One of the distinctive aspects of my experience in the course pertained to the dynamics of my design team.... Early in the process, some tensions within the group became apparent. One student wanted to use the group as an opportunity to pursue a particular technological idea that she had in mind.... I needed to emphasize constantly that the pedagogical goals I had set should not be overshadowed by a technical solution.... I appreciated her efforts while also emphasizing the particular goals I was trying to achieve in the Proseminar.

This relationship between individuals and communities is not only relevant to the participants in these projects; it is also true for the students they taught. For example, Austin's account describes PhD study as taking on a new identity through participation in a community:

> In my experience, new Ph.D. students often anticipate doctoral study as a process of fulfilling a set of requirements, rather than as an experience of entering a community that involves mutual responsibilities to and benefits from interacting over time with others interested in similar problems of scholarship and practice.

Central to this is Austin's repositioning of writing as a form of practice:

> My intention is to help new doctoral students see their writing as a process rather than only a product, as a means to gain understanding and engage in creative thought processes as well as evidence of the final outcome of sustained work over time. I want students to move from the notion of writing a paper as a task done once and considered complete to the notion of scholarly writing as involving sustained thinking, effort, collegial critique, and revising that occurs over a period of time.

The process of learning, as well as identity formation, can also be seen in the discussion of students' activities. Burns and Koziol (chapter 4) argue, for example, that:

> Because teaching must be particularized for unique contexts (Ball & Cohen, 1999), preservice candidates should have as much experience as possible [with these environments through work] in simulated laboratory contexts (Berliner, 1985; Howey, 1996; Rentel, 1992), as well as real classrooms. Digital video recording should make all of this much easier.

This experience can be interpreted as legitimate peripheral participation—a concept integral to Wenger's explanation of learning. This example involves interpreting teaching episodes in a way that is considered meaningful by peers. It is not full participation in practice, but it does permit the development of a shared repertoire through exposure to new approaches and the requirement to imagine what they meant to those involved. Burns and Koziol contrast this with the traditional approach of 'transmitting' codified knowledge that is to be applied in practice, since such decontextualized reifications are fundamentally meaningless: "a program based on codified knowledge for teaching can never fully prescribe or convey the qualities of wise practice."

Equally important is the experience of "multi-membership"—the ubiquitous situation of belonging to multiple communities and needing to reconcile the competing demands each places upon you. This experience is exploited pedagogically by Austin (chapter 9), who uses a "focus on literature and theory ... to inform participants' professional practice as well as their ability to work within and contribute to the processes of scholarly inquiry in the field of postsecondary education." Dirkx (chapter 8) also makes use of this experience, although his emphasis is upon how other communities influence participation in the course, rather than the other way around:

> PBL relies on extensive collaborative group work, from defining the problem to conducting the inquiry, to completing the final group product. Design of the instructional environment needs to provide opportunities for participants to continuously negotiate the meaning of assigned problems or cases and how they relate or do not relate to their various life contexts. This process of negotiation involves identifying, naming, and giving voice to the differences that mediate this sense-making process, and learning to work across these differences in a collaborative manner to address the problem or case at hand.

Such processes are not always easy, however, leading to tensions and delays as different meanings and practices are negotiated.

> While we were actually in the work it felt at times that the broader community might actually be holding us up. In retrospect, however, I now recognize the tension that developed between our small group and the larger community as healthy.... While we could have as a larger community addressed some of these tensions in a more explicit manner, each community finds its own way within its own context. We learn from these experiences and we move on. (Dirkx, chapter 8)

Wenger (1998) describes how our participation in communities shapes our identity: we come to be identified as part of one group and not part of others. The processes described in this book illustrate how this was achieved, even through modest actions:

Students also provided support for their collaborating teachers, thus shifting roles regarding who was considered to be an expert or novice. (Rosaen & Hobson, chapter 2)

Aganostopolous et al. (chapter 5) also explore this process, looking at how these dualisms were experienced and also transcended, both in terms of the split between producers and consumers of digital texts and between "teachers" and "learners" within the context of the media workshop.

Perhaps the relevance of this particular analytical framework should be unsurprising, given that this work was envisaged as the efforts of a community of designers. Nonetheless, it is striking how vividly these accounts illustrate Wenger's (1998) theories on identity formation.

Project as Autobiography

Millen's (1997) account of curriculum design describes how artefacts such as course reading lists contribute to the development of an 'autobiography' of the tutor, showing their interests and allegiances and how these develop over time. Similar processes were visible here, most explicitly in Austin's account (chapter 9), which takes the form of a developmental narrative.

For example, Austin describes how her values came to be inscribed upon her course and practice through her engagement with this project:

> I noted that I take my teaching very seriously, and, that for several years, I had had a growing realization that my low level of knowledge and skill with technology meant that I was not able to take advantage of some of the available resources that would benefit my students and their learning. I noted that I often teach courses on teaching and learning issues in higher education, and believe these courses should model innovative uses of technology to enhance learning. I hoped that participating in the design course would help me gain the knowledge and skills needed to fulfill these expectations.

In effect, this project provided an opportunity to rewrite an element of her autobiography that she was dissatisfied with. This two-way process continues throughout her account. On the one hand she "writes" her autobiography through the design of the course and its materials that come to represent some aspect of her identity:

It became increasingly clear that I wanted the most simple, least cluttered Web site possible. Perhaps because of my own uncertainties about using technology, I did not want a technology solution that would frustrate my students who were unfamiliar with technological strategies.

At the same time, her identity develops as a result of the experiences she has gained and the choices she has made:

By working with the team on the course Web site design, I had lost much of my anxiety about using technology in teaching. I had become more familiar with various terms and processes associated with technology use and comfortable with exploring and experimenting with new options. I had also gained some sense of the ways in which technology could support my pedagogical goals.... I also felt more confident in my ability to make decisions about technical options as they relate to my pedagogical goals. While I have not yet taught a fully online course, I believe that my experience in the Professional Development Course has made me more comfortable with this possibility.

This vignette illustrates neatly how value-laden and personal such design processes are, and how we come to be represented through the courses we develop.

Changing Conceptions of Technology

One important theme within these accounts is how individuals' understanding of technology changed through their engagement in the projects. Little's (chapter 7) initial comments are familiar to many who support staff in the use of technology:

One did not require much technology to teach either in 1000 AD or in 1963 AD. True, we had some cranky 16mm movie projectors, but films were in short supply and educational films were ... well, we all remember most of them for what they were. In the scant 37 years since we began to teach, a technological revolution in education has occurred before our wondering eyes. First, overhead projectors appeared in our classrooms. Then came the VCRs. Computers arrived in the 80s. Computer projectors came hard on their heels. And now the Internet. What's more, the rate of change keeps accelerating.

This account is helpful, in that it reminds readers that this is not the first wave of technology to influence teaching. It is simply the most recent in an ongoing process. However, the key word in Little's account is "we": a different list would be provided for those who had previously been exposed to the new technology of audio recording, broadcast television and so on; another list again would be given by those appointed after the Internet became commonplace.

Importantly, it is clear from these accounts that a focus upon hardware (and even upon software) is unhelpful and misleading.

> The look of those new cameras, computers, and software programs may cause lust at first sight, but achieving any long-term benefit from their use requires that teachers and teacher educators work hard to make it a part of the whole process rather than the entire process all by itself. (Burns & Koziol, chapter 4)

Although the "boxes" (including software) might be the most visible sign of change, the impact of technology is far subtler. Rosaen and Hobson (chapter 2) cite Burbules and Callister's assertion (2000, p. 7) that "what is most 'new' may not be the technology, the thing itself, but a whole host of other changes that accompany it." In their case, the most obvious change (the presence of the laptop) hid a host of other complex but subtle alterations, for example in coursework management and patterns of communication. This realization is important, both professionally as well as by virtue of being a research finding: it illustrates a more nuanced appreciation of what counts as "technology" (a tool's relationship to practice, rather than the tool per se) that is fundamental to understanding the pedagogic impact of the arrival of this new resource.

The Role of the Design Team

While previous research documented the practices of groups like learning technologists, the experience of the academics they work with has remained largely unexplored. These accounts provide several useful insights into this.

The clearest descriptions of this involvement form part of Austin's account (chapter 9); here, she illustrates how this approach achieves its relevance and credibility:

> The design team approach builds on an established tradition in faculty development—the use of peer feedback and support. Such peer work has long been part of successful faculty development strategies.... Colleagues note that building faculty development strategies on faculty members' expressed needs tends to lead to success. The design strategy used in the

Professional Development Course relies on such a "bottom up" approach
(building on faculty members' needs) very successfully.

Specifically, she explores her experience of the pedagogy of collaboration involved in such support work.

> They acted simultaneously as colleagues who shared similar pedagogical
> problems and as experts who had good ideas for possible solutions. They
> knew when to ask questions to draw out the thinking of the course partici-
> pants, and when to step in to offer an idea or a word of support to counter
> moments of rising frustration. They were colleagues and teachers at the
> same time.

Importantly, however, while previous accounts have portrayed learning
technologists as a discrete role, the individuals described in these
accounts varied in the degree to which they took up this role. Punya
Mishra, for example, clearly has this role within the project described by
Aganostopolous et al. (chapter 5). In Segall and Landauer-Menchik's
account, Gayathri Santhana was a programmer pure and simple.

The previous portrayals of learning technologists as a clear-cut group
may reflect the way in which new groups establish their identity by distin-
guishing themselves from others—since they are currently seeking recognition in their own right, they may well feel an unease about being
identified alongside technical support staff (Oliver et al., 2004). These
accounts reveal that no such clear division is perceived by the staff that
work in such teams.

What is interesting, however, is to reflect upon the way in which the
teachers within these accounts describe their relationship with technology.
Where there was a clear-cut division of labour, there appeared to be little
conceptual change in relation to technology (although other kinds of
learning are apparent). Where the boundaries are less clear-cut, this blurring supports the kinds of boundary crossing described above, allowing
new perspectives to be gained on practice. This may prove to be less efficient (in terms of short-term resources), but with its educative potential it
may well be more effective (in terms of the development of capacity in the
longer term).

In spite of presenting a more complex picture, these accounts do illustrate the way in which the work of "learning technologist"-like individuals
involves support staff acting as boundary crossers, developing credible
identities within multiple communities of practice. They have to be credible both as teachers and as support staff; once they have achieved this
themselves, they can then support teachers in the process of becoming
credible pedagogic designers too.

DISCUSSION

The accounts within this book provide valuable insight into the processes of curriculum design, drawing out the educational and political aspects of working within a community of designers. However, any interpretation should proceed with caution. The preceding chapters are, after all, *accounts*; in Wenger's terms (1998) they are reifications of practice, not the practice itself. Apol and Rop (chapter 3), for example, are strikingly honest about the status of their chapter as "the story of our work":

> This, then, was the story of our project. We have imposed order and tidied much of its chaos in order to create meaning, in order to draw out a narrative line that would move the telling forward in comprehensible ways. We have created a tale with an identifiable problem, a setting, characters, a plot with a resolution, and a theme, drawing on what we know from the world of literature to help make sense of what we are learning in the world of technology and education.

These accounts thus provide only a partial and provisional insight into the experience of working within such communities. This is a particular problem for those seeking to learn vicariously from them.

Nonetheless, in spite of these epistemological concerns, this work remains valuable for two reasons. First, for the most part, reifications of such practice in other institutions will be all we can gain access to. There may be no real substitute for experience, but pragmatically such reifications are better than nothing, particularly when they can be interpreted in the light of comparable experiences of our own. Second, while these accounts may not provide the "truth" of the practice of working in a community of designers, they can be interpreted as a form of practice in their own right: the practice of contributing (through writing) to the scholarly discussions of a community who cares about design and teaching practice. They, thus, provide an example of how we, too, can take up this form of practice, contributing to discussions of design, curriculum and pedagogy, and developing a shared appreciation of the experience of academic development.

CONCLUSIONS

The purpose of this chapter was to provide a wider perspective on the accounts within this book. Doing so has shown that, in spite of their status as reifications of practice, they are valuable in three ways.

First, they have intrinsic value as cases, each providing a resource from which other practitioners working in a related context can learn. Whilst they provide a story, rather than a direct experience of practice, those with comparable experiences will be able to use this narrative to illuminate and inform their own work.

Second, they have extended what we know about several important aspects of the process of curriculum design:

- They have confirmed that such work involves viewing the curriculum both as a plan and as a performance, designing both interventions and spaces for improvisation.

- Previous research suggested that academics design curricula by thinking of "types" of students, in the abstract; these accounts suggest that such "types" normally reflect experience with real individuals, not just prejudices.

- They have emphasized the iterative, cyclic process of curriculum design—that it is typically a process of redesign, working from an existing ground of practices and resources, rather than being a rational process proceeding from a blank slate.

- They have illustrated how curriculum design requires academics to take a principled position on the topics they teach, choosing either to conform to or resist the dominant conceptions within the discipline. Through this process, academic identities are forged.

- They have demonstrated the importance of understanding the relationship between technology and specific forms of practice rather than focusing on technology per se.

- Perhaps most importantly, given the theme of this book, the communal nature of learning to design has been explored. Rather than simply endorsing a community-oriented approach, the accounts demonstrated the value of this process, highlighting the possibilities it provides for divisions of labour and learning through engagement in new forms of practice. They have also explored the nature of this process, highlighting the experience of conflict and tension within communities and the need for individuals to reconcile the demands of multiple communities. These processes also contribute to the shaping of academic identities, through the adoption of new forms of practice (such as academic writing) and the positioning of individuals within or against particular groups. Traces of involvement in the design communities (materials, these accounts, etc.) can thus be reinterpreted as academic autobiographies.

- Finally, they have developed our understanding of the way in which academics experience working with such design teams. Although learning technologists may seek to distinguish themselves from other kinds of support staff the situation is actually more complex, with individuals taking up their own position that may be purely technical or involve pedagogic support as well. It seems, however, that the mixed forms of support, where boundaries between the roles of teacher and support staff are blurred, encourage those involved to develop their identities in new directions by engaging with the practices of others.

Third, they act as an agenda for action. By providing a form and a precedent, these accounts invite an ongoing dialogue about the forms of support that can best support the integration of technology through communities of design. What remains to be seen is whether this good start can be built upon to create an ongoing scholarly body of work on this topic.

REFERENCES

Ball, D., & Cohen, D. (1999). Developing practice, developing practitioners: Toward a practice-based theory of professional education. In L. Darling-Hammond & G. Sykes (Eds.), *Teaching as the learning profession: Handbook ofpolicy and practice* (pp. 3-32). San Francisco: Jossey-Bass

Barnett, R. (1994). *The limits of competence*. Buckingham, England: Open University Press.

Burbules, N. C., & Callister, T. A. (2000). *Watch IT: The risks and promises of information technologies for education*. Boulder, CO: Westview Press.

Berliner, D. (1985). Laboratory settings and the study of teacher education. *Journal of Teacher Education, 36*(6), 2-8.

Henkel, M. (2000). *Academic identities and policy change in higher education*. London: Jessica Kingsley.

Holley, D., & Oliver, M. (2000). Pedagogy and new power relationships. *International Journal of Management Education, 1*(1), 11-21.

Lave, J., & Wenger, E. (1991). *Situated learning: Legitimate peripheral participation*. Cambridge, MA: Cambridge University Press.

Howey, K. (1996). Designing coherent and effective teacher education programs. In J. Sikula, T. J. Buttery, & E. Guyton (Eds.), *Handbook of research on teacher education* (pp. 143-170). New York: MacMillan.

Merrill, M. (2001). Components of instruction toward a theoretical tool for instructional design. *Instructional Science, 29*(4), 291-310.

Millen, J. (1997). Par for the course: Designing course outlines and feminist freedoms. *Curriculum Studies, 5*(1), 9-27.

Oliver, M. (2002). What do learning technologists do? *Innovations in Education and Training International, 39*(4), 1-8.

Oliver, M. (2003, April). *Curriculum design as acquired social practice: A case study.* Paper presented at the 84th annual meeting of the American Educational Research Association, Chicago.

Oliver, M., Sharpe, R., Duggleby, J., Jennings, D., & Kay, D. (2004). Accrediting learning technologists: a review of the literature, schemes and programmes. *Association for Learning Technology Project Report.* Retrieved July 21, 2006, from http://www.ucl.ac.uk/epd/alt-accreditation/Initial_review.doc.

Rentel, V. M. (1992, May). *Preparing clinical faculty: Research on teacher reasoning.* Paper presented at the conference on faculty development, Washington, DC.

Walker, M. (2001). *Reconstructing professionalism in university teaching.* London: SRHE/Open University Press.

Wenger, E. (1998). *Communities of practice.* Cambridge, MA: Cambridge University Press.

CHAPTER 11

COMMUNITIES OF DESIGNERS

Transforming a Situation Into a Unified Whole

Bertram C. Bruce

Simple things should be simple and complex things should be possible.
—Alan Kay

A new player, digital technology, has entered into the already variegated and often contentious world of teaching and teacher education. This new player promises to disrupt existing practices in some as yet undefined way. It is not surprising that its eventual impact on learning or on educational equity is uncertain, when there is still great uncertainty around basic questions such as which digital tools ought to be considered or what they cost.

The previous chapters in this book make a major contribution to the conversation about digital technology in education. They address three large questions: How should we integrate technology into learning? What happens when we do? How do we learn to do it possibly better than before?

Faculty Development by Design: Integrating Technology in Higher Education, 205–220
Copyright © 2007 by Information Age Publishing
All rights of reproduction in any form reserved.

As Mishra, Koehler, and Zhao (chapter 1) say, the book "documents the stories, in their own voices, of a group of faculty members and graduate students ... as they struggled to learn about, and implement, technology in their own teaching." One might expect that having the participants tell their own stories entails a certain amount of self-promotion, and every story relates accomplishments. Yet these tales also include details of the context, the participants' perspectives and the difficulties encountered in a rich way one rarely sees in books about technology use.

As a sort of distant relative who dropped in from time to time, I had the privilege of seeing these experiences more closely than most people other than the direct participants. At the same time, I had a distance that afforded a perspective distinct from that of those doing all the hard work. In the present chapter, I share my capsule interpretation of what occurred in this large, multiyear project, with the aim of addressing questions such as the three posed above.

I draw on Dewey's theory of situation (Dewey, 1896/1972, 1938/1991, 1939/1991) as a lens for examining these multifaceted *communities of designers* project. Dewey's theory is consistent with the underlying philosophy for the project, and as such provides a means for identifying its most significant contributions, as well as its limitations. It also helps us to see possible future directions.

DEWEY'S DEFINITION OF SITUATION

The work of John Dewey and other pragmatists, such as Jane Addams, Charles Sanders Peirce, and William James, undergoes periodic rejections and resurgences. Dewey in particular, appears to be in resurgence now, drawing attention from diverse quarters of social and political theory, education, feminism, aesthetics, logic, and ethics. In education, his works are once again widely and unapologetically cited, especially in reference to inquiry-based learning.

In general, these citations are justified and appropriate, but their wide acceptance actually precludes a close examination of some of the more interesting implications of Dewey's theories. Some writers (Burke, 1994; Dwight & Garrison, 2003; Hickman, 1990; Koschmann, 2001) have explored these implications in more depth (and certainly in more depth than I can here), but in general many readings of Dewey miss some points that are generative, and perhaps controversial. One reason that much educational discourse glides over these points is that Dewey takes ordinary words and stretches their meaning or asks us to think about implications we normally overlook.

An example is the word, "situation." In common use, attention to situation means thinking about context, being grounded in real phenomena, or recognizing sociocultural aspects of learning and understanding. These elements are all there for Dewey as well, but his use of the term goes significantly beyond that. For Dewey, situation is not something we enter into, nor does it really exist independent of inquiry. Thus, we cannot speak of a student investigating; say a concept in history within a situation comprising a textbook, an essay assignment, group work, and primary source materials. A situation instead is an interconnected functional relation involving the inquirer and the environment. It is a dialectical situation of which we are a part, not a spectator. We change that situation and are changed through our actions. In his classic reflex arc paper Dewey (1896/1972) shows that under this view, conventional distinctions between organism and environment, stimulus and response, body and mind, or cause and effect need to be reconsidered. In his 1941 paper, "The Human Skin: Philosophy's Last Line Of Defense." Bentley goes further to show that even the distinction between "knower" and the "known" relies on an incomplete understanding of situation, positing the knower as separate from the environment.

While eliding some conventional distinctions, Dewey introduces new ones, such as that between indeterminate and determinate situations. His definition of *inquiry* uses this distinction to provide a descriptive account of how we survive in the world:

> Inquiry is the controlled or directed transformation of an indeterminate situation into one that is so determinate in its constituent distinctions and relations as to convert the elements of the original situation into a unified whole. (Dewey, 1938/1991, p. 108)

It is important to note that this account is descriptive, not prescriptive. That is, Dewey does not argue that we should transform indeterminate situations, or that a good way to help people learn is to have them do that. Instead, the controlled or directed transformation of indeterminate situations is what we do as purposive organisms. In that sense, inquiry-based learning is not a method or an option to consider for teaching and learning; instead, it is what happens when people do learn.

The resolution of a problematic situation may involve transforming the inquirer, the environment, and often both. This means that inquiry is a concrete, embodied process. Viewed this way, action in the world is not a follow-on to thinking, nor simply a means to foster cognitive development (e.g., hands-on learning to get a concept across), but along with thinking, it is an integral part of inquiry. Following out the implications of this perspective, one can see that the usual splits between theory and practice, or between work and education, make little sense.

The emphasis in Dewey's definition of inquiry and his use of situation is on transformation, on remaking the world along with ourselves. Because situations include others, inquiry involves at its core collaborative practices in real communities. The usual categories (teacher/student, technology/concept, knowledge/skill) are replaced with a need to understand the process of transformation: What means are employed to transform an indeterminate situation? What are the varied roles played by tools, ideas, and people in inquiry? How does an inquirer evaluate the unity of a situation? How do multiple inquirers coordinate their activities? How do people frame the discourse around technology in education?

HOW DO FACULTY LEARN ABOUT EDUCATIONAL TECHNOLOGY?

Situation, as used by Dewey, provides us with a perspective on teaching and teacher education, and its dialectic with technology. We can begin to see this as we look at conventional approaches to faculty development around technology in contrast with the communities of designers approach.

THE CONVENTIONAL APPROACH TO FACULTY DEVELOPMENT

The conventional approach to faculty development around new technologies is expressed well on the "Preparing Tomorrow's Teachers To Use Technology (PT3)" Web site (Advanced Learning Technologies-Center for Research on Learning, 2002):

> PT3 grantees have worked to transform teacher education so that technology is integrated throughout teaching and learning. Their goal has been to ensure that new teachers enter the classroom prepared to effectively use the computers that await them.

This apparently noncontroversial and all-positive conception builds upon several assumptions, which pervade the Web sites, brochures, training workshops, and services of most university offices of instructional technology:

- the primary goal is to encourage faculty to use more technology in their classrooms

- the use of technology will lead to a change in instructional practice that will bring about increases in student learning and motivation;
- Technology is a relatively autonomous means for improving instruction across disciplines and settings;
- the focus is on developing facility (fluency) with the tools;
- learning to teach with technology may be difficult, requiring training, workshops, and support;
- Resistance to technology use represents simply a misunderstanding of its potential;
- Difficulties in adoption are simply challenges for technology advocates and faculty to overcome together.

This is a linear model in which technology is assumed to be a good that should be incorporated more fully into teaching, that technology skills are on the critical path to success, and that resistance to technology needs to be overcome. Despite the widespread acceptance of these assumptions, none of them are supported by the research literature on the subject. Much of that literature is divided between inspiring stories of educational transformation and accounts of failed technologies, limited support, faculty resistance, bureaucratic inertia, and divergent interpretations of outcomes. For the case of inspiring stories, it is debatable whether the faculty involved changed instructional practices because of the technologies or that their path of development looked anything like that implied in typical institutionalized faculty development models. The accounts of challenged implementations suggest further that the linear model of transformation does not work. In Dewey's terms, these assumptions fail to see the situation of the faculty learner, instead focusing on isolated elements. Other studies (e.g., Becker & Ravitz, 2001; Bruce, 2003; Ferneding, 2003; Haertel & Means, 2000; Hawisher & Selfe, 1999) show that the process of change takes on a different shape depending on a variety of factors including the pedagogical history, administrative and technical support, and teachers' assumptions about the role of technology in learning.

THE "COMMUNITIES OF DESIGNERS" APPROACH

The "communities of designers" model addresses technology integration in teaching and learning in a different way. It argues that good teaching requires a "thoughtful interweaving of all three key sources of knowledge — technology, pedagogy and content" (chapter 1). This interweaving paradoxically shifts the focus away from technology by demanding a deeper commitment to understanding its possibilities, characteristics, and limitations. Rather than working "to transform teacher education so that technology is integrated throughout teaching and learning" it sets up collaborative inquiry into the relations among technology, pedagogy and content. This entails a rejection of the assumption that faculty *should* use more technology in their classrooms, instead calling first for a critical assessment of the goals, values, and contexts for learning. Whether that critical assessment leads to the use of a particular tool, and how that tool might be employed are questions viewed as aspects of the inquiry, not a priori objectives.

In contrast to the assumptions listed above, the "communities of designers" model builds upon a set of principles (chapter 1), which reflect a greater attention to situation as historical, constructed, and embodied. Consequently technology is conceived, not as an unalloyed good to be added unproblematically to a given situation, but as an element of that situation, one that is subject to interpretation and transformation.

The first principle is that a teacher's ability to use technology must be closely connected to the ability to teach. "Understanding of technology must be grounded in ... understanding of teaching and learning in subject-specific and learner-specific contexts." This principle implies that technology use alone will not lead to "a change in instructional practice that will bring about increases in student learning and motivation." Moreover, resistance may not be a misunderstanding of the potential of technology, but instead a critical judgment of its relation to pedagogical goals and characteristics of the content.

A second principle is that technology "is a medium for expression, communication, inquiry and construction that can help teachers solve pedagogical problems in classrooms." This means that far from being a desirable end in itself, technology is but one element within the problem-solving environment, what Dewey terms an "indeterminate situation" (Dewey, 1938/1991, p. 108).

A third principle is that "the implementation of technology is the reinvention of technology. The realization of technological potential in educational settings is socially constructed and highly situational." Because the resolution of a problematic situation may involve transforming the inquirer, the environment, or both, technology must also be seen as an element subject to transformation.

A final principle is that "the relationship between technological innovation and established educational practices is dialogical." This principle contradicts the prevalent deficit view implicit in many faculty development models, that is, that the faculty lack knowledge and skills, have corresponding fears and resistance, and need coaxing and training to be transformed.

HOW CAN WE INTERPRET THE COMMUNITIES OF DESIGN EXPERIENCES?

Reading through the chapters in this book, as well as thinking about other communities of design work reported only tangentially here, I am struck by the diversity of topics, approaches, settings, and pedagogies. Cheryl Rosaen and Sharon Hobson (chapter 2) write about a large variety of ways that technology, guided by considerations of learning, can infuse both teaching and teacher education. Laura Apol and Sheryl Rop (chapter 3) seek ways to use video to make literary response come alive for future literacy teachers. Leslie David Burns and Stephen Koziol (chapter 4) seek ways to help students use their own video in an English methods course. Dorothea Anagnostopoulos, Jory Brass, and Dipendra Subedi (chapter 5) work with high-school students to explore video production and in the process examine their own conceptions of literacy. Avner Segall and Bettie Landauer-Menchik (chapter 6) work with teachers to design ways to foster critical reading of maps. Timothy Little (chapter 7) explores collaborative development of social studies materials. John Dirkx (chapter 18) studies how to use technology to address existing limitations with Problem-Based Learning in face-to-face environments. Ann Austin (chapter 9) talks freely about challenges for both her students and herself in incorporating technology into the Higher, Adult, and Lifelong Education Program.

What can we learn from the communities of design approach and the experiences of those involved? How does it achieve the things it does? How can it be improved? These questions can be examined from the perspective of situation as discussed above, and specifically, by employing Dewey's definition of inquiry. Implicit in that rather compact and somewhat obscure definition (one of the few that Dewey provides explicitly, by the way), are a number of powerful ideas. One is that inquiry is not simply a process of accumulation of knowledge, but rather, a process, that is, a *story* involving recognition of a problem, physical and mental actions to address it, and a repeated cycle of evaluating and further transforming a situation. A second key notion is that of *indeterminacy*, along with its opposite, *a unified whole*. What is important here is the way that evaluation is integral to inquiry, that is, a continual assessment of the situation by the inquirer. (In Dewey's model, self-evaluation is the paradigm case, not a fringe approach). A third concept, *community* is not obvious in the definition, but when that definition is taken within the larger framework of pragmatism, it is clear that situations encompass social life, and the process of transformation typically involves collective action, including that of changing the community per se. A fourth idea, *design* is also not explicitly in the definition. But in the sense of design used in this book, one might do well to substitute it for inquiry, which in some circles has been reduced to a cognitive activity. Design encompasses both an enlarged understanding of situation as well as action to transform it. In that sense it accords well with Dewey's definition of inquiry. A final concept relates to the contradiction inherent in community-based design: How can individuals with unique experiences, attitudes, perspectives, values, and goals work together to design in a way that builds on their unique situations, if different situations require different designs? This is not easily resolvable, but it can be negotiated through *boundary objects*, which allow readings different enough to accommodate different situations, yet are similar enough to allow collective action. In what follows, I apply the notions of Story, Indeterminacy, Communities of Action, Learning by Design, and Boundary Objects to the experiences reported in this book.

STORY

Despite the diversity of these accounts, there are a number of common elements. Each tells a story, and not only because that was an agreed-upon genre. There is also a story to be told, one of initial expectations, approach, problems encountered, problems overcome or accepted, and plans for a new day. Any account that simply assessed the status at a given point would miss the important transformations of the situation. In Dewey's terms, each chapter describes an indeterminate situation and the directed transformation of that towards a more unified whole. The transformation in nearly every case involves not only "interweaving," but changes in all three of the key sources of knowledge identified in the model: technology, pedagogy and content. Moreover, there is always some degree of transformation of the participants as well.

For example, Segall and Landauer-Menchik talk about their initial goal to help students move beyond the interpretation of maps as natural, to see instead the rhetoric of maps. As they work with new technologies, social studies materials, teachers, and the divergent contexts of university and school, they are forced to confront a variety of technical, institutional, and social issues. One consequence is to understand more deeply the situation of the schoolteachers in terms of preparation time, testing, and mandated curricula. Another was to shift technologies, from Web-based to CD-ROM. The process of this transformation of the indeterminate situation is a key aspect to understanding both their own learning and the resultant nexus of technology/content/pedagogy.

INDETERMINACY

In contrast to much of the rhetoric about technology in education, the authors here are quite frank about the challenges they encountered, even in the context of a generally positive disposition towards the new technologies. Words such as "frustration," "problem," "challenge," "difficulty," or "disappointment" occur often throughout. In some cases these are disappointments of the faculty involved; in others they are of K-12 students, cooperating teachers, teacher candidates, technology facilitators, or support staff. Most often they relate to the intersection of pedagogy, content, and technology, and how the technology does not meet expectations. For example, Timothy Little (chapter 7) relates how new versions of PowerPoint software were installed on the classroom computers, which do not recognize earlier versions of curricular materials. He also talks about how graphics/branching heavy programs rendered floppy disks inadequate. They moved then to zip disks and later, CD-ROMs. As he says, "the need to repeatedly transfer and retransfer data coupled with the need to reformat after the programs are transferred can diminish the intellectual ardor of even the most devoted technophile."

Throughout the communities of design project, much time was spent on the technology in the sense of simply getting it to perform promised functions. This raises a question, which can be expressed in terms of the inquiry definition: What is the indeterminate situation here? Ideally within teacher education, that might be to focus on creating a unified whole of pedagogy/content/technology, but in many cases a large proportion of the effort appears to be to find a way that computer user and computer can live in harmony. Thus, technology may have been an equal partner in principle, but it often demanded more than its equal share.

COMMUNITIES OF ACTION

When automobiles were first introduced, they were of little use to most people. Although the machine itself did not carry much nor go very fast, that was not the problem. The greater difficulty was that roads were unpaved, service stations nonexistent, laws inadequate, auto components unreliable and difficult to find, and alternatives were too convenient. Only later, when the ecology for automobiles developed did we see them coming into widespread use. Later, as suburbs developed, downtowns died, workplaces became more far-flung, and passenger railroads disappeared, the car went from novelty, to possibility, to necessity.

One of the challenges for technology integration is that we do not have a supportive ecology, so the effectiveness of a particular technology is almost moot. In this project, that ecology was more present than is often the case. As a result, every chapter shows ways that affordances of the technologies were realized as improvements to practice. Participants were able to overcome the challenges encountered to transform their situation into a unified whole–because that situation included a supportive ecology. Every chapter refers to the multiple levels of collaboration involved. Ann Austin (chapter 9) articulates this quite well as she discusses communities and collaborations for the Proseminar project through the College of Education, the Higher, Adult, and Lifelong Education Program, the Professional Development Course, the specific design team organized within the context of the Professional Development Course, and the Proseminar itself. Others discuss the importance, and the challenges, of collaborations with communities of university students, K-12 students, and cooperating teachers (for instance see chapter 5 by Anagnostopoulos, Brass, and Subedi).

Invoking Dewey's definition of inquiry again, it is not surprising to see the importance of these multiple teams, groups, and communities to the design process. Other people, particularly those who are collaborators or clients, are integral parts of the design situation, whether that situation is indeterminate or determinate. But the definition also highlights something that is usually absent or at best implicit in the stories: Communities are not simply static surrounds for design or inquiry. We do not merely situate the triad of pedagogy/content/technology within a community, or rely on a group to support us in the design. To the contrary, communities are themselves part of the situation which is being transformed.

In the chapters, accounts of the consequence as new members are added to or leave a team are frequent. Others talk about the negotiations between university faculty and cooperating teachers (Segall & Landauer-Menchik), between high school students and researchers or among team members (Anagnostopoulos, Brass, & Subedi), and between educators and technologies (all). But these accounts tend to be positioned as happenstances that affect the design process, which itself is focused on pedagogy/content/technology. The idea that participants are actively transforming the social aspects of their situations is not conceived as a design problem, but as part of the context for design. This positioning is in part due to the focus on communities as historically constituted, geographically-based, and in a sense larger than the task at hand.

However, the pragmatist view of inquiry leads us to see communities themselves as actively constructed (as they are in fact in the communities of design project). A useful construct here is what Zacklad (2003, p. 193) calls "community of action." Zacklad argues for this term (over community of practice) for dealing with small groups which actively and thus to some extent rationally pursue explicit goals while relying on a tightly woven fabric of relationships to promote mutual sympathy and the mimetic learning that is assumed to characterize primary groups and communities of practice. (p. 194)

Communities of action work towards two kinds of goals simultaneously. The first are *service goals*, which involve transforming an external situation, for example, designing a new use of technology for learning. The second are *integration goals*, which involve constructing an internal social milieu allowing its members to develop mutual knowledge and identities. These two categories of goals reflect the fact that community is a necessary means for transformation of the situation, but as a part of that situation, it, too, is transformed.

LEARNING BY DESIGN

Issues of design pervade this book. We see individual faculty designing new ways to incorporate technology into teaching and learning. Within each project, issues of design recur whether it is for PowerPoint presentations, English lessons, maps, or problem-based learning. In the process of design, faculty conceives of pedagogy, content, and technology as designable entities. Several of the projects extend the process of design to include university students, cooperating teachers and their students as designers in a collaborative process. All of this occurs within a project that is consciously designed and continually evaluated.

The result of this attention to design is that individual teams have developed excellent activities, programs, and curriculum modules. Another paper could profitably be devoted to discussing the details of those creations. In addition, there is strong evidence now that faculty learning is deeper, more critical, more connected to use, more lasting, and more engaged. This book and the various research projects faculty has undertaken testify to its substantial impact. Moreover, the inquiry model that underlies learning by design supports that, because *learning by design* is active, embodied, and situated. It matches closely to the full sense of inquiry as defined.

One way to describe the difference between learning by design and more conventional approaches is in terms of *binding time* (Wegner, 1968). This concept, out of programming language theory, refers to the time that terms (such as variables and function designators), in a computer program are assigned values. Somewhat surprisingly, it is useful for thinking about issues of technology use in education (Bruce, 2004). For example, a learning by design approach postpones the binding of technology

choice and use from the perspective of the faculty in a faculty development program. Rather than settling on a particular technology, or a fixed
way of using it, as some programs do, learning by design engages the faculty in making those decisions. That contributes to their learning being
deeper, more critical, more connected to use, more lasting, and more
engaged. The faculty members are active creators of meaning, not passive
recipients of the inquiry of others.

Binding time also helps us see an important potential problem. To the
extent that faculty do become deeply engaged in learning and committed
to their designs, they may create early, and even rigid, binding from the
perspective of their students. Do those students have the same opportunity to experience the learning that comes through taking responsibility
for one's own decisions, encountering and overcoming challenges, negotiating among competing demands of pedagogy, content, technology, and
community, or do they become passive recipients of technologies
designed and created by someone else? How easily can faculty let go of
approaches they spend years designing? Moreover, if their students
become teachers themselves, do their students in turn have the opportunity to design, and learn by design?

Analogous second- and third-order issues such as this are endemic to
teaching and teacher education, but the use of new technologies highlights the challenge. It brings us back to the communities of action issue:
How can our situated design work come to include reflective design of the
communities that need to engage in further design?

BOUNDARY OBJECTS

Boundary objects allow computer programs to communicate, to work with
the same data, even if they interpret it differently. For example, a set of
data may be interpreted as a list of events by one program, which calcu-
lates the activity level of a group and as pointers to publications by
another program, which compiles a bibliography. For the programmer,
the challenge is to design the data in such a way that it can serve multiple
purposes, thereby facilitating communication among the programs.

Star and Griesemer (1989) extend this term to human activities.
Boundary objects allow readings different enough to accommodate different situations, yet are similar enough to allow collective action to transform those situations into more unified wholes. In Berkeley's Museum of
Vertebrate Zoology, biologists, administrators, and amateurs were collecting specimens of flora and fauna to record what existed in California in
the early twentieth century. Although they shared the goal to "preserve
California's nature," they had different means and motives for achieving

this. Standardized forms were devised to facilitate communication across dispersed work groups thus acting as boundary objects for the different participants. State maps and other artifacts also served this role, as did the museum itself.

In the current project, participants likewise came from many different disciplines (Social studies education, English education, elementary education, educational technology), and different institutional roles (university faculty, programmer, graduate student, teacher candidate, etc.). They needed to find ways to work together on a common project while maintaining the value of their diverse backgrounds, knowledge, skills, and personal connections. To reach complete agreement on every concept would have paralyzed the project. On the other hand, not to have common bases would have precluded collaboration.

The solution was boundary objects, though they may not have been conceived in that way. For example, the faculty development course is one; it has different meanings for each participant, yet it indexes a common set of experiences. One participant may conceive the course as a way to get needed technical advice, while another conceives it as a way to improve his or her own teaching. People may come for a variety of professional, social, or institutional reasons. Even during the course, specific activities, such as sharing a discovery about use of a technology may happily allow divergent interpretations while furthering the sense of a common goal, common challenges, and common experiences. This dual function of key objects may be essential for successful collaboration.

We can go one step further to see the entire communities of design project as itself a boundary object. It is true that it has a programmatic agenda, objects, people, and physical spaces. But it is also a resource by its very existence. As such, it is a site for community building, a means of political action, a medium for connecting university and school, and an impetus to software design. Rather than viewing the project as a collection of design teams, a funded grant, or a reform program, one can see it as a situation in Dewey's sense, that participants seek to take through a series of transformations to a more unified whole.

CONCLUSION

Dewey's concept of inquiry, embedded within his theory of situation, provides a standpoint for examining the communities of design project. It also provides questions for the future. For example, Dewey argues that every voice needs to be heard in a democracy, not only to be fair, but because we all need to learn from the unique experiences that each of us has. In this book, we see those unique experiences through accounts of

the conflicts between school and university, school and after-school, or
university course learning and the role of teacher in K-12. These conflicts
are not easily resolved, yet may be the source of the greatest insights for
design. How can communities of design be extended to include more of
the participants in the larger educational system? Who else belongs in the
community of design—University students? Teachers? Children? Parents?
Administrators? Citizens in general?

The pragmatist concept of inquiry also calls us to look at the multiple
forms of experience. This project is unusual and commendable for its
inclusion of aesthetic aspects of experience, critical thinking, and self-
assessment. But new technologies invite us to consider ideas for extending learning, well beyond the use of new media for organizing and presenting content. In that sense, the triad of pedagogy, content, and
technology may limit us, because it suggests looking most closely at the
intersection of these activities, rather than the ways that each may be
transformed through the processes of inquiry. How might new technologies extend learning beyond the classroom to social action? How could/
should they promote global thinking by direct connections across
nations? How are disciplines themselves being transformed in ways that
demand we think not of teaching the old more effectively, but of teaching
entirely new things? How might the use of new technologies promote a
more effective critique of the very technologies we use and the technological work we inhabit?

The communities of design project exemplifies important aspects of
inquiry in the sense intended by Dewey and other pragmatists. Those
early theorists saw inquiry, not simply as a means to learn something, but
as the action of purposive organisms engaged in both understanding and
changing the world around them. Faculty in the project could not be content with trivial uses of new technologies, nor could they spend time
studying techniques that had little relevance to the pedagogy and content
of their disciplines. Instead, they had to become active creators of meaning.

In much earlier work, Andee Rubin and I argued as follows (1993,
p. 218):

> Our study shows that the process of re-creation of the innovation is not only
> unavoidable, but a vital part of the process of educational change. Critical
> analysis of re-creations needs to be an important part of any evaluation. We
> believe that a deeper understanding of this process will highlight the fact
> that teachers need more support in attempting these re-creations. Their
> role in the innovation process is as innovators, not as recipients of com-
> pleted products.

The project shows how faculty can recreate, not simply accept innovations, even powerful ones such as digital video or problem-based learning. It shows the value of engaging learners as full participants in the learning process—as designers, evaluators, and decision makers. These engaged inquirers come to understand details of the technology, the value of a support system, the choices inherent in balancing technology with other educational needs, and the potentials for learning in a much deeper way than would otherwise be possible.

REFERENCES

Advanced Learning Technologies-Center for Research on Learning (2002). *Preparing tomorrow's teachers to use technology* (PT3). Retrieved August 3, 2004, from http://www.pt3.org

Becker, H. J., & Ravitz, J. L. (2001, April). *Computer use by teachers: Are Cuban's predictions correct?* Paper presented at the 2001 annual meeting of the American Educational Research Association, Seattle, WA. Retrieved August 8, 2004, from http://www.crito.uci.edu/tlc/findings/conferences-pdf/aera_2001.pdf

Bentley, A. F. (1941). The human skin: Philosophy's last line of defense. *Philosophy of Science, 8*(1), 1-19.

Bruce, B. C. (Ed.). (2003). *Literacy in the information age: Inquiries into meaning making with new technologies.* Newark, DE: International Reading Association.

Bruce, B. (2004). Maintaining the affordances of traditional education long distance. In C. Haythornthwaite & M. Kazmer (Eds.), *Learning, culture and community in online education: Research and practice* (pp. 19-32). New York: Peter Lang.

Burke, T. (1994). *Dewey's new logic: A reply to Russell.* Chicago: University of Chicago Press.

Dewey, J. (1972). The reflex arc concept in psychology. In J. A. Boydston (Ed.), *John Dewey: The early works, 1882-1898* (Vol. 5, pp. 96-109). Carbondale, IL: Southern Illinois University Press. (Originally published in 1896)

Dewey, J. (1991). Logic: The theory of inquiry. In J. A. Boydston (Ed.), *John Dewey: The later works, 1925-1953* (Vol. 12.) Carbondale, IL: SIU Press. (Originally published in 1938)

Dewey, J. (1991). Experience and education. In J. A. Boydston (Ed.), *John Dewey: The later works, 1938—1939,* (Vol. 13, pp. 1-62). Carbondale, IL: SIU Press. (Originally published in 1939)

Dwight, J., & Garrison, J. (2003). A manifesto for instructional technology: Hyperpedagogy. *Teachers College Record, 105*(5), 699-728.

Ferneding, K. A. (2003). *Questioning technology: Electronic technologies and educational reform.* New York: Counterpoints.

Haertel, G., & Means, B. (2000). *Stronger designs for research on educational uses of technology: Conclusions and implications.* SRI International: Menlo Park, CA. Retrieved August 8, 2004, from http://www.sri.com/policy/designkt/found.html

Hawisher, G. E., & Selfe. C. (Eds.). (1999). *Passions, pedagogies, and 21st century technologies.* Logan: Utah State University Press.

Hickman, L. A. (1990). *John Dewey's pragmatic technology.* Bloomington: Indiana University Press.

Koschmann, T. D. (2001). Dewey's contribution to a standard of problem-based learning practice. In P. Dillenbourg, A. Eurlings, & K. Hakkarainen (Eds.), *European perspectives on computer-supported collaborative learning: Proceedings of Euro-CSCL* (pp. 355-363). Maastricht: Euro-CSCL.

Star, S. L., & Griesemer, J. (1989). Institutional ecology, "translations," and boundary objects: Amateurs and professionals in Berkeley's Museum of Vertebrate Zoology, 1907-1939. *Social Studies of Science, 19,* 387-420. (Reprinted in *The science studies reader,* pp. 505-524, by M. Biagioli, Ed. London: Routledge).

Wegner, P. (1968). *Programming languages, information structures and machine organization.* New York: McGraw-Hill.

Zacklad, M. (2003). Communities of action: A cognitive and social approach to the design of CSCW systems. In M. Pendergast, K. Schmidt, C. Simone, M., & Tremaine, M. (Eds.), *Proceedings of the 2003 international ACM SIGGROUP conference on Supporting group work* (pp. 190-197). New York: ACM.

ABOUT THE AUTHORS

Dorothea Anagnostopoulos (danagnos@msu.edu) is an assistant professor in the department of Teacher Education at Michigan State University. Her research interests include educational policy, urban high schools, and the teaching of secondary English. Her work has been published in a wide range of journals, including *Research in the Teaching of English, American Journal of Education Research,* and *Journal of Teacher Education.*

Laura Apol (apol@msu.edu) is an associate professor in the College of Education at Michigan State University. She teaches children's literature and writing to undergraduates and graduate students in face-to-face, international, and online environments. This PT3 project represents her first attempt to combine her work in children's literature, literary theory, and literature response with her growing understandings of technology and teacher education.

Ann E. Austin (aaustin@msu.edu) is the Mildred B. Erickson distinguished professor of higher, adult, and lifelong education at Michigan State University. Her research and teaching are focused on faculty careers, roles, and professional development; reform in graduate education; the improvement of teaching and learning; and organizational change and transformation in higher education. Currently, she is coprincipal investigator of the Center for the Integration of Research, Teaching, and Learning (CIRTL), a 5-year National Science Foundation-funded project focused on improving teaching and learning in higher education in science, technology, engineering, and mathematics.

Jory Brass is assistant professor of English education at the University of Cincinnati. His research interests include the political, moral, and ethical dimensions of English teaching, literacy practices, and schooling.

Bertram C. Bruce (chip@uiuc.edu) is professor in Library And Information Science and codirector of the Community Informatics Initiative at the University of Illinois at Urbana-Champaign. He also has appointments with the Departments of Curriculum and Instruction, Bioengineering, Writing Studies, and the Center for East Asian and Pacific Studies. His central interest is in learning—the constructive process whereby individuals and organizations develop as they adapt to new circumstances. His most recent book is *Libr@ries: Changing information Space and Practice.*

Leslie Burns (L.burns@uky.edu) is an assistant professor of literacy in the University of Kentucky's Department of Curriculum and Instruction, where he serves as the program chair for secondary English education and directs the Bluegrass Writing Project. His research interests involve discourse analysis of literacy policy and standards, the use of new literacy studies theories for curriculum design, the politics of English education, and the standardization of teaching.

John M. Dirkx is professor of higher, adult, and lifelong education and director of the Michigan Center for Education and Work (formerly the Michigan Center for Career and Technical Education) at Michigan State University. He teaches courses on adult learning, transformative learning, program planning, teaching methods, training and professional development, group dynamics, and qualitative research. His primary research interests focus on the emotional, psychosocial, transformative, and spiritual dimensions of teaching and learning in adult and higher education. He has a particular interest in the group, interpersonal, and intrapersonal dynamics associated with online collaborative learning. He is the coauthor of *A Guide to Planning and Implementing Instruction for Adults: A Theme-based Approach,* and numerous book chapters and journal articles on adult learning.

Sharon Hobson (hobson@msu.edu) is an experienced teacher and educational consultant. For 5 years she taught methods courses in mathematics education in Michigan State University's 5-year Teacher Preparation Program. She was also a field instructor in the program for 2 years. Her research interests include integration of technology in teacher education and learning to use technology in K-8 schools.

Matthew J. Koehler (mkoehler@msu.edu) is an associate professor with appointments in the Educational Psychology and Educational Technology program and in the Teacher Education program in the College of Education at Michigan State University. His background includes undergraduate degrees in computer science and mathematics, a masters degree in Computer Science, and a PhD in educational psychology. His research and teaching focus on understanding the affordances and constraints of new technologies; the design of technology-rich, innovative learning environments; and the professional development of teachers. He has collaborated with Punya Mishra to develop theoretical, pedagogical, and methodological perspectives that characterize teachers who effectively integrate content, pedagogy, and technology.

Stephen Koziol (skoziol@umd.edu) is a professor and Chair of the Department of Curriculum and Instruction at the University of Maryland. Prior to this he was a faculty member and department Chair (1985-93) of the Department of Instruction and Learning at the University of Pittsburgh (1970-97) before becoming professor and Chair of the Department of Teacher Education at Michigan State University (1997-03). He has published widely on topics such as, English teaching practices and teacher education; the design and use of drama activities for active learning in classrooms; policy, practice, and design in teacher education programs; and, the development and use of teacher performance assessment using self-report instruments and video-supported, school-based performance tasks. He has participated in professional development or reform initiatives with major national groups such as the Holmes Group, the National Board for Professional Teaching Standards and INTASC, and with World Bank and UNICEF-sponsored reform projects in Egypt and Bosnia-Herzegovina.

Bettie Landauer-Menchik (menchikb@msu.edu) is the director of the Data Services Unit of K-12 Outreach in the College of Education at Michigan State University. Previously, she was a social studies teacher in Philadelphia, New Jersey, and Michigan. As an applied demographer, she helps schools use social, economic, and demographic information to understand the characteristics of their communities. Her most recent publication *How to Use School District Demographics for Effective Schools and School Districts* is available from the U.S. Department of Education Web site.

Timothy H. Little is a professor emeritus of teacher education at Michigan State University who specializes in history/social studies education. His career in education has spanned a period of some 43 years. During that time he has served as a high school classroom teacher, a demonstration teacher for Northwestern University, a guest instructor/curriculum designer for 12 years at Holt High School in Michigan, and a tenured faculty member at Michigan State University. His teaching, research, and service interests focus on the application of technology to school subject matter instruction and the definition and design of law-related citizenship education programs. He has authored numerous textbooks and articles in the field of social studies, directed and published two computer-driven curriculum projects for *Newsweek Magazine*, served as a bylined columnist for a computer publication for some 12 years writing about *Computers in the Social Studies Classroom*. He also served two terms as the elected president of the board of directors of the Michigan Center for Civic Education. He received the Michigan Supreme Court Justice Mary Coleman Award for his service to law-related education in 1984. He was selected to receive an all university Amoco Foundation Excellence in Teaching Award at Michigan State University in 1998.

Punya Mishra (punya@msu.edu) is an associate professor of educational technology in the Educational Psychology and Educational Technology program in the College of Education at Michigan State University. He has an undergraduate degree in electrical engineering, masters degrees in visual and mass communications, and a PhD in educational psychology. His research interests are in the area of educational technology, teacher preparation and faculty development around educational technology, online learning, and educational software development. He has been working with Matthew J. Koehler, to develop theoretical, pedagogical, and methodological perspectives to understand the process and nature of teacher knowledge as it develops through design.

Martin Oliver (m.oliver@ioe.ac.uk) is a senior lecturer at the Institute of Education, University of London, England, where he leads the MA in ICT in Education. His research addresses issues of curriculum design, the evaluation of ICT, the impact of change (such as the adoption of new technology) on roles and practices in higher education and the relationship between pedagogy and technology. He is also interested in the philosophy of technology use in education and what people learn from playing computer games. Martin is deputy editor of *ALT-J*, the *Journal of the Association for Learning Technology*.

Sheri K. Rop spent many years teaching in elementary classrooms and working as a reading teacher. Since obtaining her PhD in literacy from Michigan State University she has taught children's literature at the undergraduate and graduate levels in the Michigan State University College of Education. This PT3 project grew out of an intersection between her work with educational technology and her desire to find ways to bridge the gap between pedagogical theory and practice for teacher education students. She currently works as a curriculum consultant and writer.

Cheryl L. Rosaen (crosaen@msu.edu) is an associate professor of teacher education at Michigan State University and a faculty team leader in a 5-year teacher preparation program. She teaches courses in literacy methods and teacher education, and conducts research on learning to teach literacy, and the role technology can play in supporting teacher learning. She is a coprincipal investigator for *Teachers As Designers: A Problem-Based Approach to Preparing Teachers* (PT3), and literacy coleader for Michigan State University's Teachers for a New Era initiative (2002-08), a project focused on making subject matter content and context central in teaching.

Avner Segall (avner@msu.edu) is an associate professor in the Department of Teacher Education at Michigan State University. He has a BA in history from the Tel Aviv University, Israel and a PhD in curriculum and instruction from the University of British Columbia, Canada. His research and teaching combine critical theory and pedagogy, teacher education, and social/cultural studies.

Dipendra Raj Subedi (subedidi@msu.edu) is a doctoral student in the Measurement and Quantitative Methods program at Michigan State University (MSU). He has a master's degree in educational technology from MSU and an undergraduate degree in electrical engineering. Before coming to MSU, he was a lecturer at the Department of Electronics and Computer Engineering, Tribhuvan University, Nepal. His research interests are multilevel modeling, item response theory, and educational technology.

Yong Zhao (zhaoyo@msu.edu) is university distinguished professor at Michigan State University. He directs The U.S.-China Center for Research on Educational Excellence and Center of Technology and Teaching at Michigan State University. His research interests include teacher education and technology, technology diffusion in schools, and the use of technology to support language education.

Printed in the United States
78871LV00003B/33